# PARIS

## and the

# ANARCHISTS

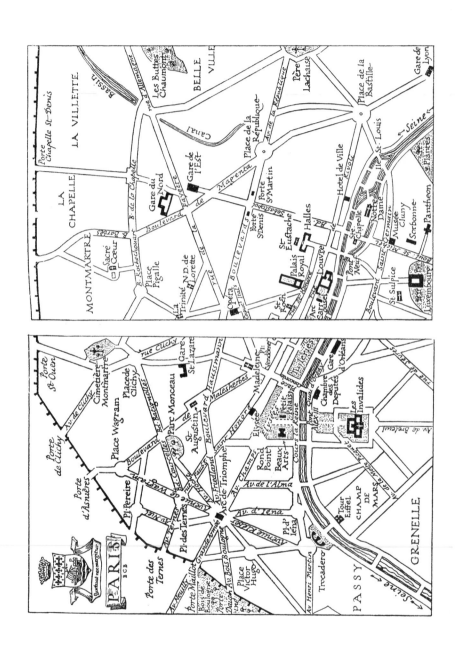

# PARIS

## and the

# ANARCHISTS

### Aesthetes and Subversives
### During the Fin de Siècle

Alexander Varias

MACMILLAN

First published 1997 by
MACMILLAN PRESS LTD
Houndmills, Basingstoke, Hampshire RG21 6XS
and London
Companies and representatives
throughout the world

ISBN 0–333–69432–5

A catalogue record for this book is available from the British Library.

10  9  8  7  6  5  4  3  2  1
06  05  04  03  02  01  00  99  98  97

Printed in the United States of America by
Haddon Craftsmen
Scranton, PA

# CONTENTS

# ACKNOWLEDGMENTS

"Mutual Aid," as Camille Pissarro said, may be but a beautiful, utopian dream. Still, I have had cause to consider its relevance during the researching and writing of this book when the support of so many people has mattered a great deal. New York University grants and the French Ministry of Cultural Services' Bourse Chateaubriand enabled me to spend the necessary time in Paris to conduct research. The late Edward Tannenbaum, Darline Levy, and Robert Scally provided the guidance and direction necessary to the organization and writing of my dissertation. Villanova University's Office of Academic Affairs was most generous in helping me obtain copyright permissions, and Donald Kelley was most extending in his enthusiastic support as chair of the Villanova history department. I thank Judy Olsen of Falvey Library at Villanova and Helen Hayes of Logue Library at Chestnut Hill College for their advice concerning illustrations and Florence Edward Sullivan, SSJ, of Chestnut Hill for her expertise with illustrations. At the same time, those on the editorial staff of St. Martins Press, particularly Maura Burnett, Jennifer Farthing, and Alan Bradshaw, have been invaluable in their diligence and dedication to this work.

I have been fortunate to have friends with reservoirs of ideas that I have often been able to visit. As it is always wise to return to the source of knowledge and inspiration, it is impossible for me to imagine my own intellectual development without Traian Stoianovich and the late Harold Poor and Warren Susman of Rutgers University. My understanding of history and culture owes much to their wonderful ideas and insights that were always expressed in the spirit of friendship and generosity. I give additional gratitude and acknowledgment to my good friends Melissa Benca, Christopher Daly, Colin Denis, Julie Hart, Dimitri Keramitas, Roy Kirvan, Seth Koven, Clara-Eugenia Nuñez, and Eric Nooter for their intellectual contributions to my ongoing work. Special thanks go to Peter Ljutich and Jeffrey Johnson for their continued interest in this project and for their critical and insightful reading of the manuscript. The comments and suggestions they made proved illuminating. I thank my mother, Evangelia Varias, and my brother, James Varias, for the love and encouragement they have shown throughout this project and my life.

For her love, support, and intellectual contributions, I dedicate this book to my wife, Lorraine Coons. From the time of our mutual research adventures in Paris, through our many shared travels, and continuing with the embarkation and completion of this book, her companionship has provided me with the greatest joy. With her help I have been able to discern the many pieces of the anarchist puzzle. I have made my way through the Parisian anarchist labyrinth with the great benefit of her intellect and scholarly gifts as she so painstakingly and critically read the entire manuscript. As a result, I confronted a number of issues and perspectives that initially escaped me. This book is dedicated to you, Lorraine, with my love.

# PARIS
## and the
# ANARCHISTS

# Introduction

A study focusing upon a subject as controversial and ill-defined as anarchism must begin by taking a partially linguistic path. In fact, the word *anarchism* has been loaded with more meanings and insinuations than most others. Its very mention arouses an immediate, but vague, picture that becomes even less distinct upon analysis and dissection. Among those who have described themselves as anarchists or have been so categorized by the public one can think of: terrorists; murderers; strikers; disorganized fomenters of chaos; Bohemians; irresponsible people refusing to work; selfish conveyers of immorality; those admiring eccentric forms of music, painting, poetry, and other artistic media; extreme egoists; excessively proud defenders of possessions; and all other asocial types. It is tempting to place quotes around many of the above adjectives, and the list threatens to lead one on to an infinite array of tangents.

Political and social definitions do not promise immediate remedy since anarchists include people of all social classes and from both wings of politics—ranging from radical to moderate interpretations of any particular idea. Anarchism can also be adjoined to altogether different political currents originally having little to do with it, including socialism, liberalism, conservatism, and fascism. The political left and right have both found delight in antigovernmental attitudes intrinsic to the ideology, and it is an interesting fact to this author that as I complete this book in 1996, I have witnessed governmental paralysis both in France (the society under scrutiny here) and the United States (my home). While strikes throughout France have been recently initiated by French unions to protest the governmental cutbacks of the new president, Jacques Chirac, right-wing Republicans running for president in the United States have made comments indicating that the American people did not miss their government—which had been shut down due to the budget impasse—a feeling that does not seem prevalent at all in the wake of threatened services on which people depend. If the French and American situations have nothing else in common, they underline the threat that antigovernmental actions and "anarchist" attitudes can pose in challenging the established order.

Uneasiness with the word as a sole unit continues, and confusion is compounded by the existence of the word *libertarian*. With the formation of contemporary libertarian movements, thoughts of people resenting taxes, gun control, and environmental standards immediately spring to mind, and such images are connected to certain new political realities of the 1990s. Most recently, popular temptation to use the title of *libertarian* or *anarchist* has been found in the cases of the Montana Freemen and the Unabomber. Of course, it is unclear whether any label can apply to these particular phenomena.

A semantic divorce could separate *anarchist* and *libertarian,* especially since the former is more frequently associated with the radical left and the latter with the far right that takes laissez-faire to an extreme. In fact, for the purposes of this study, context matters a great deal as interpretation of a concept takes on a relative meaning. It is necessary to leave our own confusions aside and attempt to understand the mentality of an age (about a century earlier) not far removed in time from the years when anarchism developed as a social, political, and cultural movement. In late nineteenth-century Paris, *anarchist* and *libertarian* were used interchangeably, and one attempting to comprehend the range of the anarchist movement must consider this fact. Keeping such linguistic and emotional debates in mind, it is possible to grasp the reasons for the nature of anarchism in that particular city and at that specific time.

During the last two decades of the nineteenth century, Paris was a city of marked contrasts and dichotomies. It basked in the light of boulevards and squares, recently created by Baron Georges Eugène Haussmann and his architects, within which the bourgeoisie pursued a sense of leisure and public pleasure reflecting its confirmed social and economic status. The architectural aura of class confidence was composed of openness, harmony, and linearity—factors that seemed to connect the recently created Third Republic to the overturned Second Empire of Louis Napoleon. These elements also served to embellish and cover the less glamorous side of bourgeois business reality.

Yet contrasts to this official facade were evident. The Eiffel Tower seemed (in the minds of some) to puncture the city's new facade with a burst of industrial mechanization and to remind the bourgeoisie of its disconcerting dependence upon that factor. Industrial suburbs surrounded the city, and certain squalid neighborhoods within official Paris continued to reflect the subversive, hostile glare of the impoverished. As the horrors of the Paris

Commune of 1871 were so recent and thus engrained in the collective memory of a city famous for its revolutionary heritage, the threat of further upheavals was never absent and political disputes often upset the tenuous balance maintained by Monarchists, Opportunists, Radicals, and other assorted parties that distanced themselves from ardent ideological fixations for the sake of governing.

Controversy also raged in the art world. If the accepted artistic conventions revolved around realism, academic style, and heroic mythological subjects, the more creative artists, inspired by the precedent set by the Romantics, sought free aesthetic expression. If they also felt committed to scientific realism, they nonetheless rebelled against the accepted forms of the Academy and the Salon and unleashed what is known as the revolt of the avant-garde. In this way, Impressionism and Post-Impressionism shook the Parisian art world in a manner akin to the Eiffel Tower's rude appearance over the western horizon of Paris.

Within this complex metropolitan matrix a rather small and loosely defined movement of anarchists spread and addressed various political, social, economic, and cultural concerns central to Parisian life. At stake was a reformulation of the city's history, culture, and politics. While never becoming an officially established movement or seriously threatening to assume power, anarchism did emerge as a vital cultural force in enclaves of late nineteenth-century Paris. Richard Sonn has pointed to anarchism as a significant subculture within Paris deriving much of its force from the popular classes.[1] Sonn has broadened our knowledge and conceptualization of the movement by considering the importance of popular slang and *mentalité* to anarchist jargon and rhetoric and demonstrating how literary and political circles were inspired by Parisian popular currents. In this unexpected manner, elites and commoners connected. Elsewhere, he has also demonstrated the anarchistic relevance to central issues of the 1990s such as feminism and ecology.[2] Likewise in analyzing a different political context and cultural setting, Temma Kaplan has pointed to the importance of popular language and imagery to the artistic currents of Barcelona during the early twentieth century.[3] Another recent study by John Hutton traces the links among anarchism, Neo-Impressionism, and science during the late nineteenth century.[4]

It is noteworthy when studying the history of Paris during the late nineteenth century to observe how anarchism served as a lens through which its adherents viewed and debated the various issues within the city. These concerns may have been envisioned in different circumstances as isolated and relevant only to their specific combatants.

In fact, the unique strength of Parisian anarchism was its diversity—a characteristic that ordinarily entailed lack of political unity. This feature allowed it to bring into close emotional proximity a variety of controversies publicized only by those most concerned. It is a paradox that anarchism (a movement alienated on the surface from conventional society) could provide forums for general assessment of the entire scope of issues troubling French society. While a multiplicity of perspectives flourished (in keeping with a movement emphasizing decentralization), continual referral to the movement's basic, original ideals enlivened political and cultural discussion with a direction and spirit that was unique and not officially evident in Paris. This was true even for those focused on single issues. Diversity within the movement facilitated debate on many issues.

This book is concerned with the ideas and concerns of those artists, poets, critics, and activists attracted to anarchism both privately and publicly and with their contributions to Parisian life. It analyzes both their subversion and hostility to the established order and the ideals they wished to further. Aesthetic questions take their place next to those concerning political dissidence.

Parisian anarchism during the fin de siècle is a subject in which one constantly senses contrasts and dichotomies. This is evident in the very nature of the study of anarchism and of Paris as both appeared during the last two decades of the nineteenth century. Given the wide range of issues and concerns to which the anarchist esteem of freedom could be applied, there was a great gap between those adherents emphasizing social goals revolving around the destruction of the state and those addressing the needs of the ego, the expressive self, or a related psychological category of the free individual. For instance, Parisian society was absorbed with many social problems (such as economic and political reform and the revelation of mass anti-Semitism within French society as witnessed in the Dreyfus Affair). Yet the city's fin-de-siècle character was also evident in the struggle for stylistic freedom and aesthetic expression that its avant-garde poets, painters, and sculptors led against the conformist demands of the Salon and the Academy. It was no coincidence that those so concerned with the demands and needs of the individual voice adopted anarchism as their appropriate ideology. Meanwhile, individuals, speaking on behalf of anarchy, exploded bombs in various official quarters of the city. Since that time, the word *anarchism* has been confused with *terrorism* because of the fallout of such random, senseless acts. Consequently, those still committed to a more systematic, community-based anarchist purpose felt it incumbent to stress the relevance of the word to their particular quest.

It is wise to take up the anarchists' linguistic challenge and to weigh the position of the Parisian phenomenon within the developing expanse of the movement. If they became entangled within the web of French politics and took publicly shocking stands, anarchists remained true to the essentially outcast position that earlier cohorts had created. What made for differences were the nature of the time in which they lived and ambiguities within the organization of Parisian anarchism. Adding to the picture was the place of anarchism within uniquely French revolutionary traditions and practices that had emerged late in the preceding century.

Anarchism was a political, social, and cultural movement with ideological roots extending to the ancient world. *Anarchos* is a Greek word literally meaning "no government," and, accordingly, the concept attached to it was of an ideal society with a lack of central authority and prescribed rules.[5] In a later era anarchism would reemerge and express an alternative mode of political thinking. During the late eighteenth and nineteenth centuries, it was increasingly developed by thinkers such as William Godwin, Pierre-Joseph Proudhon, Mikhail Bakunin, and Peter Kropotkin to attract artisans, peasants, and other segments of the population resisting the lure of modernizing tendencies. Not surprisingly, anarchism also acquired a Romantic aura and was defined by streamlined political movements as being partially reactionary in inspiration. Others saw it as progressive because of the same factors.

As the political movements of the nineteenth century (chiefly liberalism, conservatism, and socialism) evolved and grew in importance, anarchism itself emerged as a more mysterious and nebulous force. The latter aspect reflected its increasing appeal to a variety of groups and individuals. Since Marxism most forwardly organized the urban proletariat against capitalist society, anarchism, in turn, grew as an alternative revolutionary movement that emphasized not only social justice and equality, but also the destruction of central authority, the preservation of individual liberty, and the esteem of those social forces scorned by Marx—namely, artisans, peasants, and the amorphous urban masses castigated as the *lumpenproletariat.*

Anarchists and those sympathizing with them criticized the Marxist stress on mechanization. Félix Fénéon, the famous art dealer/war office bureaucrat/anarchist, stated that socialists were obsessed with the efficiency of the clock while anarchists esteemed the living organism. In the 1930s, George Orwell, in his *Homage to Catalonia,* fervently contrasted Marxists and anarchists by noting the obsession of the former with centralization and control while praising the anarchists' devotion to liberty and individualism. Orwell arrived at his generalization during the Spanish Civil War when he fought on the loyalist side in the struggle against General Francisco Franco. As one of the most important creative thinkers of the twentieth century, he formulated not only an oppositional attitude to the reactionary forces of the right wing (such as threatened democracies throughout Europe during the 1930s), but also a hostile stance against the rigid forces of the left that refused to listen to any alternative revolutionary visions. Obviously, Orwell principally directed his wrath at Stalinism, and his sentiments reflect the critical position of anarchism in the resistance to the lure of dogmas and party-dominated movements—even those on the left. We can discern within this unfolding political movement a current that gave it at once a potential for greater expansion and yet a vulnerability to marginalization. At stake was a set of ideals emphasizing political freedom and social justice, issues that invited a wide range of activists to take a number of mutually conflicting stands.

In underlining the need for complete individuality and nonconformity, Max Stirner gave a more elusive, but equally vivid, interpretation of anarchism in his *The Ego and His Own* of 1845.[6] Stirner was more concerned with the unrestrained expression of the human personality and with self-fulfillment. While maintaining Bakunin's and Kropotkin's hostility to the state, he almost completely neglected social problems. Furthermore, he envisioned nothing greater than a society of egoists in mutual conflict such as perhaps would not have surprised Charles Darwin. Life ceased to have any purpose higher than struggle and egoism, and such a conclusion imbued Stirner's thought with a nihilistic and pessimistic quality that gathered increasing influence during the 1890s when avant-garde artists read Friedrich Nietzsche's books and intensified the tone and rhetoric of their opposition to and defiance of the Academy and Salon. Increasingly, they and their critics viewed this struggle as pitting the values of youth against those of their elders.

It is important to keep in mind that the variety of anarchist trends mentioned above were circulating during a period of political, cultural, and intellectual change. As the elitist liberal political order began to break down on the continent, new mass movements emerged and seemed to presage the political history of the first half of the twentieth century. At the same time, liberal humanism was also challenged by irrational forms of thought. Painting and poetry especially were conceived in ways that departed from the familiar styles of the past and seemed to underline the fact of a cultural seismic break. While Sigmund Freud and Albert Einstein were among those to introduce even more unfamiliar ideas and methods of thought in the years to come, the signs were already there that the "banquet years" of the end of the century would be highlighted by more than frivolous leisure.[7] Life in its accustomed patterns was not to be taken for granted amidst unconventional and unpredictable discoveries and new sources of tension and anxiety.

While anarchism was one of a series of movements challenging the established capitalist order, it was unique in its ability to absorb and express a wide range of ideas and emotions. By the fin de siècle, socialism could be depicted as staid, bourgeois, and part of the familiar daily world of Parisians and Europeans. In contrast, terrorists were hurling bombs, syndicalists were attempting to organize general strikes intended to bring down the system, and artists were creating works perceived as hurling anathemas at the traditional concept of monumental art. These activities could be and often were justified in the name of anarchism—even when many of those committed to this movement scorned such efforts. Despite the efforts of organized anarchists to maintain an internal dynamic and keep clear of such unorthodox methods and goals, the concept of anarchism proved to be too flexible and easily accommodated to the desires of the movement's admirers. As a result, the Parisian movement acquired a broader cultural sweep that was evident at the turn of the century.

Anarchism in France did not have the same social character displayed in Spain, Italy, and other less developed nations. France was more advanced economically and with a different demographic structure. This made for an anarchist movement that was far more complex in its composition. The enthusiastic embrace of anarchism in Spain and Italy by an impoverished, desperate peasantry was renowned and especially evocative of Andalusia. Urban variations were no less noticeable and scholarly attention has recently focused upon unique anarchist workers' quarters that flourished in the Catalonian cities (especially Barcelona) as magnets for anarchist workers' quarters.

French syndicalism offered the most vivid example of a mass movement revolving around anarchism. Exponents of this controversial union movement loosely modeled their ideas on anarchism and endeavored to organize urban workers, not in hopes of negotiating with capitalist leaders to achieve reforms, but of destroying the system. Nevertheless, they were disappointed as the numbers of participants did not approach those found in Spain. Generally speaking, French anarchism was less of a mass movement and more likely to attract intellectuals or isolated individuals who could be receptive to popular rhetoric. As Sonn has concluded, the movement itself became part of an extensive Parisian subculture.[8] Mentalité and mores appear equally significant factors of the French anarchist topography as do tactical and political considerations. It is the contention of this book that with its particular features, French anarchism assumed a different, more complex character and addressed uniquely French concerns especially centered in and around the city of Paris.

By 1890, France had already experienced a century of revolutionary upheavals beginning with the French Revolution and most recently concluding with the Commune of 1871. As such, a revolutionary tradition had taken hold in France, and socialists and anarchists alike confronted nostalgia for its emotional appeals. The Communards themselves had organized in small clubs reminiscent of those of the "Great Revolution" and of 1848.[9] The term "neo-Jacobin" continued to be in use. While some saw this sense of tradition as retarding the progress of the French opposition,[10] it nonetheless added an element of élan. French revolutionaries may have been less dependent upon the support of an advanced working class, but they drew from the common well of revolutionary inspiration. In so doing, they reflected the common preference evident at the turn of the century for emotional and intuitive forces over rational theory.

Paris's central importance to the revolt of the avant-garde was also a key factor in its status as a city of change at the fin-de-siècle. The note of dissonance provided by these experimental artists was complemented by other expressions of disruption. Even before the French Revolution, Paris had its share of subversive writers of the literary underground[11] who used the pen to make war upon the political and cultural elites directing the establishment. During the nineteenth century, this tradition continued and was strengthened by the emergence of an avant-garde. By the fin de siècle, many artists and intellectuals arrived in Paris expecting to find fame and renown outside of the official centers of culture. Of course, their chances for success were not necessarily good. Those wishing to pursue cultural conflict to its furthest extent perceived estrangement and alienation as positive traits.

Some artists succeeded in integrating their anarchist *engagement* (activism) into their work. In the forefront of these was Camille Pissarro, one of the founders of the Impressionist movement. As seen in the recent exhibition of his later work (shown in Dallas, Philadelphia, and London),[12] Pissarro shifted his focus from open-air rural landscapes to scenes of Rouen, Paris, and other vibrant cities where people moved busily among the streets and squares. Not only did Pissarro use such cityscapes to display his Impressionist mastery of light and color, but he also expressed his anarchist mystique of communal interaction. By the 1880s and 1890s (the time when he painted these scenes), anarchism was not only a rurally focused movement; it was organized in cities as well. Paris with its fusion of modern and traditional features was ripe for the organization and myriad activities conceived by a variety of revolutionaries and intellectuals seeking to relate their concerns to the great city around them.

In chapter 1, I will examine the makeup of anarchistic Paris with regard to the areas of the city where the movement was most visible and public. This depiction will focus upon the cultural setting of the various anarchist enclaves and will especially center on the Latin Quarter, Montmartre, and Belleville.

Chapter 2 will focus upon the revolutionary tradition of Paris as a factor that shaped anarchism locally and provoked continual discussion and discourse on the movement's relevance to that heritage. The key question concerned the manner in which the anarchists continued to reflect a tradition begun a century earlier as they adapted to the new times.

Chapter 3 will discuss some of the most contentious issues in Paris that anarchists felt compelled to confront. Issues like the Third Republic's legitimacy, terrorism, the Dreyfus Affair, and revolutionary syndicalism were among the most publicized questions, but underlying problems having to do with education and language, the ego, Romantic views of nature, and vegetarianism also found their way into the debate.

Finally, in chapter 4 I will analyze the relationship between artists and anarchists and the manner in which art was viewed as a revolutionary tool. This question will be set against the great changes transforming the Parisian art world. My study was based on a wide variety of primary sources found in the libraries and archives of Paris as well as on relevant secondary sources. I have also rendered the translations of original French archival sources.

In this fourfold analysis and in the confrontation with figures like Pissarro, Louise Michel, Jean Grave, Emile Pouget, Sébastien Faure, and others, the diversity and flexibility of the anarchist movement (as well as its flaws) will be apparent. The wide degree of variety will be evident in the complex texture of debates over the myriad concerns that emerged around the anarchists and raged at the heart of the movement. This diversity would be matched only by that of the historic city of Paris, in which the movement was cast.

# The Anarchist Enclaves of Fin-de-Siècle Paris

It was not until the 1880s that Paris emerged as the principal center of French anarchism. By this time, the Third Republic had been in place for over a decade and interest in the city's revolutionary past reawakened within subversive circles. Among the factors contributing to this resurgence of interest were the approaching centennial of the "great" French Revolution of 1789 and the subsequent festivities planned in its honor—early indicators of the modern obsession with commemorating centennial anniversaries of significant events.[1] In this light, the French public's fascination with the Revolution—albeit at a safe, removed distance in time—found physical expression in preparations for the Universal Exhibition of 1889 and the construction of the Eiffel Tower.[2]

The dispersed anarchist groups of Paris expressed feelings of awe for the city's past when considering their own revolutionary goals. In giving in to their historical zeal, they believed themselves to be inaugurating a new phase of French anarchist activity centered in the national capital and consistently commemorated the importance of Paris to their cause.

Since the official inception of the anarchist movement under Mikhail Bakunin's guidance, French participants had lived and worked in areas clustered near the Swiss border such as the Jura or in Lyons. It was in Switzerland, after all, that the two most prominent anarchist intellectuals, Peter Kropotkin and Elisée Reclus, lived. From there, Paul Brousse organized militant anarchists under the inspiring banner of the Paris Commune. He would later moderate his ideas and develop the moderate, revisionist version of socialism called "possibilism."[3] Reclus and Kropotkin especially influenced French anarchists who wanted to be near their inspiring presence and have the comfort of being able to flee at a moment's notice across the border away from pursuing police authorities. Anarchists in Switzerland also favored the natural setting of the area where artisanal culture remained prevalent and the complexities of modern urban life were largely absent. In this way, the anarchist emotional inclination for Romantic, anti-urban, and agrarian ways was very strong indeed.

This would not last. An alternative soon would emerge, especially after police suppression of the Lyonnaise anarchist movement in 1883 when *compagnons* (fellow rebels) fled for Paris—the French political and intellectual center. They were followed by Kropotkin and the anarchist editor Jean Grave. Displacement, however, was followed by the immediate realization that the great city offered a stimulating and inspiring atmosphere for the contemplation of future revolt. Anarchists only had to walk along the streets and plazas to glimpse evidence of the Parisian revolutionary tradition. Most dramatic was place de la Concorde (formerly place de la Révolution), the site where Louis XVI, Marie Antoinette, and many others had been guillotined. They also remembered the years 1789, 1793, 1848, and 1871 for their famous popular outbursts and revolutionary spectacles that by now were linked to the city's history in as evident a manner as the court rituals of the Capetian, Valois, and Bourbon dynasties and the high masses at Notre Dame. In addition to place de la Concorde, Saint-Antoine, Père Lachaise Cemetery, the Champ-de-Mars, and many other places were steeped in the revolutionary past where memories of the guillotine, barricades, battles, and brutality still flourished and were enjoyed by the more macabrely inclined as thoroughly as a full-course French dinner.

Anarchists became particularly enthusiastic about the reawakened Parisian revolutionary tradition once exiled Communards began returning from New Caledonia in the 1870s and entered the anarchist ranks. Heartened by this emotional boost, activists in the movement emphasized the importance of Paris as the rebellious city par excellence and their own place within that unfolding, evolving, "great revolutionary chain of being"—but they made no reference or connection to the medieval intellectual tradition later analyzed by Arthur Lovejoy. Accordingly, anarchists envisioned a mental and physical place for themselves within an entire context of revolution and pictured their cause as continuing a struggle begun at least a century earlier. They pictured Paris and its neighborhoods as central to this vision and were transfixed by the rich popular history of the local quarters where they lived and conspired. In fact, they viewed localities as microcosms of the whole. Kropotkin and Grave evoked the significance and relevance of the Parisian past by pointing to the continuing strength of the city's artisanal life.

Nevertheless, in focusing their attention on historic Parisian enclaves, the anarchists still confronted changes within the city's urban structure and fin-de-siècle culture. Such encounters evoked a realization that the revolutionary purpose they pursued differed from those of the past.

By 1880, Paris had been transformed in appearance and structure. Baron Georges Eugène Haussmann's project had given its new places, boulevards, monuments, and buildings a more streamlined and homogeneous character. In the process, traditional Parisian quarters fell victim to the urban metamorphosis. Neighborhoods located especially on the right bank and the western sectors lost out, their narrow, meandering alleyways swept away by the new avenues and boulevards. Most dramatically, medieval town character was displaced and the city expanded as a metropolitan area. Paris was larger than ever as its "control" now extended to such outerlying districts as Montmartre. As such changes intensified the pace of communication among Parisians, formerly enclosed localities lost their identities as distinct enclaves. Nevertheless, enough of the older city stood for a myth of Paris to flourish among those attracted to its past of crafts, local life, and revolution. Indeed, a tone of urgency regarding Parisian traditions emerged from those fearing the onslaught of rapid change. Among such devotees of Paris were anarchists who admired its revolutionary heritage— as felt, for instance, in the great quarter of Saint-Antoine, minus its now demolished famous monument, the Bastille.[4]

The anarchists felt that the unique quality of local life had contributed to Parisian centrality to the French revolutionary past in that the city's many neighborhoods were self-enclosed worlds that fostered a local sense of intimacy among their inhabitants. Kropotkin believed that such uninhibited communication among Parisians encouraged their pursuit of complete local control of political and economic matters directly concerning them, causing the great revolution of 1789.[5]

Mutuality (or communal association) marked the ideals of anarchists— most notably Kropotkin who viewed its centrality to Parisian popular life as extending back at least to the previous century. The energetic activity of a myriad of sectional clubs gave the French Revolution its vibrant, popular character, and the tendency toward intimate association reflected the people's mutual familiarity and supported their independent efforts at organizing industry and commerce on the one hand and constant conspiracies against the authorities on the other. This was especially true of the famous sans-culottes of the early 1790s who had exhibited the great strength of neighborhood clubs.[6] By 1880, the club and the barricade had attained symbolic status as revolutionary tools enabling the Parisian people to rebel during the French Revolution, the 1848 Revolution, and the Commune. Kropotkin endorsed these symbols so heartily that he held communal intimacy to be a necessary prerequisite for revolutionary action, believing that the neighborhood club and the barricade were one in possessing the power to instigate people to unite within close, intimate quarters and offer a sense of "us" versus "them." Anarchists, thus, envisioned a Romantic setting that differed from what they conceived to be the abstract backdrop of Marx's proletarian revolt. It is also evident that they were disturbed at the thought that modernizing tendencies of the late nineteenth century were besieging their mythically envisioned Paris and leaving it in danger of obsolescence.

Within this vision of French mythic history, Kropotkin and other anarchists sought to support the tradition of communal clubs and intimate discussion and its role in resisting trends toward urban anonymity. Such gatherings had obvious political overtones, but Kropotkin also felt that this atmosphere reflected Parisian economic character, which was perhaps most evident in the persistent artisanal traditions resisting the leveling effects of centralized industrialization. As he wrote:

> Paris is a great beehive where hundreds of thousands of men and women fabricate in small workshops all possible varieties of goods which require skill, taste, and invention. These small workshops, in which artistic finish and rapidity of work are so much praised, necessarily stimulate the mental powers of the producers; and we may safely admit that if the Paris workmen are generally considered, and really are, more developed intellectually than the workers of any other European capital, this is due to a great extent to the character of the work they are engaged in—a work which implies artistic taste, skill, and especially inventiveness, always wide awake in order to invent new patterns of goods and steadily to increase and to perfect the technical methods of production.[7]

The tendency toward "mutuality" was a consequence of Parisian workshops that, in turn, enhanced the quality of production. As Kropotkin described the medieval system of work, he expressed a mystique of the refined craftsmanship of the artisan—in contrast to the shoddy products issuing forth from large factories. Kropotkin believed that artisans were superior workers and sharper in their wits than their modern industrial counterparts.

Kroptkin was not completely hostile to mechanization. He believed that it promised benefits for people if carried out on a small scale that allowed for human control and intimate contacts among workers—an implicit criticism of the huge enterprises then emerging in German and American industries. In his view, Parisian neighborhoods were unique in facilitating both fine workmanship and the pursuit of social equality. The city's traditional structure gave it a status as one of the few large cities preserving the sense of community. Mutual aid and cooperation were possible among Parisian workers in ways that they were not for other metropolitan inhabitants. This meant that Paris would provide an ideal stage for anarchist communes. Kropotkin believed that Paris was a late reflection of the medieval commune in its preservation and, indeed, reinvigoration of self-governing communities—an ebbing reality elsewhere. The Italian city state and the ancient Greek polis provided other parallel models for his anarchistically inclined urban vision. The large scale of baroque cities (as initiated during the seventeenth century) eroded such intimacy and subordinated cities to nation states,[8] and nineteenth-century urban areas had become even more monstrous in their implications for those desiring the closest proximity to small-scale town living. Nevertheless, as he pointed to Paris as a model anarchist urban commune, Kropotkin looked not only to the past, he also saw much potential for industrialization to help create an equitable society in which urban and rural forces would be balanced.

Paris had changed in other ways. A variety of factors helped to account for a fivefold increase in the city's population from 1801 to 1880. The Parisian population stood at roughly two million by the latter date.[9] Immigration especially from northern provinces was also causing disturbance to Parisian neighborhoods.[10] Crowded quarters, poor housing, and urban dislocation, thus, became prevalent within the city—a reality evident as well in other large European cities of the time.

Arrondissements on the outer edge of Paris grew at the fastest rate. Most notable were the 10th, 11th, 12th, 14th, 17th, 18th, 19th, and 20th arrondissements.[11] Not surprisingly, these areas tended to have a heavy concentration of workers. While Paris was not dominated by industrial life, factories were found in greater numbers in some of the surrounding suburbs such as St. Denis, Clichy, Pantin, Aubervilliers, Puteaux, and Batignolles.[12] Textile, metallurgical, and petroleum-based industries were especially prominent.[13] Many of those employed there, however, lived in the 11th, 12th, 18th, 19th, and 20th districts. Still, as Kropotkin liked to emphasize, while Paris may have held its share of workers' quarters, it did not exemplify the modern industrial city as did Manchester or Dusseldorf.[14] The "beehive" of artisans living there enabled a medieval character to survive transformations brought on by the modern world.

This was reflected in the mentality of Parisian workers. Generally, local laborers preferred a small workplace. Few of the 98,000 workshops in the city employed more than six workers.[15] According to Kropotkin, the small scale of

Parisian factories reinforced workers' skill, freedom, and resistance against trends toward piecemeal factory work so strong elsewhere. Paris would not be dominated by anonymous, industrial settings. It would remain primarily a metropolis of government bureaucracy, commerce, culture, petty trades, and workshops—though not necessarily reflecting the strict order demanded by an anarchist like Kropotkin.

Throughout the nineteenth century Paris exerted a strong influence upon a myriad of revolutionaries fascinated with its recent tumultuous past. Alexander Herzen described his feelings about the Parisian myth as he experienced it during the 1840s— the time when he first arrived in the great city in exile from Russia.

> And so I was really in Paris, not in a dream but in reality; this was the Vendôme column and the rue de la Paix. In Paris—the word meant scarcely less to me than the word "Moscow"! Of that minute I had been dreaming since my childhood. If I might only see the Hôtel de Ville, the Café Foy in the Palais Royal, where Camille Desmoulins [the famous French Revolutionary and victim of Robespierre's reign] picked a green leaf, stuck it on his hat for a cockade and shouted "à la Bastille!" I could not stay indoors; I dressed and went out to stroll about at random . . . here was rue St. Honoré, the Champs-Elysées—all of those names to which I had felt akin for long years.[16]

Herzen's exuberance in following the revolutionary's historical map of Paris as a foreign traveler and visitor is striking. His mind and memory reverberated with the resonance of the revolutionary past as he located key landmarks. As Herzen came from Moscow, where tsarist despotism and brutality were omnipresent, he could not help but react with excitement when confronting the mythic revolutionary atmosphere of Paris, seemingly crystallized in streets and neighborhoods. In giving way to his enthusiasm, Herzen visualized the city simultaneously in a spatial and historical manner. He dedicated himself to completing the work of the revolution (as did the later anarchists studied in the next chapter), and despite intense disillusionment with the failure of 1848 and frustration at the entrenched resistance to revolutionary ideas in Russia, he continued to feel excitement from ideas formed before his first trip to the city and devoted himself to work on behalf of its seditious traditions.

The anarchists gathering in Paris also came predisposed with emotions toward the city and its famous quarters. They viewed the city's history with awe. By the fin de siècle, however, Paris was seditious in more than just a political sense. Not only were revolutionary outbursts directed against traditional social and political institutions, but Paris was also in the midst of a cultural rebellion against artistic and moral traditions. Bohemians and avant-garde artists pursued eccentric individual ways and created works of art increasingly intended to baffle and shock traditional audiences. Such efforts were undoubtedly shaped by political currents and ambiguous feelings toward the bourgeoisie.[17] However, bohemians and the avant-garde directed their revolt essentially through non-political channels. Any political effects were indirect or unintended. By the end of the century, such cultural rebels were in the public limelight and strongly influencing the anarchist movement.

The anarchists of this time, then, lived in a very complex Paris. Artisanal labor continued to flourish. Governmental, educational, and religious institutions still made official culture powerful, but oppositional social and cultural forces grew. Anarchists followed their own sets of revolutionary guidelines in opposing official institutions, influenced both by the ideals and anger of workers and by Bohemians and artists.

The term "anarchist neighborhoods" is used here only in a vague manner and does not necessarily imply majority status for anarchists among the local population. They did not even form a significant demographic component. What is suggested, however, is the reality that the temporary or permanent presence of subversives in a particular quarter influenced its character and direction. As we have seen, such subversion could be political or cultural in nature—centered around artisans and Bohemians.

Anarchists attempted to mobilize support from traditional workers and, in so doing, were highly conscious of the contrasting hues and tones of Paris. Kropotkin felt that the "beehives" of the city were model building blocks for the construction of a Parisian anarchist commune, which was a plausible reality due to the countless workshops traditionally found in the many intimate neighborhoods of the city.

Kropotkin's hopes were to be disappointed. Anarchists never succeeded in creating autonomous communes within a city being integrated and connected to a degree that threatened the local sense of separate enclaves. Instead anarchists continued to remain virtually isolated and estranged from their neighbors. Due to their inability to challenge the political structure of the Third Republic and the consolidation of capitalism, they were increasingly condemned to working within the circle. As a result, they did not succeed in bringing about radical change. The state and capitalism both grew despite the reality of anarchist stances. Still, it is noteworthy that anarchists felt more comfortable with certain types of people and chose to operate in distinct areas.

A police report of August 20, 1887 declared that at least 150 revolutionary groups existed in Paris. The report listed Blanquists, Collectivists, Possibilists, and Anarchists as the most prominent of these.[18] The information on anarchists is far from exact, but it is estimated that about fifteen anarchist groups were found in Paris between 1880 and 1900. These held collectively roughly 500 members. There were, in addition, 800 to 1,000 sympathizers.[19] Few groups endured for long. Police reported that old groups continually disappeared to be replaced by new ones.[20] The Parisian anarchist world was necessarily one of change and chaos and caused bewilderment among those attempting to comprehend it.

Such groups sought to publicize anarchist ideas. They often would emerge while responding to new issues and historical developments. One sees the same assortment of names in the gatherings and, in the forefront, the same personalities who could not resist the constant urge to speak and harangue because they coveted leadership and dominance within the movement.

There was no true sense of organization, nor a unified plan of action. As one anarchist leader, Emile Gauthier, explained, meetings were conducted for the sake of conversation and socializing.[21] Anarchist patience was thin and groups were formed spontaneously while disappearing as suddenly, leaving little trace behind. Anarchists left their greatest impression when addressing crowds at large rallies publicized by newspapers, reviews, posters, and placards.

Parisian anarchists never really organized into a movement or party beholden to a central authority. As a result, adherents were never unified under one doctrine and plan of action. Then again, one would expect much resistance from anarchists to ideas implying regimentation and compromise. Such rebels sought instead to maintain radical positions, avoiding accommodation with the established system or with the methods of other revolutionaries. Nevertheless, lack of cooperation and common action among these groups is striking. Groups were presumed to depend upon the volition of their individual adherents. Such a fact entailed a recurrent lack of concord and amiability. As will be seen, the syndicalists stood out in their call for creation of a federated union oriented around anarchist lines. They convinced certain anarchists to join their cause but also confronted a great deal of suspicion. Anarchists preferred instead to maintain their loose framework and tradition of debating views within the small meeting place.

If organization was generally wanting, Parisian anarchism still exhibited some structure—most notably in the clusters anarchists formed within distinct areas of the city. Many anarchists chose to live, work, or meet in generally crowded quarters with a heavy worker concentration. Among these were the 12th, 13th, 17th, 18th, and 19th arrondissements—ringing the northern edge of the city, close to the industrial *banlieus* (suburbs), and attracting newly arrived immigrants. Anarchists preferred these districts and seemed to echo Kropotkin's enthusiasm for the traditional character of the Parisian work world even when such settings did not completely align with his mythic image.

Other areas, however, were equally significant although for different reasons. They revealed the symbiosis between anarchists and local inhabitants that made the movement as complex and diverse as it was. Anarchism was not, after all, found in isolation but within an intricate setting where a myriad of concerns and mores coexisted.

Most notable in its complexity was the 5th arrondissement with its collection of students and Bohemians gathered in the Latin Quarter and the streets around the Panthéon. On the one hand, the words "Liberté," "egalité", "fraternité" carved on the facade of the famous mortuary monument seemed an austere remnant of the Republic of Virtue pronounced about a century earlier. The excitement generated in the area was of an intellectual, philosophical kind centering around the thought of the Enlightenment and its repurcussions and the neoclassical architecture complementing it. As the Sorbonne perfectly encapsulated the district's historic character, the students and professors gathered there during the nineteenth century gained romantic renown. It became common for reformers and revolutionaries to measure their intellect by gauging the extent to which they understood the Revolution's meaning.

There was an additional feature to the Latin Quarter. Bohemian cafes and restaurants prominently displayed absinthe-drinking and other forms of unconventional behavior. Frequenters of such establishments interested themselves less in the political rebellion encouraged nearby and more in the expressive revolution emanating from anarchist circles. Two contrasting anarchist types can be discerned—the popular, congenial, hot-tempered rebel and the "highbrow" intellectual/Bohemian. These two types made for contrasting anarchist enclaves and influenced the direction of the Parisian movement. Discussion of the locales and their inhabitants will bring into focus the mental topography of Parisian anarchism and its correspondence to the city's political and cultural terrain. At its heart was the complexity and variety central to the anarchists' immersion within the great city and to the many issues disturbing them during the late nineteenth century.

## THE LATIN QUARTER AND RUE MOEFFETARD

The first Parisian anarchist centers formed in the Latin Quarter in two stages. During the early 1880s, Emile Gauthier established several anarchist groups near the Panthéon. Consequently, in 1887, Jean Grave moved his headquarters to the famous market street, rue Mouffetard, and began editing the review, *Le Révolté* (The Revolutionary). Gauthier and Grave both made the Latin

Quarter/rue Mouffetard area central to their plans because they so esteemed its cultural and social features.

Grave came to the anarchist elite intelligentsia from a humble background. His father was a miller in Auvergne who had moved to Paris in 1857 when the young Grave was three years old. After working briefly as an apprentice to a *cordonnier* (shoemaker), Jean opened a shoe-repair business with his father. This was not to last: Jean's increasing sense of independence conflicted with his father's strict paternal authority, and the two severed their business connection.[22] From this point, Jean took to printing, which he used to supplement his own shoe repair business. Printing also brought him into further contact with letters and a continual drift into leftist political circles. As was the case with other workers drawn into the printing business, Jean became literate and entranced by political ideas. Such a literary bent would bring Grave further into opposition politics.

By 1871, father and son were reunited as republican rebels in the Paris Commune. After its suppression, Jean was imprisoned, and during that time his mother died of tuberculosis while his father disappeared without explanation. Jean confronted these tragedies directly upon his release from prison, and he faced the additional reality of poverty and hardship. From that time, he devoted himself further to radical ideas and began an active involvement in the "Parti des travailleurs" (the Workers' Party), particularly working within its anarchist wing. Grave, thus, dedicated himself to opposing the more orthodox socialists and to furthering the destruction of the state. His revolutionary path was to be taken along the anarchist margins.

At about this time, Grave befriended the famous geographer and anarchist, Elisée Reclus, whom he impressed with the depth of his rationally held convictions. Accordingly, Reclus appointed him to the editorship of *Le Révolté*—which had been launched in Geneva and then moved to Paris in 1887. In doing so, Reclus confirmed Grave's road to revolutionary prominence—a road marked by sharp turns and surprises and highlighted by the Commune experience, imprisonment, and immersion in party politics. It was Grave's engaging personality that facilitated this career move by enabling him to impress people like Reclus. Working together, the two intellectual anarchists oriented *Le Révolté* around Kropotkin's internationalist anarchism, which emphasized mutualism and community life. As a consequence, police came to regard Grave as the "right arm" of Reclus and Kropotkin and the central coordinator among all Parisian anarchist groups operating during the 1880s and 1890s. They described his headquarters at rue Mouffetard as the nerve center of the movement.[23] Grave himself considered his version of internationalist anarchism to be the purest variant of the ideology, therefore justifying his imperative that fellow anarchists learn proper theory through his publications.

Other anarchists learned to resent Grave's focal position and to instigate rebellion against it. The young Communard, Charles Malato, for instance, referred to Grave contemptuously as "the pope of rue Mouffetard"[24]—a statement not considered a compliment in anticlerical circles. Henri Zisly, a member of the nature-worshipping anarchist group, the Naturiens, accused Grave of authoritarianism.[25] Such labels expressed the anarchists' intuitive and impulsive rejection of any guidance and their innate desire to follow their own volitions.

Since several anarchists expressed suspicion about Grave, he must have attempted to impose his own imprint upon a movement spreading beyond the contours of the Kropotkin-Reclus anarchist strand and absorbing other currents of Parisian life. During the 1890s Grave criticized revisionists of the movement and scorned Fernand Pelloutier's anarcho-syndicalist movement. He was also reluctant to defend Captain Alfred Dreyfus in the court-martial for treason engineered by rival military officers with anti-Semitic motives. By then, Grave's role as the principal anarchist publicist was much in doubt, and the anarchist writer Max Nettlau attributed this to his excessive, narrowly drawn professionalism and distance from ordinary popular language.[26]

Nevertheless, Grave drew mostly upon the support and involvement of artists and writers. His publications, *Le Révolté, La Révolte* (The Revolt), and *Les Temps Nouveaux* (The New Age) included both theoretical articles (written by intellectuals in a variety of specialized fields) and artistic works. Among the artists working for Grave were Camille Pissarro, Paul Signac, and Adolphe Retté. In this way, Grave served as the most crucial link connecting revolutionary art and thought during the last two decades of the nineteenth century. Due to such prominence, Grave was imprisoned in 1894 following the wave of terrorist bombings in Paris. This was followed by the "trial of the thirty"—in which thirty anarchists were selected for prosecution, including Grave. The crackdown was followed by a general acquittal and Grave's resumption of work.

Eventually, Grave became a political moderate even to the point of supporting the French war effort in 1914. His marriage to an aristocratic woman also gave him enough financial support to sustain his publications. Of all Parisian anarchists, Grave most took on the stance of official spokesperson. Yet his position within the Latin Quarter's collegiate setting also brought him intellectual isolation from libertarians organizing elsewhere. As will be reiterated later, Grave was frustrated in attempting to steer a course for Parisian anarchism. This can only underline how fruitless it was to conceive of a central direction for a movement conceiving as its main raison d'être the rejection of all controlling agencies and the tolerance of an infinity of voices.

The Latin Quarter itself was vaster and more complex than was first apparent. In addition to a large student population, it embraced a multitude of shopowners and independent artisans who contributed to the area's commercial vitality.[27] The rue Mouffetard, meandering behind the Pantheon, was known for its busy, noisy work areas, the market there renowned as one of the best in Paris.[28] Since Grave himself originally had been a local cordonnier, he was highly conscious of the other side of life in the quarter. His goals were to enable workers to gain greater awareness of their position and to convince students and intellectuals of the importance of labor. In this way, he would connect the two worlds as Kropotkin had urged and prepare the way for vigorous collective action.[29] This may sound like the Marxist notion of "praxis" (or, "action"), but certain theoretical anarchists did believe that the masses could act to bring down the established system only through a sense of self-consciousness that was forceful enough to evoke correct action. Kropotkin and Grave continued to cling to this belief during the 1880s and 1890s. They felt it crucial to reach not only intellectuals but also workers and the *menu peuple*. Nevertheless, as Grave was to discover from his dealings with other anarchists, it was impossible to employ a universally accessible language. Anarchists could unify neither under a certain "pitch" of rhetoric nor under the same system of ideas. Intellectual theory and workers' issues were not as evidently connected to others as they were to Grave and his circle. Many compagnons were impatient with theory and thought Grave aloof, remote, and attached to elitist language.

Intellectual and aesthetic outcasts cultivating the way of life called "Bohemia" were certainly prominent to the Latin Quarter's profile. In particular, they strengthened the mythic aura of the area for those rebelling against traditional mores and expressing inclinations for the bizarre and unconventional. The poet Adolphe Retté was among those who saw potential for anarchism to serve as a vehicle and ideology to further the avant-garde's aesthetic and intellectual revolt against the Salon's tastes and to justify nonconformity at all levels.

We can gather the mental universe (if not always the physical settings) of Bohemians embarking upon their Parisian adventure. One such Bohemian, Edouard Crueuel, described the life he led after moving into an atelier on the rue St. André des Arts (near boulevard St. Michel) that cost him about two hundred francs a year. He felt that "the studio walls were delightfully dirty."[30] His goal was to live in as Spartan and austere a setting as possible in order to focus his devotion to art, letters, and the café. Crueuel believed of the Bohemians' merriment that:

> their noisy and joyous manifestations of healthy young animal life were the other side of the coin of a life of hard work, of hope, of aspiration, and often of pinching poverty and cruel self-denial. The stress upon them of many kinds is great. The utter absence of an effort to reorganize their lives

upon conventional lives is from a philosophical belief that if they fail to pose unscathed through it all, they lack the fine, strong metal from which worthy artists are made.[31]

This passage underlines both the belief in the artist's potential redemption through suffering and the self-indulgent decadence intrinsic to those seeking the artificial surroundings of Bohemia. The Bohemians' indifference to everyday concerns and comforts was manifested in their display of the most unconventional moral codes and living quarters. In pursuing this squalor-ridden lifestyle, Bohemians expressed their scorn for the bourgeoisie whose outrage they attempted at all costs to provoke. The cabaret "Le Boul' Mich" offered many such opportunities. It was:

the students' highway to relaxation. Mention of it at once recalls whirling visions of brilliant cafes, with their clattering of saveurs and glasses, the shouting of their white-aproned garçons, their hordes of gay and wicked damsels dressed in the costliest and most fashionable gowns, and a multitude of riotous students howling class songs and dancing and parading to the different cafés as only students can. This is the headquarters of the Bohemians of real Bohème, whose poets haunt the dim and quaint cabarets and read their compositions to admiring friends.[32]

One could be reading of the life within the establishments represented by Toulouse-Lautrec. Here, however, students and Bohemians display enthusiastic revelry rather than the airs of jaded cynicism exuded by the figures within Toulousse-Lautrec's field of vision—focused most acutely on Montmartre. Crueuel's stress upon "wicked damsels" and the expensive prices of their fashionable gowns seems to contradict the esteem for sparse decor. In other passages, he describes the Café d'Harcourt near the Sorbonne as the wickedest cafe in Paris and the Café Banette as highlighted by the "fluffy demi-mondaines and dusty market people" found within. The reader is struck by the apparently aimless wandering through Parisian neighborhoods intended to bring Bohemians in touch with their preferred environment—especially if dusty, wicked, or decadent. It was most important, however, to avoid conventional bourgeois appearance. Such a stress upon urban wandering parallels the image of the strolling *flâneur* (city-wanderer) described so vividly by the twentieth-century cultural critic Walter Benjamin.[33]

Nonetheless, Bohemians' class orientation was not so clear cut. Historians have pointed to nineteenth-century cafés and cabarets as disruptive settings, jarring to the sense of traditional social hierarchy. Upper and lower classes mingled there in evident defiance of cultural propriety.[34] This is certainly true of the conflicting descriptions given above. Bohemians fit into such a world though they exhibited a lack of traditional social identity. They were at home and yet out of harmony both with the bourgeoisie and the working classes. These outcasts were up-to-date on the latest trends and fashions of the upper classes and still insisted on their status as oppressed and disinherited laborers. At all times, they were borderline figures in the contemporary social world and justified their position through art and aesthetic pose.

If they belonged to neither world, Bohemians still expressed ambitions and aspirations connecting them more to the affluent than to the poor. Even their attempts at self-denial reinforced this fact. Throughout the later nineteenth century, many Bohemians chose the Latin Quarter as their home and naturally were drawn to anarchism as the political cause most providing a foundation to their calling—freedom. Bohemians were not as noted on the left bank as they were in Montmartre where so many clubs dominated by "egoists" (individuals devoted to the worship of the self) and antimodern Romantics intruded upon the turf of the local anarchists. Nevertheless, Bohemians were significant enough in Latin Quarter anarchist circles to enliven debate about the movement's true purpose.

As has already been seen, Grave's immediate locale was far from uniform. Rue Mouffetard had an artisanal character, but workers, students, and Bohemians flourished throughout the quarter in abundance. Standing out, however, was the Sorbonne and its collegiate centers. Local anarchists sought to exploit the setting by emphasizing particular slants to their views. The tone set at meetings was consistently intellectual and scholarly—despite active participation on the part of those who were less cerebrally inclined and more interested in action and violence. This same pattern is revealed on the subscription lists to Grave's reviews where intellectuals and artists seemed predominant.[35]

At the same time, however, the formation of local groups revealed great discord among district anarchists. Some were established under the guidance of Gauthier and Grave as forums for the discussion of theory and the nature of European social and economic problems. Such compagnons sought to emphasize anarchism's connection to the Workingman's International and the spirit of the mid-nineteenth century as connected to progress, science, technology, and rational discourse. They felt far removed from the excessively impulsive and volatile character of Montmartrian anarchism. Obviously, their chief address was intended for students, intellectuals, and workers. Other local anarchists, however, criticized this rational approach and accused Grave and Gauthier of aloofness from the true language of the oppressed.[36] They also questioned Grave's comprehension of the workers' true mentality and dilemmas.[37] At times, such criticism grew into a general call for action. The groups

Germinal and l'Internationaliste were composed primarily of members not inclined to prolonged theorizing and intended to counter the more moderate Vengeance.[38] Those in Germinal spoke of the need for immediate, drastic action, and their rallying-cry consisted of shouts of "dynamite."[39] The Communard and alleged incendiary Louise Michel attempted to alert such potential terrorists to the possibilities inherent in strikes as alternative methods of pursuing effective revolutionary action.[40] Ambiguous exclamations heard in meetings of l'Internationaliste reflected impatience with Vengeance. One member referred to as "Delaware" exclaimed that the latter group had remained chained to the bounds of theory for too long and that "it was time at last to occupy itself more with deeds."[41] He did not get more specific, but the possibilities were obviously tantalizing.

Other groups in the district reflected the vague aspirations of youth and evade easy categorization. Among these were La Jeunesse Cosmopolite, Les Greux, Le Tocsin, and Les Négateurs. The latter was mostly composed of students "who reject all theory and philosophy; they only want to be destroyers and dream of beginning a revolutionary movement among the unemployed."[42] Police agents considered them to be a harmless lot, capable only of indulgence in meaningless debate. In fact, the vague ambitions of these groups corresponded to the nebulous motivations of Bohemians and other unclassifiable outcasts who rallied to the anarchist cause. In attaching their dreams and thoughts to anarchism, they esteemed the Latin Quarter as the perfect setting for their travails and struggles. The complexity of the area's character, shaped by eighteenth- and nineteenth-century cultural and political currents, affected the local texture and tone of anarchism found within its boundaries. As Jean Grave attempted to capture a local audience, he found it necessary to confront the multitude of intellectual forces, aesthete-dominated cafes flourishing with the new mores, and workers' enclaves that most reflected its contemporary personality. The controlled disorder he sought threatened, in the process, to assume a dissonant quality.

## BELLEVILLE

A contrasting Parisian character was found in the right bank enclave of Belleville. Like other areas it had undergone a great degree of social and economic transformation. Traditionally, a large number of artisans and skilled laborers lived and worked in Belleville, and jewelry and bronzework ranked as the most prominent and famous local crafts. As these trades were passed down from father to son, family traditions gathered around them, giving Bellevillian artisans an elite standing among Parisian workers.[43]

By the mid-nineteenth century, however, increased competition from factories caused decreased wages and unemployment among these artisans—a reality motivating local inhabitants in 1873 to open a school of apprenticeship for the traditional crafts. In this way, they hoped to preserve and reinvigorate artisan workmanship and to maintain its centrality to Belleville. These hopes were not to be realized as the quarter continued to decline. During the period from the 1871 Commune until 1900, Belleville became known for its high rates of alcoholism, crime, prostitution, vagabondage, and begging—all consequences of increased poverty and unemployment. Although not restricted to Belleville, they caused an upsurge in the local level of distress and misery. Robberies of stores and hotels were common, and arrests increased 173 percent.[44] We can detect a transformation in the very nature of crime related to the many social and economic changes that had occurred. Vendettas and personal quarrels intrinsic to traditional Bellevillian life gave way to the modern type of anonymous crime in which strangers afflict each other.[45] This was but another instance of local familiarity being displaced by modern metropolitan anomie as envisioned by the sociologist Emile Durkheim.

Belleville was also renowned for its festive cultural life. Popular theater and vaudeville there were vibrant and active,[46] and travel guides noted the remarkable numbers of street performers including musicians, comedians, jugglers, and puppeteers.[47] Problems abounded, however, as many of these pedestrian entertainers were unable to find regular work and became a part of the "miserable." Their plight was described as:

> the hard existence of young comedians . . . paid in a derisory manner, condemned to repeat five acts each day and to play five others at night; these "declassés"; whom no one can console for their misery . . . These are the carefree Bohemians.[48]

There was no frivolity nor the joyous, self-indulgent world of the "Boul' Mich" in Bellevillian Bohemia. While the district certainly had its share of cabarets contributing to a busy night life, the particular type of intellectual and aesthetic atmosphere flourishing in the Latin Quarter was absent and reflected the social and economic desperation of its inhabitants. A large part of Belleville's population indeed lived on the margins of society. This was evident in the prevalence of obsolete occupations and in the large numbers of people forced to live on the streets. Those finding work frequently were confined to the dangerous rigors of construction, and their occupations rarely provided any security and stability.

Belleville's troubles and the nature of local events evoked a tradition of social protest. This was especially true for the area around the cemetery of Père Lachaise. Holding the remains of so many Parisians, the burial ground had more recently gained lasting notoriety when the surviving insurgents of the Commune were gunned down against the "Mur des Fédérés"(the Wall of the Commune soldiers)—an event that caused Parisians to shudder in horror when they remembered the famous urban revolution of 1871. Memories of that event still lingered and endowed Belleville with its monumental equivalent to the Latin Quarter's Pantheon. However, the mood evoked by the latter's enlightened stoic image starkly contrasted with the sense of horror and tragedy hovering above the cemetery grounds. Père Lachaise continued to inspire revolt and revenge, and its dangerous aura was intensified by the presence within its walls of many derelicts and criminals.[49]

Anarchists formed groups within the famous quarter and sought to recruit such outcasts of the "dangerous classes." They rarely were successful in gathering more than thirty or forty activists. Nevertheless, police spies pointed to cafés and halls on the rue Menilmontant, rue Belleville, boulevard Charonne (the Café de Nation), rue du Faubourg-du Temple (la Maison du Peuple), and rue de la République as regular anarchist meeting places. Les Libertaires, Les Travilleurs Communistes Libertaires, Le Drapeau Noir[50], Le Groupe Anarchiste du Père Lachaise, and Le Groupe Anarchiste de Belleville were among the more prominent anarchist groups in the area. Among other things, police agents noted that anarchists continually discussed "the legitimacy of work"—an unusual topic given the problem of local unemployment.[51]

Local anarchists quickly reacted to issues raised by leaders of the movement elsewhere. This was vividly evident during the Dreyfus Affair when Sébastien Faure's strong defense of the wrongly accused Captain Dreyfus indirectly intensified discord and acrimony among the Bellevillian anarchists. Such tension already was dividing an educated elite cadre emphasizing reason and moderation from those preferring popular vengeance focused on local animosities. The latter believed that Faure, through excessive involvement within the larger fabric of official French politics, had neglected the anarchists' mission to destroy the state and capitalism. Their view was that anarchists should only pursue goals directly relevant to the needs of Belleville's constituents and, in keeping to a revolutionary course, "inculcate within the audience a hatred of exploitation and of governments."[52] Such enthusiasts felt that Faure's pursuit of justice for a military official and downplaying of the movement's intrinsic goals would ultimately trivialize anarchist ideas emphasizing radical action intended to end poverty and social misery.

The Dreyfus Affair was one of the issues troubling not only Parisian society at the end of the century but also the anarchist movement itself. Captain Dreyfus's court-martial and imprisonment on charges of treasonous grants of military secrets to the Germans was eventually unmasked by Emile Zola in his polemic article "J'accuse" as a blatant act of injustice motivated largely by anti-Semitism and jealousy. The ensuing controversy created a highly charged emotional atmosphere and a deeply divided populace. Parisian anarchists were no different in displaying their many reactions. The range and nature of these will be examined in greater detail in chapter 3. For the purposes of this chapter, it is necessary to keep in mind the effect of rhetorical fallout from the controversy upon the structure and emotional landscape of Parisian anarchism.

This was most obvious in the opposition between extremism and moderation within Bellevillian anarchism. The Dreyfus Affair intensified these differences and helped mold them into three-dimensional form. Anarchists had already, during the 1880s, used the terms "extremism" and "moderation" to address a variety of concerns. Faure was in the forefront of "moderate" anarchists and fiercely opposed by others. At one meeting in 1887, an anarchist called Espagnac proclaimed a great disgust for the very concept of moderation. Espagnac depicted all moderating inclinations as betrayals of the *enragés,* the radical, angry revolutionaries of the previous century who most ardently pushed the sans-culottes' desires for direct democracy and vengeance. Espagnac and other Bellevillian anarchists believed that the term "compagnon" necessarily was synonymous with "enragé" and implied a radical revolutionary character consisting of intense emotional commitment and an instinctual avoidance of compromise. They resisted Faure and other "elite moderates" whom they accused of betraying radical principles by pursuing justice for a bourgeois military officer.[53]

We can detect within such rhetoric a division between Faure's intellectual anarchism and the "enraged" violent polemic of those oriented around the local club in the sans-culottian manner. The radicals resented intrusions into their affairs from a larger metropolitan force and sought control of their own movement. They were aware of the conflict between the enragés of 1793 and 1794 and the leaders of the Revolution and thought that a similar tragedy was in the making. Consistently, as they angrily denounced moderates within the movement, they emphasized the stark and deep schism in Bellevillian anarchism between elites and enragés. This condition reflected an earlier eighteenth century conflict between the sans-culottes and leaders of the Terror who had co-opted the movement. In meetings, they expressed fears that certain past episodes would be repeated. The history of Paris was, after all, entangled in the concerns of the moment and bitter divisions among a revolutionary body that had already overthrown a despotic leadership were clearly a part of that history.

Of course, this was but another instance of a revolutionary movement troubled by the contrasting aspirations of leaders and constituents. While the former attempted to shape the movement within a metropolitan and national context, the latter found comfort in the local club enclosed within the neighborhood section. They hoped to find within the club an identity and a means by which they could address their unique problems. In the case of Bellevillian anarchism, feelings were also very strong regarding the quarter's role within the context of the new Paris and the various issues relevant to its future.

## MONTMARTRE

By the end of the nineteenth century the area around place Clichy and Montmartre generated as much renown and publicity as any other in Paris. This was due both to the village-like atmosphere flourishing in "la Butte" and to the exotic cabarets exhibiting the latest Parisian social and sexual mores. Avant-garde artists stood out further as they made the area the center for their aesthetic experiments. People perceived Montmartre as removed from the main currents of Paris because of its high location at the northern end of the city and its traditional position as a pilgrimage site—for the commemoration of Christian *and* revolutionary "saints" (like Jean Paul Marat). This continued to be the case after the quarter was absorbed into the city of Paris in 1860 during the great urban changes of the Second Empire.

While divisions among elitist and popular anarchist groups distinguished the Latin Quarter and Belleville, Montmartre exhibited a complex series of anarchist movements reflecting the robust, vibrant life found there. As so many avant-garde artists lived and worked in Montmartre, it is not surprising that some were drawn to anarchism. In contrast, however, stood the variety of popular revolutionary groups reflecting the concerns of local workers. There were also groups emphasizing alternate ways of life and suggesting that atop the Butte it was possible to remove oneself from the pressures exerted by the Parisians and their false ways. It was perhaps possible in Montmartre to find harmony and composure.

Despite the general sense of economic decline in the area, Montmartre was in the forefront of public attention because of its social and cultural life during the 1890s. It was constantly in the news. The mores and popular culture flourishing there made it a center of curiosity for Parisians and outsiders. Avant garde artists and Bohemians were drawn to its offerings. A guide noted:

> Montmartre has become . . . a small city inside the large city. Despite the six floor buildings, which now rise in place of the small houses and gardens of other days, it has preserved an allure, a life, mores, an originality that you look for in vain in any other quarter of Paris.[54]

This guide's perception of six-floor buildings as "high" may seem strange when compared to twentieth century architectural standards that center around skyscrapers. Yet clearly Montmartre was unique. The Metro's presence there by 1900 did little to change that fact, although it made transportation to the center of Paris so much easier and faster.[55]

The presence there of so many small proprietors and artisanal workers was striking and reinforced Montmartre's village atmosphere.[56] Many changes had occurred, however, during the century and had altered the area's character. To begin, its incorporation into Paris had meant loss of status as an independent town and amalgamation into a large, modern metropolis.[57] Just ten years following its inclusion into Parisian history, Montmartre, as one of the strongholds of Commune rebels, was the setting for bloody, bitter battles fought by surviving Communards in a losing cause against the troops of Adolphe Thiers's provisional government. Consequently, the quarter assumed a position within the revolutionary history of the city to which it had so recently been attached and, through the mere mention of its name, could arouse emotions approaching those surrounding the Bastille or place de la Révolution. During the last two decades of the century, Montmartre emerged as an area of extravagant behavior and crime.[58] The bourgeoisie and Bohemians gathered in smoke-filled cabarets reeking of alcohol while the problems of unemployment and crime ran rampant outside the walls of pleasure.

Nevertheless, the continued strength of an artisan population marked Montmartre's complex life even more vividly. The radical journalist Emile Pouget inspired a social anarchist movement unique to the Butte.[59] This interesting figure had been born in Pont-de-Salars in the Averyron in 1860 into a family that was bourgeois both in its economic status and its mentality. The father was a notary. At age fifteen, Pouget worked in a small shop in Paris and was influenced by radical republican ideas in circulation following the Commune. In 1878, he helped establish a union of textile workers and began participating in workers' revolutionary movements. After attending a meeting of the International in London in 1881, Pouget returned an anarchist.

Pouget's first public prominence as an anarchist came two years later when he and Louise Michel led a demonstration at les Invalides to protest the exploitation of workers and mass unemployment. As this episode occurred at the famous military school holding Napoléon Bonaparte's sarcophagus, both the press and the police immediately interested themselves in the leaders of the march. Michel and Pouget were arrested, and a police search of the latter's house ended in the discovery of chemical explosives.[60] This incident and others revealed Pouget's concern for the precarious position of artisanal workers in modern conditions and his endorsement of radical action, even violence, to remedy the situation. In assuming an anarchist stance, Pouget echoed the movement's esteem of traditional, nonindustrial crafts and, in this case, especially Montmartre's cabinetmakers, shoemakers, carpenters, and textile workers. The historian Max Nettlau contrasted Pouget's vision of unions to that of his British counterparts by pointing to the anarchists' hopes to destroy the state through threatening, violent positions and British labor's use of organization and strikes to achieve bargaining positions for wage increases.[61] This inclination would lead Pouget in the direction of the syndicalist position pushed so powerfully by Fernand Pelloutier and others.

Pouget's most famous anarchist involvement was derived from his journalistic bent. He used newspapers and pamphlets to express ideas directly addressed to workers' demands. In 1889, he commenced work on *Père Peinard* (Father Peinard)—a review that was published in Montmartre and modeled upon the prominent and notorious newspaper of the French Revolution *Père Duchesne* (Father Duchesne). As Nettlau nostalgically wrote, *Père Peinard* was

> an anarchist paper, which closely approached popular sentiment, and by Pouget's consciousness of the movement of ideas, by intelligent social and political criticism, his review resembles the great voice of the French Revolutionary press . . . Pouget was converted into the Marat of anarchy and like Marat, Blanqui, Proudhon, and Varlin, I considered him one of the most intelligent minds of French socialism, one of the rarer men who really wanted popular revolution.[62]

Pouget attempted for five years to raise the level of workers' resentment and anger by printing works filled with violent rhetoric. He carried out this task largely through the adoption of workers' slang and illustrated caricature. In his use of the latter, Pouget was the first anarchist journalist to employ artists. Regarding his enthusiasm for slang, Félix Dubois noted that Pouget's ordinary penchant was for standard French. However, he was resourceful in exploiting street language in order to attract the notice of the working classes who found a source of inspiration and sympathy in his rhetoric.[63]

Police considered Pouget a dangerous and violent man who fostered corresponding traits among his "coreligionnaires" (fellow worshippers).[64] In supporting their assessment, they pointed to Pouget's seeming delight in advocating violence—both verbally and pictorially. Certainly, he made no attempt to disguise his denunciations of the military and of capitalism. Pouget endorsed violence as a necessary revolutionary tool and, because of this position, like other anarchists, he was compelled to leave for Britain during the famous police crackdown of 1894. While residing there, he became fascinated with the possibilities offered by trade unions for revolutionary action and, upon returning to Paris, decided to focus his energy upon workers' organizations. However, as already noted, Pouget was dissatisfied with the reformist aims of British unions and wished to maintain anarchists' strict adherence to the French revolutionary tradition and the demands of Parisian artisans.

From this point, Pouget urged workers to join the emerging syndicalist movement and published such sentiments in his reviews. The same immersion into workers' issues that had inspired him to become an anarchist in the first place was now pushing him to join Pelloutier's cause. Other anarchists such as Jacques Prolo and Grave would condemn syndicalism because of its apparent attachment to organization and structure. They would opt for immediate, violent mass actions. Nevertheless, Pouget's success in reaching workers' emotions through anger-provoking slang made him less suspect than other syndicalists. At the same time, he succeeded in furthering Montmartre's importance as a workers' district and in publicizing the anarchist cause throughout Paris.

Montmartre, however, was famous for activities evading easy political classification. Bohemians felt the area's nightlife to be the most interesting and bizarre in Paris. The Moulin Rouge was celebrated for its great liveliness intensified, no doubt, by the mutual associating and mingling within of people of diverse backgrounds. Such clubs contributed to the blurring of social boundaries demarcating both class and "proper" conduct as popular classes and the bourgeoisie stood and drank next to each other. Drunkenness and promiscuity flourished in such settings, and cabarets only differed in the degree to which they advertised their temptations. (An already high rate of prostitution was evident in the quarter.)

Crueuel described the Moulin Rouge, marked by its novel electrical lighting, as a refuge for diversion-seeking artists. "The poets of Bohemia were there, and gayly attired 'cocottes' assisted them in their fun at the café tables." Artists such as Toulouse-Lautrec, experimenting with the latest styles, used the setting to express ironic amusement at the ways of Parisian society. Crueuel described the ritual bacchanal of the Moulin Rouge that:

> was indeed a wild scene of joyous abandonment, and from an artistic point of view grand, a luminous point in the history of modern times. Here were the life, the color, the grace of the living picture with a noble background of surrounding temples, altars, statues—a wonderful spectacle, that artists can understand and appreciate.[65]

Bohemians could set aside their ordinary inclinations for severe, Spartan settings and suddenly embrace a world filled with sensation-stimulating objects and backdrops. The Moulin Rouge seemed to embody all the outrageous, frivolous, and promiscuous currents running through Parisian life and endowed them with a ritual character. Nonetheless, it did not quite capture them all. The cabaret emphasized celebration and joy in contrast to the Café du Néant, which was more focused upon macabre and supernatural themes. This strange establishment was influenced by contemporary spiritualist movements centered around theosophy that were found both in Paris and London. Conversations in the "Néant" (meaning "nothing") mostly consisted of musings on ghosts, hauntings, and death. Seances were commonplace occurrences there—although with an unknown degree of success! The café's setting suggested a mortuary with coffins providing the tables upon which drinks were served. "Spirits," thus, flourished in an ambiguous world of double entendre. Images and depictions of spirits and devils lurked on the enveloping walls and reinforced belief in the supernatural's omnipresence.[66] Crueuel's final assessment of Montmartre focuses upon its bizarre, extreme Bohemian form. It was a place, he felt, that had gone too far:

> Montmartre presents the extravagant side of Parisian Bohemianism. If there is a thing to be mocked, a convention to be outraged, an idol to be destroyed, Montmartre will find the way. But it has a taint of sordidness that the real Bohemianism of the Latin Quarter lacks—for it is not the Bohemianism of students.[67]

Even for those dedicated to the Bohemian way, there was such a thing as excess. Some discerned amidst all of the tumult and eccentricity a genuine standard for regulating their conduct. It was best represented by the idealized austere and restrained ways of students in their unconventional devotion to aesthetic ends. Bohemianism and anarchism were, in fact, parallel both in attracting nonconforming individuals from all walks of life and in placing nebulous bounds around their "proper" ways. Their shared challenge was to provide social expression for such vigorous currents of nonconformity.

The complexity of life in Montmartre made the quarter ideal for the flourishing of excessive and infinite varieties of behavior. Those accustomed to the more intellectual setting of the Pantheon and Sorbonne areas expressed shock and dismay. They believed that Montmartre had become too removed from conventional life and saturated with too much destructive energy. The Butte and its surroundings were special to Paris. Even those segments of society attracted to it were unable to classify the area. Nevertheless, this only held for pockets within Montmartre. In fact, a great deal of continuity was also present there, and anarchists did not neglect that fact. As noted above, Pouget fostered the growth of a workers' anarchist movement in acknowledging the traditional artisan sector still holding sway in areas adjoining the cabarets and nihilistic cafes. Anarchists living and organizing in Montmartre and vicinity took on the shades and tones of the contrasting local ways. Consequently, dichotomies and juxtapositions noted there were even more striking than in other sections of Paris, and Montmartrian anarchists were torn between the social and aesthetic sides of their movement far more than their compagnons in the Latin Quarter or Belleville were. They were a different lot altogether.

As an avant-garde center, Montmartre enticed anarchists immersed in the advanced culture of the age. This was true both of artists and critics. During the fin de siècle and the "belle epoque," the area became synonymous with experiments in the pictorial arts revealing new modes of perception. For instance, Cubism, as later created simultaneously by Pablo Picasso and Georges Braques, was in the forefront of such movements. Picasso himself lived and worked in Montmartre and publicized the Butte as a center for artistic innovators who confronted a sneering public unable to understand, even remotely, their efforts.[68] Montmartre seemed to offer all of the support of mutual communication and accepted mores needed by such artists. Anarchists in the area were, thus, exposed to the wide variety of culture emanating from the meandering streets intersecting it. Politics, culture, and art there were highly volatile, and their exponents approached revolutionary positions within their respective visions—sometimes meeting on common ground, oftentimes not.

Individual anarchists attracted to the possibilities for artistic or political revolt lived in Montmartre, refusing to become a part of any official group or movement. Such a figure was the important art critic Félix Fénéon. This enigmatic figure was originally from Turino, Italy, having been born there in 1860 to a father working as an advertising agent, a copyist, and a traveling salesman and a Swiss mother formerly employed in a Burgundian post office. Félix Fénéon attended the Ecole Normale in Cluny in 1877 and 1878 but never completed his studies, deciding to enroll instead at the Lycée Lamartine in the Mâcon where he met the future art critic Georges Lecomte.[69] Lecomte would eventually be an enthusiast for Post-Impressionist art and an admirer in particular of Camille Pissarro's work.

In 1889, Fénéon embarked on a paradoxical phase of his life when he entered the military and passed an examination for a bureaucratic position in the War Ministry—a post that was not too out of line with the professional background of his family. Soon afterward, he moved to Paris where he worked for the next thirteen years in that governmental department. He would eventually live on rue Lépic situated in Montmartre.

Fénéon's life between 1880 and 1894 was filled with strangely contrasting experiences. While working diligently and regularly at the War Ministry, he also became an anarchist and immersed himself in the art of the avant-garde. It was certainly not unusual for one to be drawn into such circles in Montmartre, but Fénéon's choice of career made him atypical as either an aesthete or an anarchist.

Fénéon became familiar with the new artists through friendships formed with the critics Jules Christophe and Louise Denise. They especially acquainted Fénéon with the works of Impressionists and Symbolists. From this newborn enthusiasm, Fénéon cultivated a unique point of view and began writing art criticism. He also began to dress like a dandy and to emulate the "decadent" manner, expressing pessimism and unconventional mores publicized so famously earlier in the century by Charles Baudelaire.[70]

His writing career progressed to the point where in 1884 he founded his own journal—*La Revue Independante* (the Independent Review)—and devoted it to the new artistic styles. Fénéon also wrote for other reviews of the time such as *Entretiens Politiques et Littéraires* (Political and Literary Dialogues) *l'Endehors* (From the Outside) and *Père Peinard* (in the pages of which he displayed an astute sense of slang). He further worked as the editor of *La Revue Blanche* (the White Review).

One striking feature of Fénéon's writing was his reliance upon a host of pseudonyms behind which he hid to express his unorthodox opinions. At the same time, it was never too difficult to discover the author's identity—especially when hinted at by "F.F." These publications were all anarchist in orientation, but Fénéon focused his attacks on the artistic establishments that refused to support painters he championed such as Georges Seurat.

Fénéon's desire to connect political and cultural trends is of further interest. Exemplifying this fact is the great influence he had upon Neo-Impressionists like Paul Signac, Maximilian Luce, and Camille Pissarro. As a critic immersed in both art and politics, Fénéon evoked political responses from such figures, and it was striking how many of the leading artists within Neo-Impressionism (also known as pointillism) were anarchists.[71] They also struggled with the problem of relating their rebellion against the Salon to their opposition against the capitalist order and the state. As will be seen in Chapter 4, these figures were unclear about the degree of symbiosis necessary for a healthy balancing of the two revolts.

Fénéon himself was not a mere intellectual anarchist who wished to avoid direct involvement. He knew the terrorist Emile Henry and was suspected of having stored in his apartment the explosives used in the infamous bombing that Henry carried out.[72] In her work on Fénéon, Joan Halperin has suggested that the aesthete, in fact, threw a bomb into a restaurant and that the subsequent explosion caused several injuries including irreparable damage to the eye of Laurent Tailhade—a fellow libertarian writer.[73] The irony involved in this incident provoked countless journalistic comments. In the trial of the thirty in 1894, Fénéon was charged with housing explosives and with performing terrorist acts. However, the critic was acquitted after a series of uproarious exchanges with prosecutors when his biting sarcasm was put to good use.

It is clear from reading Fénéon's work that his anarchist commitment originated in enthusiasm for the avant-garde's rebellion. Such hatred and contempt for the Salons are evident in his statement:

> we should applaud a conflagration that should cleanse the Luxembourgian stables if there were not in that museum a collection of documents indispensable for future monographs on the stupidity of the nineteenth century.[74]

This passage, focusing upon the Luxembourg Museum (adjoining the famous gardens) and its tradition of rejecting avant-garde art, reveals the ire, passion, and "explosive" humor of the man who worked so regularly and nonchalantly at the War Ministry.

Artists, in responding to the different facets of Fénéon's personality and gaining inspiration to pursue their work, accepted his call for rebellion. Given the general hostility with which most critics and the public greeted their work, such artists appreciated his ardor and wit as he defended their cause. Pissarro, for instance, felt that Fénéon's laughter at "the expense of the bourgeoisie" was invaluable to his work.[75]

Like other Bohemians, Fénéon comes across as Walter Benjamin's symbolic flâneur.[76] He drifted through all sectors of Paris keeping his official position distinct from his more enthusiastic involvements. Beneath the facade of the bureaucrat, lurked the enigmatic dandy, art critic, and anarchist. Fénéon was accustomed to juggling these contrasting roles as he pursued his multifaceted life. If he did not commit any terrorist act (a question about which there is yet no sure answer), he certainly did not recoil in horror at expressing the language of terrorism. He connected avant-garde art to anarchism and believed the two to be the most advanced "creative" movements of the nineteenth century. Fénéon viewed both as simultaneously furthering the search for social justice and new aesthetic standards. As the art historian John Rewald later wrote:

> Fénéon was an anarchist. All his friends were anarchists at heart, Signac and Pissarro, Kahn and Tailhade, Luce and Regnier and Lecomte; so had been Seurat. How could they accept without protest a social order . . . in which the artist had no real place, in which he had to struggle all his life for recognition, in which the role of the bourgeoisie went to reaction in politics and in art as well?[77]

Fénéon connected the two areas of commitment central to Parisian anarchism: rebellion against institutions and devotion to elusive nonconformity. He viewed the surrounding world both through the lens of social protest and of Bohemian dandyism while restricting himself to neither. This confirmed for him an air of mystery and wonder. As such an unclassifiable figure, Fénéon seemed to embody the anarchists' most fundamental aim—freedom—and, in this role, he presented an individual challenge to the established order as loudly as did his more group-oriented compagnons.

Other pockets of anarchists were also found within Montmartre, and their role in intensifying the level of debate on relevant issues will be discussed in chapter 3. Sébastien Faure was deeply influenced by the social vision espoused by Pouget, and for that reason he first worked in the Montmartrian world. Nevertheless, he moved away from Pouget's social radicalism and focused instead on concerns of individual justice and liberty.

Placed like an unexpected object within a cubist collage painting, the puzzling anarchist group Les Naturiens was also situated in Montmartre under the guidance of Henri Zisly. While Montmartre was complex enough already, Zisly and his cohorts there pursued anarchism in relative isolation and without much reference to other Parisian groups. Their presence in Montmartre only served to baffle those attempting to decipher the entire range of the phenomenon.

Influenced by the ideas of Charles Fourier and Jean-Jacques Rousseau, Zisly not only loathed cities and industrialization, but also civilization itself. He expressed this worldview within the largely amorphous setting of Montmartre. The quarter's ambiguity assumed a different form for Zisly. While located on the fringes of metropolitan Paris, Montmartre also seemed like a distinct enclave with an antique, rustic charm. It still resembled a village, and Zisly found it a convenient setting for proclaiming his conscious preference for pre-civilized humanity.

The implications of this lifestyle option would cause angry exchanges with other anarchists who decided that, after all, there were several advantages to be gained from civilization. Police referred to Zisly's Naturiens as the *Sauvagistes*. In fact, the Naturiens were but one facet of the Romantic, nature-loving movement found elsewhere in Europe during the 1890s. Within a decade, the German *Wandervögel* (wandering birds) organized excursions into nature in hopes of developing and reinvigorating the German *Volk*.[78] Racial identity and mythology, however, were not the issues here. The Naturiens pushed for a more radical retreat from cities, industrialization, and civilization. At the same time, the movement was fostered in the midst of Montmartre and Paris, not in a desolate wilderness or a rural commune. The Naturiens' rejection of modernization was expressed uncomfortably in a setting made possible only by forces set in motion by it. The positions they assumed, therefore, could only seem puzzling and counterproductive to other libertarian activists who sought revolutionary goals but not a dismantling of civilization.

The Naturiens' limited contacts with other anarchists were confined to the Libertarires and Pouget's circle. They especially embraced Pouget's violently-inclined rhetoric. Otherwise, they existed as a distinct pocket of cultural resistance within Montmartre.[79] Like the Bohemians of this area, the Naturiens maintained a pose of social defiance embodied in their eccentric community within the Butte's confines. Nevertheless, as indicated above, they were never accepted by the anarchist Parisian establishment but remained on the extreme margins of the movement—just as they lived on those of Paris. Theirs was a constant state of struggle and antagonism with anarchist leaders like Grave, whom they considered an elitist.

In addition to the various cafés and cabarets catering to the many varieties of Montmartrian diversion and entertainment, others were centered around political subversion. Among the cabarets singled out by police spies as notorious centers of rebellion and sedition were Chat Noir and Café de Conservatoire where the famous singer Xavier Privas performed.[80] Privas was known for, among other things, his lyrical social commentary on the lives and experiences of Parisian garment workers.[81] The bitter criticism expressed in his songs made them powerful weapons for opponents of the social and political establishment.

In addition, the Cabaret du Chat Rouge on the rue de l'Ouest was a favorite meeting place for artists and anarchists wishing to congregate in a place offering coffee, alcohol, and seditious song. (It also seems evident that cats of various colors attained symbolic status as culturally subversive rebels, given the number of clubs attached to the name "chat.") At first, police saw the Chat Rouge as a center of "dangerous libertarians"; however, they later concluded that the anarchists meeting there were largely harmless and not prone to violence.[82] Nevertheless, police had to take note of the potentially dangerous emotions stirred by a spontaneous performance of the song "Dame Dynamite." Music had ways of yielding actions through the power of inspiration. Perhaps the French could especially understand this as they remembered the effects of the "Marseillaise" during the French revolutionary wars when the tide of war was turned against invading Austrian and Prussian armies. Even songs with more subtle themes could provoke violence. All of this meant that police spies had to be vigilant in surveying the various cafes of Montmartre, even betraying excessively paranoid inclinations.

Within the world of Parisian anarchism, Montmartre and its environs certainly offered the greatest number of categorical gradations. This was due to the complexity of life in and around the Butte. While the anarchists of Belleville and the Latin Quarter were divided along elitist and popular lines, the Montmartrian movement was intersected by a network of political, cultural, and artistic subversive currents evoking the sense of a world spinning out of control. As the poet William Butler Yeats would state a few decades later "the center does not hold." This does not seem surprising for a movement basing itself upon individual initiative and suspicion of authority. Yet as noted already, anarchists like Grave did attempt to impose some sense of shape and structure on the groups they organized.

While Belleville was marked by the decline of its traditions, Montmartre was truly in the forefront of Parisian culture and seemed to be leading the way into the next century. Artistic prominence there and the flourishing of cabarets gave Montmartre an air of innovation and vitality. At the same time, traditional crafts remained strong in the quarter and generated an impetus to workers' organizations. Pouget, thus, found a strong base of support among the artisans living and working in the vicinity.

Montmartre's contemporary image was formed by the unique combination of old and new forces flourishing alongside each other. Art and social mores cast an aura of modernity over the quarter, but traditional ways of work and street culture remained strong and ensured continuity with the past. These complexities affected the organization of anarchism itself as a symbiotic relationship across vague boundaries developed between culture and politics. Such ambivalent anarchistic tones were perhaps nowhere more dramatically evidenced than in the life and example of Félix Fénéon noted above.

More than other modern political movements, anarchism has been unsuccessful in presenting a united front. Political, labor-related, and national factors worked to divide anarchism in its ideology and organization and to impair its effectiveness as a movement. The divisions were obvious even at the neighborhood level in Paris during the fin de siècle. Social, economic, cultural, and intellectual forces evident within each arrondissement affected the anarchists' attempt to form a base. While such organizers wanted to forge a citywide movement, they worked alongside local compagnons with ideas of their own—for instance, the need to address local concerns like unemployment, inflation, and taxation.

At the same time, differences in social and educational background surfaced as locals tended to distrust the motives of those they regarded as a literate, cosmopolitan elite. If such an elite was able at times to enhance the sense of a Paris-wide anarchist movement, the reality was that local problems and cultural phenomena such as Bohemia and cabarets limited the extent of this possibility. Consequently, anarchist groups were ensconced and self-enclosed within particular locales. This was but an indication of the difficulties faced by anarchists in organizing in a city both traditional and modernizing at the same time. Such was Paris.

## 2

# Anarchists and the Parisian Revolutionary Tradition

As seen above, Parisian anarchist intentions and goals differed in how they reflected the complex facets that composed contemporary Parisian culture and politics. Additionally, however, the great city's past cast a large shadow over anarchists' efforts and molded the direction of the movement. If there was a theme that anarchists had to echo continually it was that of revolution. After all, revolution was the one ideal and goal central to anarchists—at least on the surface. The Great Revolution (as entitled by Peter Kropotkin) had taken its place alongside the monarchy and the Catholic Church as one of the principal historical forces in Paris and absorbed anarchists' zeal as it had that of other radical movements. Unlike many reformist socialists of the time, anarchists still believed that revolution was inevitable and crucial for the establishment of their ideals. Perhaps they could never agree upon the time when revolution would sweep away the vestiges of the capitalist, statist order, but libertarians felt that its leveling results and destructive forces would provide the only means by which their envisioned egalitarian, just society could emerge. Consequently, anarchists dedicated themselves to revolution, doing everything to promote its development and to hasten its occurrence. Their main passion and devotion was to revolution, even when it seemed more of an abstraction than a pending reality. As Mikhail Bakunin wrote:

> The revolutionary is a man under vow. He ought to occupy himself entirely with one exclusive passion: the Revolution. . . . He has only one

aim, one science: destruction . . . . Between him and society, there is war
to the death, incessant, irreconcilable.[1]

Such rhetoric was irresistible and had an enduring allure for subsequent
anarchists. Bakunin's view underlines the anarchist devotion to revolution,
which, at times, seemed to place the need for destruction above the nature of
specific goals. In any case, it could be assumed that no matter the result of the
revolution, the consequences would be positive because the path would be
cleared of oppression and inequality. This nineteenth-century view now seems
naive to current cynical observers of more recent revolutionary cataclysms.
Nevertheless, it reflects the aspiration for progress—among all circles—linked
to the mentality of the age. Some anarchists believed that social upheaval would
be beneficial because it would yield a utopian new order. It would provide a
cleansing and purification rite essential for the emergence of paradise. On the
other hand, many within the movement took a more cautious view and pointed
to the continual work that would need to be performed in the wake of the
revolution. It was evident that the complexity underlying Parisian anarchism
would affect its constituents' esteem for revolution.

Anarchists viewed the subject against the background of a century of
revolutionary activity and failure—a span long enough to engender a sense of
tradition and myth. "Scientific" and "realistic" explanations were bound to such
a heritage. Karl Marx had interpreted the French Revolution of 1789 as
bourgeois and a conclusive defeat of the feudal, aristocratic order. If the
bourgeoisie had ended aristocratic practices and prejudices (not necessarily a
completely accurate assessment of European society after 1815),[2] the capitalist
order created new inequities and exploitation. Marx believed that such realities
as the oppressive and brutal enslavement of the proletarian class complemented
capitalist industrial production. He also felt that the proletariat would acquire
increasing consciousness of its position, destroy the capitalist bourgeois order
in a revolution of its own making, and pave the way for a new era of equality
and justice. The Marxist view was that revolution was inevitable because of the
horrendous social and economic conditions imposed by capitalists.

Anarchists viewed the past a bit differently. They also believed that their
revolutionary tradition descended from all others and that it would correct
these revolutions' failures. Nevertheless, they pointed to different aspects of
those past events and stressed their most appealing features. Thus, they
depicted 1789 as the year of bourgeois triumph but 1793 as the time when
the popular classes made their deepest imprint upon the revolution. Socialist
and anarchist commentators perceived similar patterns in the developments
of 1848 and 1871.

Anarchists, however, did not believe that revolutions necessarily had to occur in stages. They criticized the Marxist pattern's emphasis on the determining role of historical and economic conditions in limiting or expanding the scale of rebellions. In contrast, anarchists believed that revolutions could succeed at any time if accidental circumstances were right. From our vantage point, a thin line may separate such accidental circumstances from historical determinants. It could also be a matter of semantics. Still, anarchists held fast to their view that revolutions were not dialectically ordained as Marx had stated and that their failures were avertible. Furthermore, anarchists did not believe the proletariat to be the only essential agent in revolutions. They also sympathized with peasants, traditional craftsmen, and individual shopkeepers and envisioned major revolutionary roles for them. Anarchists, thus, were enthusiastic in mobilizing such groups and countering the scorn cast their way by Marx.

The years 1789, 1793, 1848, and 1871 provided many lessons for later nineteenth-century revolutionaries desiring to carry on these revolutions' frustrated work. An accumulation of events that anarchists passionately attached to these years had also created a mythic revolutionary atmosphere. In their enthusiasm for the romantic, rebellion-inspiring myth, few revolutionaries would have questioned the relevance of these lessons to their own aspirations. Parisian anarchists of the 1880s and 1890s depicted the drama inherent in these years as part of a historical web needing further scrutiny. In doing so they intended not only to further knowledge but also to create historical connections to the past. Several compagnons actually had participated in either the 1848 or the 1871 upheaval (or known others who had) and had access to powerful memories of struggle and sacrifice. They sought to communicate their emotions to younger rebels whose subsequent enthusiasm, élan, and determination would find them a place in this heroic process.

Historians have often discussed the effect of the "great" French Revolution upon other French popular revolts of the nineteenth century. Stewart Edwards has noted that in its reliance upon revolutionary festivities and diverse social groups, the Commune of 1871 "belonged more to the past tradition of Paris revolutionaries than presaging the industrial struggles of the future."[3] Richard Cobb has focused upon the influence of the sans-culottes upon revolutionary movements of the nineteenth century—both in the sense of their serving as a political model and in their evocation of revolutionary celebration. Cobb feels that the revolution left:

> the example of the Revolutionary Passion Play . . . . During the Commune, there were pseudo-Heberts, the communards had discovered *hébertisme*, they had not rediscovered *sans-culottisme*; but among the *fédérés,* there

were many who preached the olde *sans-culottes* remedies . . . and believed too in the same myths.[4]

Cobb refers here to Jacques Hébert—the leader of one of the radical popular factions in 1793. In another vein, Mona Ozouf has written about the importance of festivals and rites during the French Revolution.[5] Nineteenth-century revolutionaries attempted to reenact that era's famous scenes because they constantly sought a place within the national revolutionary tradition.[6] Cobb points also to the flourishing number of clubs during 1848 and 1871 and the subsequent demands for local and decentralized "direct democracy." He concludes that "the most permanent memorial to the poor *sans-culottes* was the evocation and the habit of violence. It was as if future generations had taken them literally, when they had spoken with threats and bluster."[7] Recurrent revolutionary outbursts had, thus, become ingrained within a long political and theatrical tradition.

If one wished to point to the Revolution of 1789 as the origin of later revolutionary activity, discourse, and proclivities toward violence, then the anarchists were part of such an inheritance. Not only can their words and actions be viewed at times as having been consciously or unconsciously modeled upon the aura of the French Revolution, but also they frequently attempted to justify their works in terms of this tradition. Bakunin himself had proclaimed the goals of that upheaval to be his own:

> What we demand is the proclamation anew of this great principle of the French Revolution, that every man must have the material and moral means to develop all his humanity, a principle which, according to us, is to be translated into the following problem: To organize society in such a fashion that every individual, man or woman, coming into life, shall find as nearly as possible equal means for the development of his or her different faculties and for their utilization by his or her labour.[8]

More than Marx, Bakunin believed that many political goals of 1789 were still relevant to his time. While Marx and his followers updated revolutionary demands, Bakunin (among other anarchists) justified his own in terms of a past still endearing to him. He was a Romantic looking back to another age.

Anarchists emphasized different aspects of the revolution and imbued them with a positive character. Much discussion at anarchist meetings concerned completion of the work begun in 1793.[9] This was in keeping with anarchist ideals since 1793 had been the year when the sans-culottes worked hardest to inaugurate popular vengeance against the aristocrats, the monarchs, and "enemies of the Revolution" such as the Girondins. Maximilien Robespierre had exploited popular sentiment to expel the Girondins from the National Convention, thus enabling the Jacobins to head a one-party state. Soon thereafter, he created the Terror to combat the national emergency posed by foreign invasions and counterrevolutionary insurrections in the Vendée, Lyons, Marseilles, and other centers. For some time, it was possible to envision parallel purposes for the sans-culottes and the Terror, but it was most notable that Robespierre and the Committee of Public Safety had used power to crush the former. The Terror was used just as much (if not more so) against revolutionaries endeavoring to push their cause in a more egalitarian direction as it was against aristocrats, monarchists, and other foes. A great many members of the sans-culottes had become victims of the guillotine. Nevertheless, this did not prevent Parisian anarchists a hundred years later from stressing the democratic and just facets of the Terror. Time had blurred the boundaries between the types of executions carried out by the "national razor."

Despite their realization that the French Revolution had not succeeded in establishing liberty, equality, and fraternity, anarchists continued to believe that it had, nonetheless, created the spark igniting nineteenth-century upheavals that would topple the capitalist order. In this way, the work of the past would be completed. Jean Grave pointed to the reality of capitalist dominance of the Revolution as evident in the National Assembly's issuance of the "Declaration of the Rights of Man and Citizen"—a document enshrining property and enabling the bourgeoisie to thwart momentum toward more radical change.[10] Despite this reality, Grave believed that the arduous efforts to achieve direct democracy and social reconstruction in 1793 would ultimately and successfully be revived.[11] He stated that the same enemies were still present since many Third Republic political officials and businessmen had descended from people who had frustrated the sans-culottes.[12] In overthrowing the power of such figures, anarchists in the next revolution would not only be acting in support of the "miserable" of the late nineteenth century, but also helping to redress the past. It then would be clear that bourgeois, authoritarian forces did not have permanent, inevitable power and were quite vulnerable before a popular uprising that would transform the entire nature of time and history.

Grave seems to have accepted the Marxist perception of the French Revolution as a stage in the consolidation of bourgeois power. Unlike Marx, Grave did not believe that the results of the Revolution had been caused inevitably by economic forces. Marx stressed that economic realities had determined the relative failure of past popular movements—the sole purpose of which was to serve as a foundation for the great future revolution destined to conclude history. Grave, in contrast, viewed with promise the waves of crowd action evident between 1789 and 1794. At the same time, he and other libertarians did not think that the future course of revolutionary action needed guidance either from a unified workers' party or by a temporarily imposed omnipotent state that Marx and his followers had emphasized as a necessity for proper action. Grave always viewed the people as the only agents for change and condemned any governmental usurpation of their power.

Libertarians instead idealized the revolutionary clubs of 1793, 1848, and 1871 as the true forces of insurrection and sought to emulate them.[13] They saw in such gatherings the correct combination of cohesion and freedom of action. At the same time, revolution resulted in the "absence of a strong government" and the acquisition of power by people organized at the neighborhood level to act simultaneously from many different directions.[14] Anarchists believed that the true realization of liberty, equality, and fraternity depended upon revolutionary action aimed at ending all centralized authority. A further level needed to be attained—anarchy.[15] This process entailed the creation of a federalist and localized society of small communes working together according to Kropotkin's notion of mutual aid and harmony. If the frustrated work of 1789-1793 were to be recommenced, libertarians needed to resurrect the Parisian revolutionary clubs. This point raises another key difference separating anarchists and Marxists—the interpretation of the Revolution. Both agreed that it held great significance for the future. Anarchists, however, were far more romantically disposed and emphasized their place in an unbroken tradition begun in 1789 and still needing completion. Marxists scorned this view and stressed the need for workers' to concentrate upon the needs of contemporary reality. A new economic and political system had emerged from the French Revolution, and there was no question of nostalgically looking back. Rather, the traditions attached to 1789 were inherently flawed and had to be destroyed and transcended by proletariat revolution. In contrast, anarchists romanticized the Revolution and portrayed Hébert, Gracchus Babeuf, even Robespierre, among others, as martyrs whose sacrifices still inspired their nineteenth-century counterparts.[16]

While some libertarians viewed themselves in the context of the past, others sought to project the structures and feelings of the earlier period onto the present. For one, they continued to refer to the calendar of the French Revolution. The *Père Peinard Almanach* (Father Peinard Almanach), with its division of the year into the months made famous by the radical phase of the Revolution rather than those of the Gregorian calendar, most publicized this tendency.[17] Its creators, thus, attempted to instill among compagnons the notion that the origin of modern times could be equated with the initial destruction of the Bourbon monarchy. Anarchists felt all the more fervently the meaning of the Revolution since they were bound to it as part of an unfolding myth binding together related events. Memories of Prairial directly stirred and mobilized their revolutionary sentiments, although they probably attached less enthusiastic feeling to the counterrevolutionary month of Thermidor.

The use of symbols was also convenient in evoking the sense of revolutionary continuity. As they praised the sought-after ideal of the Republic, anarchists referred to Louise Michel as "Marianne" (the symbol of revolutionary republicanism). As Maurice Agulhon has demonstrated, the image of Marianne retained a powerful force throughout the nineteenth century and served to arouse ardent revolutionary sentiments.[18] Not only would republicans respond to this symbol, but so would all rebels contesting the various unpalatable French regimes of the time. They felt, in this response, an intrinsic affinity to the first attempt at placing Marianne in power.

The anarchist response to Marianne did not demonstrate the movement's support for republicanism but its adherence to the revolutionary spirit that the bare-breasted Marianne nourished. After the many earlier struggles carried out against authoritarian regimes, anarchists now felt that the heritage of revolt had been passed on to them as they fought against the "corrupt and debased" republic entrenched in power in the 1880s and 1890s. The titles of Jean Grave's first two papers conveyed that message: *Le Révolte* and *La Révolté* Anarchists believed that the regime, which had begun by crushing the Commune in 1871 (the Third Republic), did not differ greatly from the systems in place before. In fact, it served as the repository of a variety of traditional and contemporary forms of exploitation and oppression. Accordingly, it had to be overthrown.

Police officials also felt apprehension about the anarchists tapping into the legacy of the French Revolution. Special Commissioner of Police A. Moreau in 1897 offered his own interpretation of the influence of that past upon rebels of the day. As he stated, the seeds of anarchism had been sown during the French Revolution—a reality that was especially reflected in the central tenets embraced by the more radical revolutionaries. Moreau referred to the French Revolution's *Manifesto of Equals* issued by Gracchus Babeuf as the first delineation of modern anarchist ideas and specifically cited the following passage:

> This equality transcribed within the Declaration of the Rights of Man and Citizen does not concern us. We want it next to us, under the roof of our house. Larger than private property, the earth belongs to no one. If one man is richer and more powerful than his equals, then the equilibrium will be broken, the crime and the disaster will be on the earth.[19]

Obviously, the bourgeoisie did not want to extend the same social mobility it had acquired during the Revolution to the lower classes. Moreau was thinking in a similar vein as he singled out this passage and relished his own sense of social superiority. It had been one thing for the bourgeoisie to attain equal status with the aristocracy, but extension of that same spirit of equality to the workers was unthinkable. Further leveling could only damage overall bourgeois prestige and wealth. This was as true during the 1890s as it had been during the French Revolution. The sans-culottes and Babeuf's followers within the Conspiracy of the Equals had already striven for equality and used the issue to radicalize the scope of the Revolution and threaten the gains already attained by upper echelons of the Third Estate.

Moreau further traced a line connecting the ideas of the manifesto to those of Etienne Cabet, Louis Blanc, and eventually Bakunin who all, according to Moreau, espoused communistic aims. As Moreau suggested (in unconsciously agreeing with Karl Marx's assessment), ideas of this kind found their initial practical application during the Commune of 1871—the first attempt at effecting complete social transformation and reversing the course of capitalist hegemony.[20] Such scrutiny indicates that the police were just as interested in detecting historical influences as were the revolutionaries. Their goal, however, was to penetrate the minds of those they pursued in order to understand their motivations and stifle their ambitions. The police and anarchists were alike in attempting to trace such historical influences, albeit from opposite sides of the political fence. Police obsession, however, was dominated by the need to demonstrate the reality of continuing historical conspiracies carried out by agents of social chaos against the order of the bourgeoisie.

As the one hundredth anniversary of the commencement of the French Revolution approached, anarchist journalists speculated on its heritage and attempted to draw parallels between the years 1789 and 1889. One article, included in an issue of Grave's La Révolte in 1888, focused on the meaning of that year and hinted that similarities with 1788 were obvious but that now "the watchword is demolition, destruction: it is social revolution and communism which must bring about Anarchy."[21] The anonymous author (presumably Grave) observed that previous revolutions had brought forward different aspirations such as: in 1789, the rights of liberty, equality, and fraternity; in 1830, republican demands for the destruction of monarchy; in 1848, Louis Blanc's Social Workshop program that would guarantee the right to work; and in 1871, the Communards' vision of complete social leveling.[22] A certain amount of idealizing and abstraction was present in such attempts at surmising the meaning of these movements. The writer also implied that revolutions were progressive in nature and worked upon the gains of the past.

Such analysis was not necessarily based upon rigorous research and study, and the conclusions are highly debatable. Yet it reveals a tendency to view the next revolution as the most advanced and successful and the culmination of all past movements. Anarchy would be at the heart of that upheaval and the ruling principle for future society. In the context of this chapter, it is not so much the historical accuracy or error of this vision that engages our attention but the anarchists' need to connect their aspirations with those of the past and, in so doing, impart to their compagnons an emotional relationship to history. This would provide both a sensation of belonging to a particular revolutionary heritage and a determination to act in confirming the reality.

Nevertheless, in attempting to determine the need for such a long process of revolutionary struggle, anarchists were compelled to consider the reasons for the failures of previous uprisings. Kropotkin wrote *La Grande Révolution: 1789-1793* in an effort to account for the Revolution's ultimate failure to shift power to the menu peuple.[23] As George Woodcock has noted, this book says just as much about the perceptions of nineteenth-century libertarians as it does about the Revolution itself. Indeed, "his anarchistic bias led him to overemphasize the libertarian elements present within the sans-culottes and the 'enragés.'"[24]

Jean Grave believed that the revolutionary armies had demonstrated the power of the Revolution's libertarian forces to arouse France and to save it temporarily from monarchy, invading foreign armies, and counterrevolutions in areas such as the Vendée and Marseilles. It is, at first, startling to realize that such nationalistic and militaristic ideas were expressed by a member of a movement despising nation-states, governments, and the army. The contradiction is glossed over by Grave's reasoning that armies are not destined to be authoritarian and repressive arms of government but could reflect the spontaneous decisions of an aroused populace to act freely and voluntarily in defense of its interests against tyrants—in the manner of a militia. The difference was that in a situation where the revolutionary community's survival was at stake the French people and not the French state should maintain control.

This was controversial emotional terrain for Grave to tread and he did so gingerly. Grave did little to raise questions about universal conscription—begun during the Revolution as the "levée en masse" and inaugurating an unparalleled era of state intervention into people's lives. This posed a difficult problem as he needed to align his anarchist beliefs with his esteem for the Revolution's patriotic currents. He escaped the dilemma by proclaiming that "a revolutionary army and a government are terms which contradict one another."[25] The Revolution had inspired the sans-culottes and other popular groups behind it to take arms and reawaken French élan. This was not a governmental matter but one of the people making their presence known. They acted to advance and safeguard the interests of the Revolution. Any army created spontaneously to act in this way, therefore, was not so much an institutional structure, but a force for justice. It was to be contrasted to armies serving as puppets of authoritarian governments and intending to crush the people's voice.

There was obviously much whitewashing here. The revolutionary government created by Robespierre and his associates on the Committee of Public Safety was tyrannical and authoritarian in nature. Its use of the army and police force was indeed demonstrative of power and had ceased to represent the people. Grave was still reacting to the recent coup attempt by Boulanger—an event that he not only considered a threat to the Third Republic but a reminder of Napoléon's coup. Indeed, the Napoleonic empire and traditions growing around it had formally ended hopes for continuous revolutionary upheavals.[26] Grave was not alone in making such points and echoed the thoughts of the socialist Jean Jaurès regarding revolutionary militias. Grave emphasized that while militias were free and spontaneous forces defending liberty and equality, armies were rigid and hierarchical and threatened to stifle the popular will. Militias had been evident between 1789 and 1794. Military systems, in contrast, were used by Napoléon and other powerful generals to enforce tyranny.

Grave was more uncertain and ambiguous about transitional states in which both revolutionary crowds and a centralized state claimed to represent liberty, equality, and fraternity. Since the Jacobins had been so instrumental in the destruction of the Bourbon monarchy, anarchists continued to embellish them with a revolutionary aura and to portray them as martyrs for the cause. Yet it was also clear that Robespierre and the Committee of Public Safety used force against those who pushed for expansion of the revolution's scope and that more members of the sans-culottes were condemned to the guillotine than were aristocrats and wealthy bourgeois. Such actions were dictated by considerations of power. Anarchists were not certain about relating such authoritarian forces to popular bases. How had governments gained increasing control over armies and detached themselves from their revolutionary origins? This question would continue to be asked many times more in the future as disappointed idealistic revolutionaries wondered about their failures.

Anarchists attributed the triumph of tyranny to the continued presence of military institutions and to the pervasiveness of upper-class property and wealth. They saw both military organization and private property as authoritarian holdovers that prevented the establishment of egalitarianism. Thoughts of self-gain and power continued to stand in the way of those aspiring to a society of equals.

Furthermore, obsession with private property corrupted revolutionary ideals and solidarity and fostered the growth of authoritarianism by helping to erode the belief that one's best interests were satisfied alongside the common interests of all. The impetus for self-gratification also implied a hunger for power that would cause the many to be subjected to the few.

It was Grave's view, thus, that Napoléon's coup was only the culmination of a process begun when private property had superceded social egalitarianism as the goal of the Revolution. Article 16 of "the Declaration of the Rights of Man and Citizen" reflected John Locke's defense of the inalienable right to property, proclaiming it to be virtuous and sacred. Anarchists could cite the article as the original source of corruption to revolutionary élan and of encouragement to the wealthy to dispose of their belongings solely as they saw fit.[27] This confirmed society as a competitive, social Darwinistic jungle in which wealth and acquisition were sought and the needs of the poor neglected. In contrast stood the goals for social transformation stressing mutuality and harmony. As they pointed to Article 16, anarchists were, in fact, suggesting that the Revolution's deterioration and drift toward authoritarian rule and social ostentatiousness had begun during the early days of its initial stage and entailed continued dependence upon state power and lack of commitment to social justice.

Grave and other libertarians saw the Revolution of 1789 as a perpetual struggle between the suffering, wretched masses longing for change and their leaders who, once in power, became more interested in clutching on to and increasing the power of their newly acquired positions. The latter merely sought to impose a new government at the expense of truly needed social and economic improvements for the poor. Anarchists may have displayed a naivete regarding the scruples of French revolutionary leaders, but this same conception of selfless leadership was at the basis of their view of revolutionary movements. In fact, they believed that divisions between leaders and the led should ultimately dissolve. This suggested a more critical perspective of Robespierre than at first was apparent.

The more emotional anarchist Charles Malato expanded on this theme by stating that all power struggles undermined original revolutionary goals. In the end, the executioners themselves were guillotined. The thirst for authority became self-consuming and led the way for others to grasp power for baser ends. Several instances reflected this trend. Hébert, Georges-Jacques Danton, Robespierre, and Antoine Louis Saint-Just had all traveled the path from revolutionary engagement to power or from influence to the scaffold.[28] Furthermore, Marat had been assassinated in his bathtub by the enraged Girondin Charlotte Corday. The only result in the end was internal collapse and Napoléon's establishment of a new authoritarian empire.

Within such developments, Malato detected conspiracies, led by moderate revolutionaries and various reactionaries and clerics, to dilute the ardor of the struggle for justice. Such plots were intended to prepare the way for counterrevolution and involved bizarre twists of political engagement. Several counterrevolutionaries in the Vendée, Malato stated, had a few years earlier in October, 1789 marched with the women on Versailles to demand the return of Louis XVI and Marie Antoinette to Paris.

Malato believed that many of the leaders of the 1848 Revolution were disguised clerics who called themselves republicans but revealed their true colors when opposing Blanc's Social Workshop reforms and urging the dispatch of French troops to Rome to protect the pope from local rebels.[29] Malato continued his diatribe and accused later rebels of posing as Communards in order to subvert and suppress the movement of 1871 in which his father had participated.

Since Malato raised the question of French involvement in the defeat of the 1848 republican uprising in Rome, it is noteworthy that he had been born in 1858 in Fougin Merthe-et-Mouvelle to Italian immigrants. His father was a Sicilian who had been active in the 1848 Italian revolutions and fled to France following their collapse. While in France, his father became further involved in revolutionary activities and participated in the Commune. Soon thereafter, disappointed and defeated, he was sent into exile accompanied by Charles. Their destination was the group of Pacific islands known as New Caledonia.

Already entranced by revolutionary ideals, the fourteen-year-old Malato had his curiosity further aroused by his fellow exiled traveler, Louise Michel. He was immediately impressed by Michel's legendary, romantic history as a Communard accused not only of fighting government troops but also of involvement in incendiary acts. The two discussed revolutionary politics on the voyage and throughout their stay in New Caledonia. By the time they returned to France in 1880, both Michel and Malato were anarchists and devoted themselves to the Parisian anarchist effort. Malato spent much of his time writing about anarchistic philosophy although he had little formal training and was primarily self-educated. He was especially drawn to the moral and emotional tone of Michel's and Kropotkin's teachings. As one who had developed a revolutionary attitude from his personal contacts, Malato continued to learn from those around him. In turn, he impressed others with his own ardent convictions. It was clear that his development as a rebel would always be shaped by family relationships and friendships. This meant that he held politics to be based upon communal experience—whether within families, neighborhoods, cities, or nations.

Malato began his political musings by stressing the nature of ideas in the abstract. Originally, they were pure, uncorrupted by experience. This situation would change as influences from national and other traditions caused deviation from the original state of purity. Such an evolutionary pattern was also evident in movements such as anarchism.

Of course, it is obvious that no ideas are pure or abstract because they are always created within the context of human situations. Malato was not a metaphysician but a political activist. As such, he placed a needless obstacle in his attempt to understand the place of anarchism. It is interesting, however, to note his conversion of this concept into an indictment of recent French revolutionary politics. He believed that the best examples of revolutionary idealism were found in other nations and that France had an especially unfortunate recent history of failing to live up to their standards. Malato felt this to be painfully true of the Third Republic, which he viewed as a false, insincere version of democracy. Missing from the scene was the enthusiasm and vigor of Giuseppe Mazzini and Giuseppe Garibaldi or the rebellious dedication of the Russian revolutionaries. The latter especially had addressed true human needs and aspirations. Not surprising to Malato was their ardent espousal of the anarchist message. Malato contrasted the cynical power-mongering of Robespierre and Saint-Just to the communal concerns of Russian anarchists stating:

> just as Greece gave us art, Rome the state—an evil which was necessary to combat and conquer gothic feudalism that the barbarians created to revive Europe . . . so it seems that successively, France was destined to give Europe the first notions of republicanism, Germany to give author-itarian communism [code for Marxism], and Russia to bring the eventual triumph of anarchy.[30]

More than other Parisian anarchists, Malato considered national character as contributing to or detracting from revolutionary élan. We can see that he expressed suspicions of the German socialist movement led by Karl Kautsky and August Bebel. In point of fact, his feelings on the subject extended much further. He viewed Marxism as too austerely philosophical and probably best suited for the Germans (a point that Marx may not have contested). In contrast, he praised the "pure" rebellious spirit found among the Russians, Spanish, and Italians. Malato was guilty of dramatic idealization since scrutiny of all three societies reveals an equal or greater dose of revolutionary disappointment as was found in France. Because of his emotional devotions, he urged the French to learn from these people who perhaps were not advanced economically and socially but who had developed noteworthy anarchist movements.

Of course, geography and culture determined French inclinations in the various parts of the nation. The heavy concentration of industry in northern France gave moderate socialism and trade unionism the same possibility evident in Britain.[31] Malato viewed in a different manner the Latin French (including most of the people outside of the far north) among whom Blanquism had fostered violent and undisciplined methods of rebellion to complement other centuries-old traditions.[32] The problem was that Blanquism had been so volatile and uncontrolled that it was unable to have a lasting impact. What was needed was a more coherent philosophy of revolution and social reconstruction that avoided the systematic excesses of Marxism. Such racialism was not new to France. During the eighteenth century, French nobles had attempted to delineate their Germanic origins as they contrasted their knightly ancestry to the docile nature of Latin French nobles.[33] This was part of an aristocratic reaction against the upcoming nobles of the robe. Despite his many differences with notions of aristocracy, Malato still believed that the understanding and consciousness of racial identity could enable the French to grasp the importance of the French Revolution and its long line of descendants. They could then decide which of their contemporary opposition forces most adhered to that tradition.

For French anarchism to reach a level of revolutionary vitality and sincerity, it would do well to learn from the example of its Italian counterpart. No doubt, Malato remembered his own father's attempt to import his Italian-born subversive activities and revolutionary ideals into France.[34] As the son of this Italian immigrant, Malato believed that his father's native culture was destined to play a special role in France. It also meant that he would be part of such engagement. In keeping to the Italian-French anarchistic connection, Malato pointed to Errico Malatesta's social criticism as having an especially relevant meaning for French revolutionaries. He felt that a combination of Malatesta's and Auguste Blanqui's ideas and emphases on violence and élan could be most powerful in furthering the movement and enabling anarchists to discover the significance of their search for true order. Malato thought it very important for France to invigorate its revolutionary spirit by receiving rebels who fled from repressive regimes and sought havens for their ideals elsewhere. French anarchists had to harbor their own "underground railroad" for them—especially as they had need of it themselves when having to go into exile. (Malato was one of those and, as will be seen in chapter 3, wrote a guide for those seeking asylum and comfort abroad.)[35] Consequently, he was active in helping Spanish and Italian refugees live secretly in France. As another expression of the movement's international character, this activity implied a high degree of communication with foreign anarchists.

Charles Malato's life and thought, in fact, reflected the internationalism inherent in nineteenth-century revolutionary circles. His attempt to connect his father's Garibaldian experiences to the existing French situation was an interesting example of revolutionary sentiments crossing national boundaries and taking on corresponding mutations. Throughout his revolutionary career, he attempted to infuse some of his father's enthusiasm and his own lessons derived from exile in New Caledonia into the French anarchist movement. As Malato perceived so much disappointment and torpor in the French revolutionary tradition and contemporary radical movements, he believed that his efforts would help rekindle anarchist élan.

As noted above, Malato viewed the right wing's determination to overturn the Third Republic as a series of ongoing conspiracies. Although feeling that France's republican character was weak and bereft of inspiration, he still saw it as a progressive force serving as a building block for further reform. Reactionaries sensed this and sought its overthrow. "Against popular sentiment, against the opinions and democratic faith of the masses, alive with hope, the clerical and MacMahonian reaction has uselessly tried its nails and teeth."[36] The presence of Marshal Patrice de MacMahon's name seems out of place at first, since he was one of the early leaders of the republic. Malato singled him out because as a staunch conservative and monarchist, MacMahon during the 1870s attempted to prevent the emergence of pure republicanism. In 1877, he contemplated an actual coup. By the time Malato was writing during the 1880s and 1890s, the name MacMahon was synonymous with authoritarianism. Malato, in fact, felt that reactionary threats were evident both within and outside the republic. He saw MacMahon's presence, the 1877 monarchist revival, the Boulanger affair of 1885, and the Dreyfus case of the 1890s all as examples of such tendencies. It was further clear that clerics, the military, and a rabid ultra-right-wing press represented the greatest challenge to the new republic's pursuit of justice.

Certainly, divisions between democratic and authoritarian factions loomed largely during the early years of the Third Republic. However, while he rightly pointed to the menace behind the ultra-right, Malato's paranoia knew no bounds in detecting patterns everywhere. It would lead him to study past events and discover the same trends evident in contemporary crises. As he traced what he perceived as relevant tendencies unfolding from 1789 to his own day, Malato was continuously attempting to discover causes and connections between past revolutions and contemporary movements. At the same time, he wished to maintain anarchists' awareness of the reactionary dangers, which had been evolving during that time span. He saw continual reactionary attempts to infiltrate rebel ranks woven into the web of French republican history. In seeking to weather social upheavals challenging their positions, clever reactionaries accommodated themselves to the challengers and then betrayed them at the first chance. As police spies constantly attended anarchist meetings, it was not so farfetched to muse upon such possible infiltration, but excessive paranoia was also irresistible.

Since Malato felt anarchism represented the most advanced and just of contemporary revolutionary movements, he also believed it was most threatened by conservative plots. Therefore, it was necessary for anarchists to be vigilant against plots being organized against them and most careful in their choice of compatriots. Study of past revolutionary failure would cause realization of just this point.

Anarchists also focused upon 1848 as another example of a revolution incompletely meeting its goals and ultimately collapsing. As they attempted to underscore the revolution's relevance to their concerns, anarchists at the turn of the century gave it much consideration and attempted to determine its historical position and the reasons for its demise. They perceived it as having unfolded in phases—beginning in bourgeois and popular stages and concluding with Louis Napoléon's election and subsequent coup against the Second Republic. The finale was marked by his coronation as emperor. Within this series of developments, a complex of interconnected forces fought for the revolution and yet worked against it as the common course splintered into its fragments. Those most adamant in their enthusiasm for the Second Republic (such as the followers of Louis Blanc) were quickly disappointed and forced off the stage of significant happenings.

The anarchists pointed to two factors as having contributed to the revolution's failure. To begin, the Parisian insurgents were unable to mobilize peasants to join in the national effort. At the same time, the bourgeoisie continued to exert its power and managed to obstruct true social change. Anarchists painfully contrasted both sets of events to the revolutionary determination of Russian peasants to join in a universal upheaval against the tsarist establishment. While this judgment may have been more revealing of anarchists' hopes than of the factual state of Russian political affairs, the model nonetheless served them well in their attempt to find a point of contrast to the failures of the French revolutionary past.

The terrible conditions of France in February, 1848, in fact, were attributed to the bourgeoisie's economic and political dominance—evident in its grip upon Louis-Philippe's July Monarchy. For the great majority of French people, daily life was marked by extreme poverty and lack of a political voice. Many anarchists already blamed "The Declaration of the Rights of Man and Citizen" for having prevented the Revolution from 1789-1794 from instituting dramatic social transformation. The new system of inequity and injustice was well in place, therefore, by the time 1848 broke out. Jean Grave wrote:

> Property, remaining in the hands of those who possess it already, under the aegis of the law, was rendered into the hands of the bourgeoisie, because they deprived the nobles of it by law and then turned their backs on the people. They were not capable of great thought nor of generous aspirations: they did proclaim the right of each man to satisfy his own

needs. They replaced purely and simply, the tyranny of the aristocrats by their own. And after the troubles of the revolution had been resolved, they found that power and property had become the privilege of a few thousand bourgeois. Law consecrated the established fact.[37]

As noted above, Grave believed that the French Revolution had molded the pattern of nineteenth-century class dominance and social antagonisms. His view did not greatly differ from that espoused by Marxists. Anarchists and Marxists shared certain ideas within a revolutionary language even though they diverged in so many respects. Both held that the new laws had reestablished injustice and novel forms of social inequality to replace those already existing prior to 1789. François Guizot's advice of "enrichissez-vous" (get rich) to those demanding suffrage during the 1840s was the most vocal and unabashed espousal of the new system's class divisions. Grave felt that Guizot's statement was only a crude reflection of the declaration's earlier implication that the most relevant rights were centered around wealth and property—in the manner of Montesquieu's belief that "privilege is the ancestor of liberty."

The bourgeoisie's power would not be overthrown so easily. In the attempt to preserve and enhance its position, this class would work with the church, the military, and all other reactionary forces amenable to it, and Grave felt that this would entail continued bourgeois suppression of the menu peuple. Despite the fact that the bourgeoisie had helped destroy monarchy once and for all in 1848, it would do all it could to protect its own interests—a fact demonstrated when it pressured the provisional government to crush in brutal fashion the workers' revolt in June, 1848. Although this action entailed betrayal of a former ally, no other bourgeois course was possible since sentiment was of no value when power and wealth were at stake.

Such class-conscious analysis did not differ greatly from the type used by Marx to examine the meaning of 1848 in France and Germany.[38] Originally, a common ground among rival groups was found in the struggle against traditional antagonists. Once the monarchy and the nobles could no longer impede bourgeois social hegemony, that class used all means at its disposal to prevent further social revolutions from threatening its gains. Such an episode also had occurred between 1789 and 1793 when "sans-culotte" demands for the expansion of democracy and enforcement of regular grain shipments to Paris were ignored. The newly entrenched oligarchy now had the power to contain popular demands.

Anarchists' views differed from the Marxists' in several key respects. In the first place, they perceived that economic and class interests alone did not account for the failure of these events. In addition, there was a political factor at work, and this invoked the anarchists' raison d'être of not only redressing social and economic ills but of eliminating government. The persistence of government, they felt, was most responsible for the legal institutionalization of property and the resulting social divisions. No matter how far the rebels of 1789, 1793, 1830, and 1848 had gone in addressing social, economic, and political problems, they clung to the notion of a central government—such as Cardinal Richelieu had sought during the seventeenth century. The irony of this point has been evoked by Alexis de Tocqueville in his classic study *The Old Regime and the French Revolution*.[39]

Experiments in decentralized government and direct local democracy had held great promise and initially had been attempted by the sans-culottes (before their betrayal by Robespierre). Such hopes approximated the anarchist ideal. Authoritarian government was restored, however, and as Elisée Reclus would suggest, the systems established after the popular upheavals of 1830 and 1848 preserved the centralized state. For this reason, revolutionary leaders at the time lost touch with the people and were fated to failure.[40] Anarchists, thus, felt that they conveyed an old and new revolutionary message. They would return to the aspirations of the sans-culottes and extend the range of their hopes and goals. Such ideals and interpretations of the past were opposed to the Marxist perception of revolutions as manifesting inevitable, historical forces found in particular eras and impossible to reverse. It was also clear to Marxists that the state could only vanish or "wither away" after the necessary amount of revolutionary activity had cleared the debris of the past. The eclipse of the state was to be reserved for a far-distant future. How different from the anarchist view holding that the state could have been terminated at any time in the past!

Anarchists also disagreed with Marxists about the importance of peasants. Marx had portrayed the peasants in insulting terms. They were reactionaries, and the failure of 1848 in France could be directly attributed to their conservative bent as they helped sweep Louis Napoléon into office.[41] These "sacks of potatoes" (as Marx described them) had ceased to be revolutionary after procuring their property rights during the waning days of feudalism in the summer of 1789. Not only did they cease to show concern for persistent political and social questions once their thirst for land had been satisfied, but they stopped caring altogether about conditions in Paris and other major cities. In a country like France, where peasants made up such a large segment of the population, their electoral participation would be crucial. Marx blamed the republican implementation of universal manhood suffrage for the election of Louis Napoléon, and, of course, for his eventual coup d'état. Marx's view was that peasants could never again play a revolutionary role so long as they maintained an independent status and resisted immersion into the proletarian class. France would, thus, be at the mercy of their reactionary tendencies and communism itself would be frustrated because of its dependence upon the presence of an overwhelming proletarian work force.

Anarchists envisioned peasants in entirely different terms. Since several in their ranks had come from Russia, where peasant insurrections against oppressive estate owners offered the most hopeful revolutionary situation, they were not quick to dismiss this group. Bakunin and Kropotkin not only envisioned an important economic function for peasants, but also bestowed upon them an important role in the massive anarchist agitations and upheavals that would overturn capitalist society and the state.

Among libertarian thinkers, Grave analyzed the position of the peasantry most directly. He again blamed the flawed outcome of the French Revolution. In particular, the legal institutionalization of private property and the partition of land to the peasants had deflected the course of the revolution from more radical ambitions. Grave still expressed the anarchist ambivalence regarding the French Revolution: as a phenomenon that had offered hope by dismantling the monarchy but remained unsatisfactory in other areas.[42] This disappointment, as already noted, revolved around the facts of bourgeois replacement of aristocrats as the new source of oppression and exploitation and the beginning of peasants' conservatism following their expropriation of noble land during and after the days of the Great Fear. In both cases, aristocratic eclipse gave way to new regrettable political patterns. Grave did not differ, therefore, from Marx in blaming the defeat of 1848 upon the combination of bourgeois and peasant forces acting in concert.

Nevertheless, important differences of interpretation existed. Unlike Marx, Grave did not dismiss the peasants as reactionaries inclined by nature toward counterrevolution. Peasants also had been upset about the way in which the provisional government confronted their problems. Those in power in Paris neglected the countryside completely and caused peasants to feel that their interests were not being taken seriously and, indeed, were being jeopardized.[43] As a result, the search for social reform evolved into a political power struggle between leaders of the centralized state and the citizens, on the one hand, and between Paris and the provinces on the other.

This had been the typical scenario Grave discerned within the society of the ancien régime. Despite their previous belief in the monarch's "royal touch" (perceived to be a direct source of miraculous healing), peasants continued to perceive Paris as the seat of the enemy that tolerated threats to their security. This perspective was still present in 1848. Following the events of February and June of that year, they felt even greater fears about an ultra-centralized state intruding upon their private affairs. Their ultimate reaction in the December elections was to vote in overwhelming numbers for Louis Napoléon as president. From a later and different perspective, this could appear to be a reactionary inclination, but peasants did not necessarily view their actions in that way. Grave felt that such an error was possible because of the government's brutality against workers in the "June Days" and Louis Napoléon's own reputation as a revolutionary republican.

As anarchist ideology dictated, peasant votes in the elections did result in error as Louis Bonaparte not only became an authoritarian but also Napoléon III. Grave described as an irony the fact that universal suffrage provided both the means for peasant vengeance and the restoration of monarchical rule.[44] With this development, all hopes for reform (as had been envisioned for the republic's National Workshop and Social Workshop programs) disappeared. Bonapartism once again replaced the Bourbons and Orleans as the new authoritarian force stifling revolutionary ambitions.

Grave believed that the republicans essential problem of 1848 was to seize power and preserve state control over all aspects of reform while preventing people from directing their own affairs. This imposed an immediate obstacle in the path of revolutionary social reform. Revolutionary leaders ended by merely changing the form of government and replacing old names with new ones. In the meantime, they managed to frighten the peasants into thinking that their security was endangered by republican rule. This came at a time when republican leaders attempted to preserve their position from the bourgeois menace. Grave contrasted the failed 1848 Revolution to the future anarchist uprising, which would not be:

> a superficial change . . . but a complete transformation of all social relations occurring at the base of their organization; a sweeping away of all present institutions. And as the anarchist tactic concerns possible action as soon as the possibility of effective action arises, the revolution created by the anarchist conceptions will reach into the remote corners of the country.[45]

It was not clear how this was to be. Grave only reiterated that anarchists had to understand the peasants' mentalité entailing an emotional attachment to land. Nevertheless, there would be a need for joint dialogue. It would be necessary to educate the peasantry in anarchist ideals and to inculcate in them an understanding of the means by which their true interests could best be secured. Peasants needed to learn the libertarian creed, cooperate with their Parisian compagnons in mutual aid, overcome the temptation to seek only their isolated interests, and grasp the possible benefits derived from machinery. Only after this had been accomplished "would the peasants understand communistic anarchism and resupply the cities."[46] Peasants educated in anarchist doctrine would no longer see their interests detached from those of people living in cities or in other provinces. Historical scrutiny of past revolutions only revealed the manner in which peasants' ignorance of their true interests caused them to cut off food supplies to cities in desperate times, and anarchists needed to help peasants overcome this pattern. It was also clear that peasants would need to part from their emotional predispositions tying them to property, and this issue would cause great problems for anarchist mobilization of French peasants.

Grave's analysis demonstrated the anarchists' desire to incorporate peasants into their movement rather than scorn and ignore their revolutionary potential in the Marxist manner. Neglecting the peasants would, as Grave felt, risk the unleashing of a contrary force capable only of reversing all hitherto-accomplished progress. One cannot help but note, however, that it is also possible to see in his historical analysis an ongoing anarchist utopian belief that greed and paranoia could be overcome by patience and reason.

Anarchists emphasized the need to celebrate the revolutionary clubs of 1848 as models and inspirations for the future. Indeed, they linked their enthusiasm for the clubs of 1848 and of 1789-1793, esteeming these groups' parallel decentralized attempts to encourage voluntary communal efforts within federations intended to topple the monarchy and the aristocratic order. Such clubs mobilized common hatred against these institutions and achieved this aim—most famously in the seizure of the Bastille by a populace described in mythic terms as having acted "spontaneously." While the clubs may have planned some crowd action, they did not act as models of Marxist revolutionary organization in which spontaneity (except in the later ideas of Rosa Luxemburg and Antonio Gramsci) had no place. Their goal was to keep the idea of insurrection in the air. When the proper atmosphere flourished, however, crowd spontaneity would turn the tide.

Nevertheless, there were still other Bastilles to conquer in 1830 and 1848 (even when the original structure no longer stood). Other Bastilles remained in 1871 and would metaphorically emerge in future years.[47] Grave suggested that prisons did not need to be constructed of the same stones standing near Saint-Antoine for so long, nor did they need resemble fortresses physically. They could evade material description and be crystallized in ideas and institutions bound to tradition and embracing all areas of life. Endless revolutionary struggle terminating in the destruction of the state entailed the existence of eternal Bastilles in some form or another, demanding eternal conquests. Evident in Grave's analysis is the anarchists' tendency to link their work both to the incomplete revolutions of the past and those that were expected to follow.

Standing out here was anarchists' devotion to a revolutionary tradition attached to the city of Paris around which they perceived a romantic aura, even a halo.

As would be expected, anarchists saw oppression, economic exploitation, and authoritarianism as the primary forces of the era of 1848-1871. Romantic idealism and republicanism had disappeared at least from the surface of political life, and Napoléon III was at the helm of a powerful state. Nevertheless, they also viewed these decades as inaugurating the International Workingman's Association through which the oppressed classes could combat the established order. Within this network, anarchism first began to be formulated as a distinct revolutionary movement. Widespread discontent, following the defeat of the French in the Franco-Prussian War, erupted in the Paris Commune of 1871. Marx and the anarchists did not disagree in their idealized views of the Commune as the first successful example of a lower-class revolt briefly resulting in a takeover of local power and social restructuring through fundamental, radical reforms.

The chief difference in their perceptions revolved around Marx's view of the Commune as an organized, planned proletarian movement commencing an age of uncontainable international revolution along lines he envisioned. Anarchists, in contrast, saw the Commune as an expression of the voluntary and spontaneous will of many people acting in concert. They felt that the Commune was, in fact, connected to the events of 1793 and 1848 and the latest in a line of phenomena originating in 1789 and still addressing similar issues. While Marxists continued to look to events signaling clear and distinct breaks from the past, anarchists esteemed the past and sought their place within an emotionalized atmosphere of tradition.

The Commune's impact would be felt for years, and the French would look back to it as the most violent social upheaval of the nineteenth century—and one perhaps leaving permanent divisions between the upper and lower classes. "1871" was invoked on the left as a rallying cry for further change within the Third Republic. Those oriented in a more nationalistic direction would relate the Commune's resistance against the Prussian armies to the defense of the Third Republic against potential enemies on the continent. This could involve both leftist and rightist interpretations. Some former Communards, like Henri Rochefort veered politically to the right and tapped into memories of the Commune to justify militaristic, patriotic, and anti-Semitic attitudes.[48] As such a recent event, the Commune was more powerful than 1793 or 1848 in its evocation of powerful emotions about the French nation. Many Communards were still alive during the 1880s and 1890s and wrote and spoke about their personal experiences. Some of these figures (or their children, as in the case of Malato) became anarchists and attempted to connect their interpretations of the Commune to their newest revolutionary mission. From such perspectives, an anarchist debate on the meaning of the "civil war" began in earnest.

An article by Grave in *La Révolte* on March 17, 1888 summarized the anarchist view of the Commune. While praising the revolt and the Communards' heroism, Grave again felt that one could detect serious flaws in revolutionary strategies, the main "fault committed by the people being that they created a government to represent them and entrusted to it the task higher than ordinary representative government—that of directing the revolutionary movement."[49] In other words, the people still lacked the confidence to direct their own movement and trusted decisions made by authorities; no matter how well-intentioned such leaders may have been, they made themselves into an enclosed, self-interested clique. Grave believed that, in this way, the revolutionary impulse was not able to overwhelm the one area of French life most in need of it—the state. A successful revolution, would, in fact, have eliminated the state and completely transferred to the people the power to direct their own affairs—as the sans-culottes ideally would have had it.

This coincided with Kropotkin's own analysis of the Commune. However, Kropotkin gave it a racial twist. In articles he wrote for *La Révolte,* Kropotkin portrayed the Commune as a revolutionary manifestation of a Latin race whose French representatives were inclined in a more anarchistic direction than were, say, German socialists. Race was a significant aspect of the history of French revolutions and partially explained their decentralized and local character.[50] While Malato saw French national character as somehow marring revolutionary spirit, Kropotkin felt it to be guiding a sincere reaction to centuries-old authoritarian traditions.

After describing the condition of Paris during the Prussian siege, Kropotkin then explained how Parisians sought to run their own affairs. As the state had collapsed and become incapable of distributing goods to people and of maintaining order, it was left to the people to assume responsibility by taking formal control of Paris and declaring it an independent commune.

As an anarchist, Kropotkin praised this proclamation since it reflected his belief that people should govern their own local needs and detach themselves from a central state. The next step in consolidating independence would have been to complement the political revolution with one in economics by seizing capital and redistributing wealth. However, during the wartime emergency this proved to be impossible. As Kropotkin explained, there was a further complication. The Communards faced the hostility not only of the Prussian army but also of the French provisional government forces directed by Adolphe Thiers.[51]

Despite these realities, Kropotkin also believed that the Communards' main fault lay in not going far enough to alter the Parisian political structure.

The transformation of the city into a separate commune was a positive step. However, Parisians continued to cling to the notion of a city government directing all districts within the commune. Centralized government, therefore, continued to be a major force when it could have been overhauled and rendered obsolete. This setup was contrary to Kropotkin's vision of a Paris managed through the federated cooperation of its many different component neighborhoods as one large "beehive." The particular size of the city would not matter since local cells would create the right sense of proportion. His hope was that not only the nation-state but also centralized city government would wind up in the "dustbin" of history. Only the voluntary wills of people could be entrusted with transcending all intermediate bodies placed between them and their affairs. The anarchist ideal was to have many communes within the Commune—the only truly binding force emanating from the peoples' moral sensitivity and sense of mutual aid as they cooperated on an intimate level.

It was not so much a political end that Kropotkin had in mind as a social revolution to be effected through the reorganization of cities:

> Paris did not seek to isolate herself from France, any more than to conquer it by force of arms; she did not care to shut herself within her walls like a nun in a convent; she was not inspired by the narrow spirit of the cloister. If she claimed her independence, if she tried to hinder the interference of the central power in her affairs, it was because she saw in that independence a means of quietly elaborating the bases of future organization and bringing about within herself a social revolution; a revolution which would have completely transformed the whole system of production and exchange by basing them on justice; which would have completely modified human relations by putting them on a footing of equality; which would have formed our social morality anew by founding it upon equality and solidarity. Communal independence was then but a means for the people of Paris; the social revolution was their end.[52]

In this passage, which includes the brief anticlerical aside, Kropotkin inferred a direct linkage among urban structure, morality, and justice. The central ideal of *Mutual Aid* is that human affairs would be arranged more efficiently and with a greater concern for the common good if the large metropolis were redesigned. A similar idea would inspire Lewis Mumford's urban vision in the later twentieth century, and it is not surprising that he enthusiastically referred to Kropotkin's ideas.[53]

Kropotkin believed that although the Commune had been unable to follow its natural course to a sound conclusion, his ideal anarchist society would be based upon its precedents. More so than 1848, the Commune was deeply imbued with the spirit of anarchy. Kropotkin felt that the reforms of the National Workshops of 1848 were far too dependent upon the prerogatives of rulers and, indeed, were only authoritarian by-products. In contrast, by 1871, "free communism, anarchistic communism was only beginning to dawn upon the minds of the workers."[54] The tragedy, according to Kropotkin, was that impulses in the direction of anarchistic communism were present in 1871. However, the Communards' uphill struggle against Thiers's troops, who increasingly placed enormous pressure upon the Parisians, prevented them from firmly implementing their program.

Kropotkin, in finally assessing the revolt's collapse, viewed the Parisian Communards' eventual all-too-eager embrace of the principle of government as significant a factor as the French troops. Thus they also gave in to a current and tradition too deeply engrained in French mentality to be overcome immediately.[55] If 1871 was the first true attempt since the Middle Ages to free France from the clutches of national government, its innovative nature was still thwarted by what Kropotkin called "the fetish worship of governments," even at the local level.[56] Consequently, "as the idea of anarchism had then but faintly dawned upon men's minds, it was checked half way, and in the midst of the Commune, the ancient principle of authority cropped up."[57]

Kropotkin believed that the Commune reflected the first attempt at creating an anarchistic society through the inspiration given it by the many local clubs and societies that revealed a popular dimension of unprecedented magnitude. Such facets of the Commune could be greatly contrasted to the machinations he viewed as intrinsic to Marxism. The ideal of the Commune, thus, kept to the heritage of the French Revolution and inflamed revolutionaries of the next two decades. Even as a Russian emigré, Kropotkin worked closely with such rebels to organize an anarchist movement, feeling a deep connection to that tradition. Despite obstacles posed by the deep-seated nature of authoritarian rule in France, Kropotkin felt that in time the movement toward anarchy would become irreversible. Nevertheless, it was necessary to study the lessons of 1871 both to learn from mistakes made at the time and to appreciate the true place of anarchism within the larger French revolutionary tradition.[58] The future revolution would succeed because it would both eliminate central government in any form and redistribute wealth and property. Once power and wealth had been properly disposed of and no longer impeded people's mutual efforts, anarchy would be an achievable goal.

In his historical analysis of the Commune, Kropotkin, thus, sought to reveal the origins of French anarchism and to inspire in the anarchists of his own day the ideals of 1871. His view of the uprising as a failure did not diminish the lessons and guidelines that his writings dispensed to future revolutionaries. Its shortcomings needed to be weighed against the background of continuous rebellion.

> If then . . . there are periods in human development when a conflict is unavoidable, and civil war breaks out quite independently of the will of particular individuals, . . . let, at least, these conflicts take place not on the ground of vague aspirations, but upon definite issues; not upon secondary points, the insignificance of which does not diminish the violence of the conflict, but upon broad ideas which inspire men by the grandness of the horizon which they bring into view. In this last case the conflict itself will depend much less upon the efficacy of firearms and guns than upon the force of the creative genius which will be brought into action in the work of reconstruction of Society.[59]

No doubt, Kropotkin held anarchy to be the descendant of such ideas and the rallying-cry for the rebuilding of contemporary civilization. The Commune's strength, in its rebellion against the ebbing authority of the Second Empire and Thiers's Provisional Government, was found in its broad base. Included in the revolutionary movement were anarchists, republicans, Blanquists, neo-Jacobins, and socialists. Such revolutionaries were only united in their hatred of the rule of Napoléon III. This reality also was the cause of their weakness. Only vague aspirations toward a republic modeled on that of 1793 or 1848 inspired their program, and they adopted no concrete plan of action to follow upon their envisioned success. Kropotkin clearly believed that their true failure consisted in not having detached themselves completely from the obsession with centralized government. Other observers could also conclude that control of Paris reinforced an emotionally based and romantic attachment to the city's past and divorced the revolutionaries from the realities of French life else-where—among them Thiers's oncoming troops.

By 1890, anarchists perceived the Third Republic to be the principal enemy and contested its legitimacy despite the democratic aura its name suggested. They perceived a connection between the persistent power of wealthy capitalists and the continued existence of centralized government. At the same time, they chastised the republic's apparent lack of devotion to the ideals of justice and liberty proclaimed by its previous two counterparts. Time now enabled opposition forces to overlook the failure of those republics to enforce these very ideals. Among the realities pointed to by anarchists and socialists as evidence of the Third Republic's unvirtuous nature were: the militaristic threat posed for some time by General Boulanger and the forces gathered around him;

the financial outrages of the Panama Canal scandal; and the Dreyfus Affair.[60] Anarchists ardently pushed for a revolution that would smash the government linked to these scandals and destroy all forms of the state and property allegedly responsible for them. In the process, previous revolutionary hopes would be fulfilled. As an anarchist named Georges Etièvant wrote: "the modern enigma 'liberty, equality, and fraternity' posed by the sphinx of the Revolution will be resolved in Anarchy."[61]

Yet direct, visible links between the Commune and the anarchists were still maintained by former Communards who relived dramatic memories for members of the libertarian movement. Charles Malato's writings on the shared exile in New Caledonia that he and his father endured have already been noted. Like Grave, Malato eventually believed that the Commune's failure had been caused by lack of mutual understanding and coordination between Parisians and peasants. Malato agreed that the peasants had become too comfortable with the results of the land settlement of 1789 and had allowed their revolutionary loyalty to atrophy. As a result, they entirely neglected their devotion to French society.[62]

At the same time, however, Malato sympathized with their traditional vulnerability to the greed of large landowners. He believed that much peasant land had been lost to such owners in the interlude and that it was incumbent for anarchists to reassure peasants about the viability of their holdings in the event of another revolution. This would involve the uncomfortable and bizarre acceptance of some form of private property on the part of anarchists. Yet something had to counter provincial reactionary trends and prevent peasant disgruntlement from assuming too prominent a position. If not, Malato felt that the anarchist revolution would suffer the same paralysis and collapse experienced in the past.[63] Malato remained an optimist, in any case, because he felt that the city-province antagonism would dissolve once anarchy replaced republicanism as the guiding principle of the French opposition. Since republicans were traditionally overly city-oriented, anarchists (with their natural admiration for rural life) would be more successful in forming harmonious bridges across all segments of French society. In fact, anarchism was the movement most able to serve as a mediating force between these two often opposed areas.[64] We can note here the anarchists' natural inclusion of agrarian and artisanal sectors within their revolutionary vision and perhaps the same tendency to exaggerate peasant devotion to general revolutionary principles that transcended their material interests.

Malato felt that during and after the Paris Commune, revolutionary sentiment had become detached from republicanism. Whereas *revolutionary* and *republican* had been nearly synonymous adjectives in describing distinct political types, their mutual association now became less probable. Thiers's brutal suppression of the Commune had begun this estrangement because the person directing the military assault was no longer a king or an emperor but one acting in the interests of a nascent republic. After the tragic events of 1871, it also became increasingly evident that the Third Republic had emerged as the new institutionalized status quo. Malato especially blamed the politicians known as Opportunists, whom he accused of governing through a variety of corrupt means.[65] In his writing, he contrasted the refreshing simplicity of primitive life in New Caledonia to the venal cynicism of French political life under the Third Republic.

Malato was reassured, however, by the continued presence of the revolutionary spirit in France—as symbolized by Marianne. He wrote how "my friends and I, remaining faithful to Marianne, continued the oral and written struggle against the government— joining to it the struggle against budding Caesarism."[66] On this latter point, Malato referred to the ambitions of Boulanger and the general resurgence of French popular enthusiasm for the military. In challenging this ominous trend, Malato wondered about the kind of revolutionary trend best expressing the spirit of Marianne. The answer was clear.

The situation of Louise Michel was similar although she had experienced a much longer period of revolutionary élan. Michel had been born out of wedlock to a châtelain and one of his servants in 1830 in Vroncourt-le-Côte in the Haute Marne. Soon after Michel's birth, her father left the château, leaving the task of bringing up the child to her mother and grandparents. She was sent to a boarding school in Chaumont to receive a liberal education. At that time, Michel developed an interest in the poetry of Victor Hugo and immersed herself in the Romantic, liberal republicanism flourishing during the 1840s. She also began to write poetry, focusing upon nature and freedom as literary themes—as she would continue to do during her later anarchist experience in the 1880s and 1890s.

While Michel's literary and political interests intensified during the period of the 1848 revolution, she became bitter after its defeat. Michel also transformed her career interests. Initially she had been interested in an educational career and sought a position as *sous-maîtresse* (school under mistress). Nevertheless, she rejected the first position offered to her due to a demand that she pledge an oath of allegiance to Napoléon III. Subsequently, she combined her interests in teaching with her devotion to republicanism. In 1853 and 1855 Michel opened free schools at Audeloncourt and Millieures in her belief that she would be able to foster republican principles in children. Police harassment forced her to close these schools, and she left finally to teach in Paris. In the capital city, she continued to write poetry and became associated with opposition groups forming around Jules Valles and Eugene Varlin—two of her future Communard compagnons. Soon afterward, she became involved in their causes and helped organize republican papers and neighborhood meetings.

Between 1869 and 1880, Michel's revolutionary career accelerated as she became first a Communard and then an anarchist. During the Commune, she was a member of the National Guard and organized the *Comité Centrale de l'Union des Femmes*.[67] She deeply believed that women were more passionate than men in the struggle for liberty and justice in that they had continually confronted and endured social constraints not encountered by men. They suffered from the same lack of political rights and economic opportunities familiar to working-class men. Yet, at the same time, their plight included further barriers formed by consistent sexual discrimination. Marriage was one such barrier Michel pictured as standing in the way of women's self-fulfillment. Those women desiring to find careers or lead unconventional lives should vigorously reject marriage and espouse freedom. (Because of her refusal to marry, she was called "The Red Virgin.") Michel felt that such struggles now had to be expanded onto the social stage. Women needed to do as much as possible in order to achieve a new social and political order. Therefore, Michel stressed the need for women to organize in furthering their aims.[68] Such a position was most pronounced during the Commune when her remarkable feats of heroism during the defense of the Commune's cannons from Thiers's threatening armies gained her a legendary revolutionary stature.

Following the Commune, Michel was imprisoned and sent into exile to New Caledonia in 1873 where, as we have seen, she became acquainted with Charles Malato. New Caledonia began the critical period when the two became anarchists. For the next ten years, Michel increasingly connected her political tenets with the anarchist creed. Local developments in New Caledonia also gave her anarchism greater fervor. Among the events to which she and Malato reacted was the series of rebellions of natives (the Canaques) against French imperial authorities. New Caledonia's colonial era had not been easy for France. French explorers had been massacred in 1851, and native feeling remained hostile—especially after formal annexation occurred in 1853. Two serious insurrections erupted in 1878 and 1881.[69] Michel and Malato witnessed the 1878 rebellion close up. Michel's desire for freedom as well as her Romantic esteem for nature are evident in her *Chant des captifs* (the Captives' Song) concerning her experiences in New Caledonia.[70] By the time Michel and Malato left the colony in 1880, they already considered themselves anarchists. They also believed that in these remote islands they had witnessed important episodes in the historic universal struggle for freedom. Yet these events held further importance in their setting within another continent. They revealed a natural, instinctual form predating the invasion of Western civilization and found universally among all people. Malato described this tendency as "ensauvage."[71]

In exile, Michel and Malato also discussed the connection between what they had observed in New Caledonia and life in France. Michel's revolutionary vision had become more global in scope than it had been before the days of the Commune. This transformation was now evident in her view of the future. The revolution to come, she felt, would be international, no longer confined to France. As she later wrote:

> the revolution is larger, it includes the world; it is not again only against caesars but against everything which limits the happiness of man . . . [it is] the new river.[72]

Michel was expressing a truly cosmopolitan vision that transcended her earlier European-centered focus. Henceforce, she identified the revolutionary struggle with people everywhere rather than with one specific culture. Michel was no longer interested in focusing solely upon the European struggle against tyranny, as seen continuously from the Roman era to 1794, and in neglecting the concerns of non-Europeans. Her revisionist attitude now focused on the creation of a new universal order. Yet, as always, Paris was central to this pursuit, and she gave the city a principal role in her revolutionary career.

Soon after their return to Paris, Michel and Malato left for London where they attended an anarchist congress and met and befriended Emile Pouget. Michel's formal anarchist career was in the initial stages. By 1883, she was meeting with anarchists in Paris, and that same year, she and Pouget led the much-publicized antigovernment demonstration from the Invalides to St. Germain-des-Près. Both anarchists were arrested and prosecuted in a trial that gave them renown and notoriety.

During the next twenty years, anarchists throughout France viewed Louise Michel as a symbol of revolutionary dedication. Such fame also made her the target of attacks, which reached their height in 1888 when she was shot and wounded in the head during a speaking engagement in Le Havre. This did not deter her revolutionary ardor; she recovered from her wound and continued a public role.[73]

Michel had to go into further exile during the early 1890s in order to avoid prosecution by French authorities during the trial of the thirty—an experience she again shared with Malato. The two friends met in London again and connected exile and anarchist engagement by joining Kropotkin's Avant-Garde group. At that time, Michel also attempted to establish an international libertarian school. However, her lifelong pursuit of revolutionary justice came into question upon her return to Paris in 1895 due to a renewed association with Henri Rochefort—a former fellow Communard who was turning strongly to the right and expressing nationalistic and anti-Semitic views. In fact, other anarchists and socialists questioned the wisdom of Michel's work for Rochefort's paper *L'Intransigeant* (the Intransigent). It was obvious that her writing for such a hate-generating publication only succeeded in demonstrating the strains between the views Michel had always represented and those that were evident in practically every other article or headline proclaiming hatred of the Jews. The episode revealed her bad judgment and lack of discrimination—tendencies already evident in leftist circles where criticism of a famous rebel, even for obvious reasons, was rigidly avoided.

This conflict became especially bitter during the Dreyfus Affair. Depending for her income upon Rochefort's commissions, she refused to support Dreyfus and oppose her publisher's racist views. Sébastien Faure, who considered himself Michel's friend, at this time led the Dreyfus cause among anarchists and publicly criticized her hesitation to speak more vocally. Michel defended herself by saying that anarchists had no business defending a bourgeois career military officer. This attitude provoked Faure to point out that she merely was allowing herself to be used by people who were really sinister militarists and nationalists and no longer revolutionaries. As will be evident later in this discussion, the anarchist debate over the Dreyfus Affair raised fundamental questions about anarchists' positions within the Third Republic and underlined their difficulty in retaining a revolutionary stance on all issues. It was also clear that revolutionaries were no longer confined to the left. New subversive types were appearing on the scene—on the fringes of the right—and Rochefort was now one of their representatives. This phenomenon would become even more obvious during the twentieth century.

Michel's career can be traced to an early enthusiasm for the revolutionary ideals of 1848 and for the Romanticism inherent in that era. Such impulses led her to become a Communard and an anarchist. As she stated in an interview in 1895:

> no one has done anything great without poetry . . . . We are all . . . the bards of the new era . . . . We march towards equality which is the sole justice, the sole liberty, the sole fraternity, which has in it, all purity and all "elevations."[74]

Michel's statement reiterates her ardent desire to reevoke the ambiance of 1789 within the society she viewed. It was now necessary to recast the slogan of the previous century in terms relevant to modern France and in such a manner as to give it a new sustaining force. Readers can gauge Michel's Romantic inclinations in her political writings. Also obvious are her consistent association of revolution with heroic action and poetic ideals and the depiction of her role as that of a bard. Nothing was more foreign to her than the cynical, scientific style of Marx. She demanded revolutionary passion, such as Marx would have deemed superfluous to the proletarian struggle. It was this passion that provoked her involvement in the Commune and later in anarchism. The revolutionary thread in her life was central to her historical and personal consciousness.

> Above everything else I am taken by the Revolution. It had to be that way. The wind that blew through the ruin where I was born, the old people who brought me up, the solitude and freedom of my childhood, the legends of the Haute-Marne, the scraps of knowledge gleaned from here and there—all that opened my ear to every harmony, my spirit to every illumination, my heart to both love and hate. Everything intermingled in a single song, a single dream, a single love: the Revolution.[75]

Michel's revolutionary ardor centered around the pursuit of justice and liberty—ideas and themes developed much earlier but to which she now attached even greater symbolic and emotional meaning. Revolution would restructure society and rid it of obstacles to the fulfillment of these ideals. This was no simple matter of strategy and realpolitik. Michel's description of her revolutionary thoughts and involvement resemble an artist's:

> Some people say I'm brave. Not really. There is no heroism; people are simply entranced by events. What happens is that in the face of danger my perceptions are submerged in my artistic sense, which is seized and charmed. Tableaux of the dangers overwhelm my thoughts, and the horrors of the struggle become poetry.[76]

While Michel attempted to equate poetry and justice, heroic action was paramount. Like other romantic rebels, Michel was consumed by the pursuit of heroic activity and espoused valor and élan as essential spurs to revolutionary radicalism.[77] Parisian history in recent years had, in fact, been molded by the activities of its heroes. As a participant, Michel stressed that this was especially true of the Commune with its symbolic, heroic barricades. Among the episodes in which Michel participated were the incendiary actions for which she gained legendary renown among fellow rebels and prosecution by police forces during the early days of the Third Republic.

Heroes had their villains. In this case, Thiers and the Versailles Provisional Government, the army, and the Bordeaux Assembly had been villainous in crushing the people's struggle. The military was an obvious choice against which Michel's anarchist wrath could be directed. Nevertheless, as with other anarchists, she equally condemned the Bordeaux Assembly, which stood as the bastion of misguided parliamentarianism, having been established in the closing days of the Franco-Prussian War when the government had fled Paris—allowing the Prussians (led by the infamous General Helmuth von Moltke) to begin their siege of the city. The Bordeaux Assembly had been intended to divert republicans from participating in any potential revolution—as indeed was appearing over the horizon in Paris. Several rebels did become co-opted, but Michel believed that they would become frustrated and eventually return to the streets alongside the people. She cited Georges Clemenceau as an example of one such frustrated republican who left the assembly in disgust after attempting to initiate radical reform from within it.[78] Of course, he would go on to other more nationalistic endeavors, leading the French cause for revanche after the First World War as the "tiger" of Versailles.

Michel never lost sight of the fact that the Commune had evolved into a conflict between Paris and the remainder of France.[79] She did not think that other French citizens were hostile to the revolutionary principles of the Paris Communards. Rather, the Versailles government (the artificial national center of baroque kings and queens) had duped the people into believing that the Communards were committing atrocities. (Of course, it was true that atrocities were committed by both sides.) Like Grave, Michel believed that lack of education and information among the peasants remained a primary problem and always would resurface to impede the progress of any future revolution. She emphasized that the Communards had attempted to address this problem by sending agents into the provinces to inform the people more concretely of the actual Parisian situation.[80] This had not worked, but it was a beginning. Therefore, anarchists needed to continue the process of educating the peasants—a cause to which Michel felt especially drawn considering her background as a teacher.

There were, in addition, some resemblances between Michel's comments on the Commune's importance and on the history of the French Revolution. As stated above, Michel was acutely aware of the conflict between the Parisian population and the government at Versailles. The memories of October, 1789 were strong. At that time the city of Paris and the monarch at Versailles stood in a tense standoff—the former under revolutionary control, the latter ensconced in baroque splendor. Consequently, the Women's March on Versailles was undertaken to bring the royal family back to Paris where it would remain under the watchful eyes of revolutionary authorities representing the people.[81]

During the Commune and less than a century later, Michel endorsed the idea of another march on Versailles, which would consolidate the new revolution and expand upon its goals. To further these ends, she proposed that someone assassinate Thiers in Versailles.[82] This went quite a bit further than the Women's March on Versailles, but it was obvious that Michel and other Communards viewed Versailles in mythical terms as the bastion of authority and the fulcrum of French hostility to Paris. Eventually, the gap between Paris and the larger French society had to be bridged. Nevertheless, such a development could only occur once the nation marched in tune to Parisian leadership in the struggle for justice. Indeed, it had to be recognized that Paris was the revolution. As the city in the forefront of French rebellion, Paris drew Michel's revolutionary ardor—a fact clearly evident when she returned there as an anarchist and gained notoriety in the Invalides demonstration of 1883.

Michel also emphasized the important role played by women in the organization and execution of the march on Versailles in 1789 and later in the Commune itself. Obviously she was thinking of her own central role. Yet she also pointed to other important episodes of women's participation. Among such examples stood women's efforts to defend Parisian cannons from government troops in March, 1871 and to instill Commune principles among people in the provinces. In the latter example, we observe one side of the effort to unite Paris and the remainder of French society in the revolutionary struggle. Michel, thus, highlighted the crucial significance of women's engagement in both struggles as well as their suitability in leading the work of revolution. This role emanated, she believed, from their more practical nature and ability to be attuned to the particular needs of urgent action. As she stated:

> If the reaction had had as many enemies among women as it did among men, the Versailles government would have had a more difficult task subduing us. Our male friends are more susceptible to faintheartedness than we women are. A supposedly weak woman knows better than any man how to say: "It must be done." She may feel ripped open to her very womb, but she remains unmoved. Without hate, without anger, without pity for herself or others, whether her heart bleeds or not, she says, "It must be done." Such were the women of the Commune.[83]

Despite masculine ideas about the "faintheartedness" of women, Michel believed the opposite to be the case. Among the actions Michel believed "had to be done" was the setting of fires, for which she and other Communard women were prosecuted by the governmental authorities of the early Third Republic. Women were central to the carrying out of these incendiary actions, and she emphasized that feminism was as important to her as any other contemporary issue. Yet women could only flourish within revolutionary movements. They needed to involve themselves in such phenomena because only in so doing could they further their emancipation from male-dominated institutions and ensure that rights and status were equally accorded to both sexes.

These instances all reflected Michel's belief in the guiding power of ideals and principles. She was especially struck by primitive life in New Caledonia where both the harshness of reality and human virtue were equally vivid. In contrast, Western civilization was dominated by distractions and superfluous extravagances that clouded one's view of true human needs. Misery and French colonial oppression in New Caledonia were harsh, but they did not eliminate the natives' harmonious cooperation. Such contrasts could provoke anarchistic aspirations. The natives, despite their situation, exhibited arduous, cooperative efforts. Anarchists (and by this time Michel could be counted among them) believed that humanity's simple goodness gave it the ability to attain the ultimate dream of a perfect society where inequity and injustice were vanquished. This was not the first time that anarchists evoked a vision seemingly indebted to the ideas of Rousseau. It was also true that the agon for that end involved the simplicity of untainted human character struggling against unscrupulous, exploitative authority. Michel, thereby, accepted all aspects of anarchist tenets by directly observing colonial oppression in action. The absence of customary European conditions disguising authoritarianism and injustice brought the situation into even greater clarity.

As noted, Michel had witnessed a native rebellion against the French in New Caledonia, and the event affected her revolutionary ideas. She felt, in fact, that the rebels there "were seeking the same liberty we had sought in the Commune."[84] Because she believed that the rebellions in both cases had a common human and global basis, she stated that "liberty" and "equality" were now universal principles relevant to all societies and at all times. Yet it was also true that because people in New Caledonia were less corrupted by the forces of modern capitalist society, they were able to verbalize and feel these principles more acutely. Like many other travelers, Michel conveyed her own beliefs and predispositions in what she considered to be objective observations. In this case, it was the perspective of the nineteenth-century Romantic attempting to revitalize the lively and vibrant legacy of the French Revolution.

While Michel herself would not deny the influence of past history upon her beliefs (as with the events of 1789 or a few lines in Hugo's verses), by 1880 she seemed to have become more ahistorical in her thinking and more concerned with the universal nature of oppression, injustice, and inequality. Geography and time alike were unable to prevent such problems from becoming serious areas of dispute. She could, thus, attune her critical focus by moving her revolutionary lens from ancient Rome to the modern world. In this way, she developed a more cosmopolitan consciousness and stressed that all cultures had to learn mutual cooperation if only because they shared similar structures.[85]

Exile had not made Michel a repentant or regretful revolutionary. If anything, after she became an anarchist in New Caledonia, her views radicalized. She returned to France determined to play a new role in fighting the established order. At the same time, she believed that France was not an isolated nation caught alone within the snare of authority and the revolutionary tradition combating it. Its famous history of rebellion most momentously inaugurated in 1789 was significant, but the chain of events begun then was finding dramatic relevance as well in other parts of the world.

The geographer and anarchist theorist Elisée Reclus attempted to prove that revolutions were part of a continual process originating in the biological and geographical spheres of existence. The clock, influenced by so many extrahistorical forces, could not be reversed.[86] Reclus defined revolution as the final and, inevitably, violent expression of change contrasted to the less abrupt form of transformation— evolution. Nevertheless, it was significant, he believed, that revolutionary scenarios were part of a determined and objective reality existing independently of their participants, who were merely puppets pulled by the strings of larger forces. Nature was the determining factor, above all, in revolutions.

This deterministic view is paradoxical considering the great esteem given by anarchists to individual freedom and spontaneous volition. Yet it was shared by many such libertarians and especially highlighted the thoughts and feelings of those drawn to the ideas of Kropotkin and Reclus. Theoretical anarchism was especially prone to this interpretation. It did not embrace the whole of the movement within which one could find examples of individuals delineating their roles and attempting as much as possible to emphasize their self-willed actions. Still, the past always served as a reservoir of great events and conflicts against authority to which anarchists of all categories could come to drink its waters of inspiration. Past, present, and future were all one and part of the same ongoing process of revolutionary struggle against oppression and great wealth.

Anarchists' dreams, thoughts, and actions for their ideal society (which they would have hesitated to call "utopia") were framed by the past and the surrounding environment, which served as sources of inspiration. Therefore, since past insurrections had paved the way for the conflicts of the present, it was necessary to study their import and relevance to the contemporary world.

It was obvious also that revolutions would continue until the end point was reached. So it was imperative that justice-seeking rebels "hitch their wagon" to the proper star. The moral imperative, however, was to learn from the goals of former rebels and discover potential limitations. Mistakes of judgment could not be repeated. This implied that, to a certain extent, history provided more than its ample share of flawed examples. It was important to minimize the criticism directed against those who had erred in the name of justice, liberty, and equality and to continue respecting their idealized status. However, it was also essential to point to any tactical mistakes they had made. The past also provided a great many assets to those dedicated to revolution. Anarchists could retrieve slogans and rallying cries shouted a century earlier and the symbolic gestures and forms accompanying them. For this reason, a march on Versailles or a street barricade provided an amazing amount of emotional ammunition. One could, for instance, lead a demonstration to the hated symbol of the Invalides and take one's place within the revolutionary heritage. This latter point was especially driven home by such figures as Louise Michel, who had participated in such a momentous event as the Paris Commune. Since memories of that event were deeply felt in the 1880s and 1890s, Michel's ability to stir emotions among anarchists cannot be minimized. Such memories transcended theory and brought forward the symbols and connecting threads of the past, giving the revolutionary struggle its deepest meaning to those engaged on its behalf. After all, anarchists scrutinized revolutions not only to learn theory and facts but most importantly to trace their movement's relation to the past in order that the revolutionary thread could continue to be woven into the future.

# The Anarchist Debate and the Third Republic

Revolutionaries sharing a common dogma frequently clash about the issues and questions that resonate from their surrounding society and on which they must state positions. Debates over tactics and strategy are often at the heart of such conflicts, which are further complicated by emotional and political predispositions. Since anarchists did not agree on a consistent program to begin with, they were especially prone to deep divisions and disputes in coming to terms with the problems facing the early years of the Third Republic. Among the issues anarchists confronted were violence and terrorism, the Dreyfus Affair and its revelation of mass French anti-Semitism, the tension of modern urban life, syndicalism, education, and the legitimacy of parliamentary democracy and capitalism in the Third Republic during the 1880s and 1890s. As anarchists addressed these issues, they inevitably reflected their own myriad of concerns centered around questions of goals and methods relevant to their movement. This chapter will focus upon the anarchist debate over key questions and the manner in which this dialogue affected the movement—both as a whole and as a splintered assortment of groups spread throughout the arrondissements of Paris during the fin de siècle.

As is evident, anarchists yearned for the elimination of social inequality and the bolstering of individual freedom. In this pursuit, they generally shared a common resistance to government, capitalist enterprise, and official institutions. Like other revolutionaries, anarchists attacked both the existing authority and potential rivals on the left whom they could accuse of inaugurating a new era of despotism. They especially singled out Marxists, in a tradition going back to Mikhail Bakunin's condemnation of Marx at the International of 1860. Revolutionaries on the left of the political spectrum have always clashed over tactics; anarchists were greatly sensitive to the authoritarian currents running in rival revolutionary circles. As noted earlier, the art critic turned anarchist Félix Fénéon attacked Marxists because of their alleged desire to create "a society in which each citizen carries a number. They prefer the complexity of a clock to that of a living body."[1] This statement has a peculiar mid-twentieth century ring to it and foreshadows Orwellian criticisms, but Fénéon's statement also implies that Marxists are too concerned with abstractions and thus capable of building a new theoretically based authoritarian order.

It was difficult, nonetheless, to maintain a united anarchist perspective on Marxism since participants tended to be divided between those emphasizing social concerns and those espousing extreme individualism, wavering at times toward decadence.[2] Throughout the 1890s, anarchists quarreled over the various questions confronting them and justified their positions by pointing to one side or the other of their vast ideological terrain. They were, accordingly, quick to accuse each other of betraying the movement and of creating a socialist organization at the expense of liberty, or, conversely, of allowing egoism to supplant community concerns. Their debates oscillated between these contrasting poles even as they confronted seemingly unrelated issues.


## ANARCHIST VIEWS OF THE THIRD REPUBLIC


Perhaps central to the anarchist debates was the relationship of the movement to the Third Republic. It has already been noted that until the 1870s, French revolutionaries had placed their hopes for change in democracy and republican government. It had, after all, not been easy to maintain stable republican government from 1792 to 1794 and in 1848. Social, economic, and political change and republicanism had been inextricably linked in the pattern of history. This was evident, for instance, in the career of Louis Blanc and his role in 1848. Bonapartism and the Restoration had halted and reversed the direction of progress achieved under the two republics. Militarism crept back into French life, and, although clerical feeling for Napoléon was lukewarm, the church assumed new prestige and power—especially during the reign of Charles X. Nevertheless, anarchists also explained that the path for these reactionary forces had been cleared by the more conservatively minded reformers who first opted for republicanism, profited from it, and then objected to its expansion. This reality was vividly evident in the actions of the bourgeoisie and the peasants.

The Boulangist phenomenon and its threat to impose an authoritarian government headed by the popular general between 1887 and 1889 was a fresh reminder of the traditional forces that could menace the Third Republic. Anarchist ambiguity about the Third Republic was, however, most noticeable. As a departure from monarchy and Bonapartism, the Third Republic was perceived as a descendant of the previous governments instituted by revolutions. Its very name made this relationship clear and unmistakable. Marianne flourished once again.

As worshippers of the French revolutionary tradition, anarchists favored the republic and contrasted it to the more overtly oppressive monarchies and imperial despotisms. Nevertheless, they were reluctant to endorse the Third Republic wholeheartedly since its political leaders had made too many concessions to the upper classes and disappointed the earlier hopes for social, economic, and political reform held by anarchists and socialists alike.

Some anarchists saw the conflict between the hopes for complete transformation and the compromising realities in the early years of the Third Republic summarized in the ambiguous historical position of Leon Gambetta. After his heroic stands during the Paris Commune, Gambetta attempted to institute republican government and found compromise with moderates an essential component of his program. This act disillusioned many of his admirers who began to view him as yet another moderate. Gambetta's premature death, while endowing him with the status of a martyr in some circles, did not diminish the acerbic criticism directed at him from others. Emile Gauthier emphasized such a sense of disappointment in a poem in which he depicted Gambetta as an enemy of the Commune's spirit. Gambetta is seen as having attempted to destroy this spirit only to be frustrated by the heroic determination of the Parisian fédérés—the last to fall at Père Lachaise.[3] Gauthier saw Gambetta's democratic republicanism by the mid-1870s as having no further revolutionary significance. The compromise intrinsic to democracy meant that it was no longer the ideal for radical goals. At the same time, anarchists could not make liberty their sole rallying-cry. They instead needed to strive for egalitarian goals in order to combat the type of excessive liberty leading to laissez-faire capitalism and limitless social exploitation.

It is true that many revolutionaries had been disappointed by the political programs of the first two republics that ignored the voices of those pushing for further change. Maximilien Robespierre's suppression of the sans-culottes and the June days of 1848 also demonstrated the determination of republican leaders to destroy popular egalitarian forces if compelled to do so. Nevertheless, these governments had not endured for long before being overthrown. Those sacrificing their lives for these governments would eventually be seen as martyrs by succeeding participants in the revolutionary struggle. The Third Republic, in contrast, was surviving and, therefore, not surrounded by the aura of tragedy coloring popular images of the former two. Furthermore, radicals bitterly recalled the Commune's final defeat at the hands of the newly installed government. Their memories reinforced the perception of the Third Republic as a militaristic regime that had put down attempts at radical government—as seen, for instance, in the efforts of the Communards. It was also no surprise that this same republic would attempt to block the anarchists from realizing their goals. Thus, anarchists opposed the Third Republic regardless of whether the governing coalition was led by Monarchists, Opportunists, Radicals, or Socialists. No established government then conceived could, as far as anarchists were concerned, confront the range of social and political problems in the just manner.

Anarchists' views of republicanism, then, were not clearly defined. They accused the republic and the parliamentary system of servicing the interests of the bourgeoisie and of betraying the lower classes. Some anarchists even pointed to the Convention of 1793 (otherwise known as a bastion of radicalism) as one example of a corrupt parliament placing personal power and prestige above the concerns of the masses.[4] Similarly, Charles Malato felt that the government of the Third Republic expressed none of the Communards' ideals. It had reversed the movement toward popular government, republicanism, and justice (the goals of any future legitimate society) and, in the lavish display of cynicism and corruption by its leaders, mocked the valiant sacrifices displayed in 1871.[5] Malato would continually recount his increasingly bitter realization that the Romantic idealism of Giuseppe Mazzini, originally inspiring his own revolutionary aims in Italy and continuing to do so after he crossed the Alps into France, was being betrayed by the creators of the Third Republic.[6] It was for such reasons that anarchists urged their comrades to abstain from voting in elections since doing so endorsed the system.[7] The radical journalist Zo d'Axa proposed that anarchists express their scorn for the republic's elections by voting for an ass. [8] He meant here a literal ass and did not use the term to describe a person. Within a completely different context, d'Axa used the ass to deride the republic as the mad emperor Caligula used a horse to mock the Senate, proclaiming it senator during the strange days of the Claudians in ancient Rome. Such action would obviously bring more discredit upon the electoral system if taken by large numbers of voters. Ridicule was an all-important weapon.

On the other hand, anarchists still viewed the Third Republic as a progressive force when compared to the autocracy of the Second Empire and the narrow elitism of the July Monarchy ruling France between 1830 and 1848.

Some anarchists came to its defense when it was attacked by reactionaries. Sébastien Faure, for example, was quick to defend the republic against leftist and rightist cries for its overthrow. Consequently, at the meetings he sponsored, Faure was often heckled by anarchists of a differing persuasion.[9] Faure was especially on guard, however, against right-wing extremists who focused upon chauvinistic nationalism and anti-Semitism in their attempts to gain popular support. Such mass agitation was mobilized to threaten the stability of the fragile democratic structure established after the Second Empire's collapse in 1870.[10] As in the case of Malato, Faure invoked memories of the Communards' ardent devotion to democratic government and accused all opponents of the republic of not only insulting the Communards' memories but of also demeaning the nature of their sacrifices. At the same time, Louise Michel resurrected the Commune's heritage to mobilize anarchists. However, "the Red Virgin" was ambivalent about the republic. While praising the efforts of those who had sacrificed their lives for the new republic, Michel viewed the actual rulers of the new order as despotic and determined to uphold the privileges of capitalists' wealth, on which they were dependent.[11]

The anarchist dialogue over the place of republicanism in the movement was relevant to a variety of questions. Some viewed republicanism against the background of a mythic past molded by revolutionary forces. Others saw it as an unpleasant compromise through which the bourgeoisie oppressed the people in new and progressive ways. Those taking the former perspective felt that the republic was a necessary step in the direction of an egalitarian and just society. Others, taking the latter view, were inclined to depict that government as a retarding force, implemented to prevent a final, apocalyptic, and revolutionary change from taking place. (Such a perspective can be found in the person of Souvarine depicted in Emile Zola's novel *Germinal.*)[12]

In a sense, the divergence revolved around the desires for reform or revolution. Even in a movement whose primary aim was revolution, the choice between the two poles was evident—especially against the backdrop of Paris with its connections to both institutionalized power and the revolutionary overthrow of it. Anarchists always portrayed themselves as part of a revolutionary tradition whose programs and dogmas reflected the historic upheavals of the past. Nevertheless, they also had choices to make regarding the central issues of the time, and, in this way, found that compromise was an alternative. Therefore, they brought to their views of contemporary questions a range of opinions concerning accommodation or rejection of the Third Republic. They felt it important to ask whether the government was a result of revolutionary change. Their complex answers to that question brought out a host of other inter-related matters, which they also had to confront.

## TERRORISM

Anarchists agreed that any revolution would entail the need for violence and suffering. As one anonymous member of the movement stated in 1885, "We must not have universal suffrage because revolutions have never been made by elections but by force."[13] Anarchists did not bypass the issue of blood since they viewed it as necessary to the revolution's final fulfillment.[14] Some even tried to guess the length of time required to end the social conflict and the amount of corpses necessary. Police spies in 1892 quoted one vocal anarchist, Jacques Prolo, as proclaiming at a meeting that ten to twenty years of perpetual war and between two to five million dead would be required for the execution of an anarchist revolution.[15] Like many anarchists, he did not ignore the need for violence and seemed to echo Jean-Paul Marat's demand a century earlier that 200,000 heads be severed for the saving of a million others. Prolo stressed the inevitability of blood and relished the chance to visualize destruction.

More problematic were the questions revolving around the nature of violence, its appropriate form, and its timing. The wave of terrorist bombings carried out from 1890 to 1894 by "inspired" individuals such as Francois-Claudius Ravachol (whose original name was Koenigstein and who also went under the name of Leon Leger), Auguste Vaillant, and Emile Henry brought these matters to the forefront of the movement itself since many of the bombers professed to be anarchists. Among such terrorist acts were the assassination of President Sadi Carnot, the detonation of a bomb in the Chamber of Deputies, and the bombing of the Café Terminus in the Gare St. Lazare. The public trials of these individuals brought forward emotional self-defending speeches in which the accused presented their crimes as justified in the name of the anarchist-inspired social struggle. This self-justification has to this day caused a blurring in popular mentality between the terms "anarchist" and "terrorist."

Anarchists subsequently found themselves troubled by the issue of whether or not such actions constituted revolutionary engagement. Were they, in other words, part of the wider movement of anarchist insurrection? Could individuals decide singlehandedly to act and carry out "propaganda by the deed" on behalf of the entire movement? Within the anarchist movement there was a deep split between those condemning and those praising the terrorist acts. Ambiguity surrounded the character of terrorists, but their claims created a problem for anarchists. Ravachol, Vaillant, and Henry had characterized themselves as sympathizers, and Henry himself worked for Zo d'Axa's review *L'Endehors* and associated with some of the leading anarchists of Paris. The three justified their deeds by appealing to anarchist doctrine and claiming it as the most precise verbalization of their cloudy aspirations. While offering some sympathy for the terrorists, organized anarchists also were prone to practice the art of distancing and exhibited caution and reluctance in accepting the terrorists as their comrades.

Some anarchists accepted the need for individuals to act spontaneously through terrorism. Individual freedom was, after all, intrinsic to the movement's goals. They also hoped that a series of such events would ultimately instigate the larger revolution that would destroy the old order and create an anarchist society. A conflagration was necessary. These libertarians tended to regard terrorists as martyrs who had been willing to sacrifice their happiness and well-being for the benefit of the entire community and had ignited the fuse. This contention could even be applied to some unexpected cases. For instance, the poet Paul Adam depicted Ravachol as a redeemer and compared his "sacrifice and offering" to Christ's in that both were nonconformists, expressed contempt for the values of their surrounding society, and represented high ideals (left undefined).[16] At meetings, anarchist writers like Laurent Tailhade praised the actions of Henry and Ravachol[17] and extolled violence against bourgeois establishments. A song called "the Ravachol" was invoked both as a danse macabre (dance of death) and as a way of rousing and inspiring anarchists much in the manner that the old "Carmagnole" had been used to stir revolutionary feelings. This was a virtual hymn to terrorism in general and to dynamite in particular.

> Dans la grande ville de Paris
> Il y a des bourgeois bien nourris
> Il y a les misereux qui ont le ventre creux
> Ceux la ont les dents longues
> Ceux la ont les dents longues,
> Dansons la Ravachol
> Dansons la Ravachol
> Vive le son, Vive le son
> Vive le son d'explosion
> Vive le son, Vive le son
> Vive le son d'explosion
> Ah ça ira, ça ira
> Ah ça ira, ça ira.

TRANSLATION:

> In the great city of Paris
> live the well-fed bourgeois
> and the desperate ones with hollow stomachs

but with long teeth.
Dance the Ravachol.
Long live the sound of explosions.
So it will be.[18]

The song takes aim at the class conflict in Paris between the "well-nourished" bourgeoisie and the hungry, miserable masses who sharpen their teeth and hope to hear the sounds of explosions. The poetic range here is obviously limited, but the sounds of modern conflict sweep along the roused audience with a ritual resonance. Such a dance of death was further celebrated in a song written by Marie Constant under the pseudonym of "Père la Purge" and entitled "Dame Dynamite." Its import can be gathered by the title alone, but it included the refrain:

Dame Dynamite
Que l'on danse vite,
Dansons et chantons
Et dynamitons

TRANSLATION:

Lady Dynamite
let us dance quickly
let us dance, sing, and dynamite.[19]

While any thought of poetic subtlety is absent also in this song, the enthusiasm and sympathy felt by anarchists for terrorists is evident, and the movement's instinctual, theatrical inclination for violence clearly influenced the nature of debate over the question.

Nevertheless, the issue was not clear-cut. Jean Grave criticized individual acts of terror even when he expressed sympathy for those committing them. Grave pointed to the frustrations and anger at existing social conditions in France that had caused such explosions. Theoretical anarchists like Grave did not completely disown Ravachol, Vaillant, and Henry. Grave himself stressed that people needed to understand that such figures had lost patience with the Third Republic's bourgeois government and saw no open avenues through which they could act other than terror. In this respect, he sympathized with terrorists.[20] Grave did not feel that anarchists should be lenient to those in power. In fact, he urged anarchists to express their anger through forceful denunciations of the system and through terroristic language employing sarcasm and irony—an advocacy possibly at odds with Grave's general image as a theoretical and overly rational journalist (anarchists indeed tended to view

Grave's style as diametrically opposite to Pouget's).[21] Still, he never suggested that anarchists should imitate acts committed by Russian and Italian terrorists (among others) because, in his view, these efforts were wasted and would be better utilized if directed through the collective revolt of workers.[22]

Grave believed that a true revolution could occur only through collective action and that terror undertaken by sole individuals would not produce anything more dramatic than police suppression. (Grave himself was persecuted and tried by the authorities in 1894.) According to his perspective, revolution would occur only when the timing and circumstances were right. If individuals attempted to hasten its outbreak under the wrong set of conditions, the collective movement itself would be harmed.

Grave's view was highly influenced by a sense of caution and restraint. He believed that revolutions needed to be planned and historically timed. As already noted, Grave urged anarchists to understand the causes of past revolutions and to realize why they had occurred at certain moments within a historical environment rather than at others. He also argued that it was imperative for anarchists to scrutinize the reasons for the failure of certain rebellions; if one looked closely, it would be evident that failed revolutionary upheavals had not been undertaken at the correct historical moment. Grave's view paralleled the Marxist emphasis upon restraint and the need to trust historical conditions as the proper fostering agents of revolution. Mistakes and disasters could ensue if people tried to overturn governments not ready for an early demise. Unlike Bakunin, Grave did not believe in immediate action, and this view was further reflected in the way he approached the issue of terrorism, which he saw as premature and fated only to produce reaction. His view, however, also brought opposing anarchists to depict him as an overly cautious theorist.

In addition to preaching patience and restraint, Grave also urged workers to learn the full range of historical issues and to distrust vague aspirations and the momentary outbursts of terrorists.[23] As would be true of a "rational anarchist" committed to the International mold of theoretical socialism, Grave stressed the need for adherents to learn historical consciousness and anarchist theory. He wanted:

> complete and perpetual revolt, in all of its forms, but not unconscious revolt which strikes out blindly under the impulse of a momentary anger and brings about a passing explosion . . . rather . . . conscious revolt which knows where it goes.[24]

Direction was all-important, and it was necessary for the workers to reach a certain collective level of consciousness concerning appropriate action. Laborers could become true revolutionaries only after becoming anarchist theorists since theory alone could enable them to learn about their rights and the proper means of revolt.[25] As we can see, Grave stressed the workers' central role as significant revolutionary instigators. Detached individuals were not in the best position to act because the knowledge and level of consciousness they could attain did not approach even remotely the awareness mass numbers of workers achieved. As with Rousseau's concept of the "general will," it will later be seen that education would have a critical role to play in effecting such a degree of consciousness. The alternative would be blind, ignorant, and futile rebellions.

Grave and the anarchists within his circle continued to believe that knowledge and reason were instrumental in the process of change. Consequently, theory preceded action, not vice versa. This current of anarchist belief was strong during the 1880s, but during the following decade it was increasingly challenged by other trends emphasizing immediate action and irrational means. This movement against rationality was most evident in the case of the Naturiens who attacked the very essence of civilization itself and sought a Romantic retreat into nature.

Other anarchists were more sympathetic to Ravachol and Vaillant and tried to explain their acts by referring to the state of injustice prevailing in the Third Republic. Often, ambiguity was the only verbal device they could use to express their sentiments. At other moments, they attempted to be more open and pronounced. For instance, the journalist and playwright Octave Mirbeau felt that the terroristic period was an unavoidable transition to an anarchist society and had been instigated by the government's violence and oppression. As he saw it, Ravachol's bomb was at least imbued with the "Idea and with Pity."[26] It had, in other words, been hurled and exploded out of indignation at social injustice and sympathy for the oppressed. Louise Michel also believed that it was more important to locate the causes of terrorism in the social abuses of the wealthy. Before terrorists ceased their actions, such abuses would have to be eradicated through a social revolution. She, thus, refused to condemn terrorist acts unconditionally, although she did imply that the actions of the collective whole would be more relevant to the cause.[27]

These divergent views perhaps did not contradict each other as is first apparent. While most of the thirty anarchists tried in 1894 denied any participation in the bombings, they all expressed an emotional affinity to and sympathy for the people carrying out such heroic deeds. Nevertheless, further thought about the possible consequences of "propaganda by the deed" to the movement brought divisions and caused some compagnons to engage in antiterrorist rhetoric and others to applaud the crimes.

The critic Camille Mauclair became an anarchist largely through his sympathy for Vaillant following the terrorist's execution. Yet he later claimed that he overcame this emotion by much afterthought and reflection. At that point, he realized that the passion for destruction and hatred needed to be replaced by more constructive acts and thoughts.[28] Mauclair developed his perspective through his immersion in the new ethics of the individual as seen in egoism. He frequently alluded to Friedrich Nietzsche's writings and especially to the concept of "self- overcoming" attained by introspection and self-knowledge. Although Nietzsche's works are filled with calls for heroic action of a different type, Mauclair believed that the strong person acted only after much reflection; he did not submit to nor act from the demands of the spontaneous will. Mauclair came to see terrorism as an impulsive, misguided program of insignificant action that contradicted his behavioral ethos. Nonetheless, observers could wonder about his own later thoughtless drift into fascist circles.

The anarchist debate about terrorism during the 1880s and 1890s was, quite literally, one between those favoring construction and those preferring destruction. Virtually all anarchists agreed in their condemnation of the system's oppression and felt the same anger that had triggered the terrorists' acts. The real question, however, was whether the revolutionary movement would be bolstered by bombings and shootings committed with such destructive intent or damaged by the ensuing backlash of public opinion and police suppression. Furthermore, would terrorism hurt the solidarity of group action that required a certain amount of individual restraint to be effective? Such anarchist critics of terrorism stressed that the movement could only progress if individuals coordinated their actions. Rash, spontaneous behavior came at the expense of the whole community. Those hating the system then in place could either revel in the destruction and chaos or urge a transcendence and catharsis of such volatile passions in more decisive revolutionary actions. While terrorism reflected the social resentment and hostility of anarchists, it nonetheless divided them as they sought to assess proper revolutionary practice. This was also true of the issues highlighted by the Dreyfus Affair and syndicalism.

## THE DREYFUS AFFAIR

Unlike Marxism, the type of anarchism originating from the International revolved around both the end of the exploitative class system and social concerns. Grave yearned for:

the complete transformation of society, well-being for all, the elimination
of inequality, and the abolition of exploitation of man by man.[29]

This statement reveals a very definite social side to anarchism and, furthermore,
in its federated and mutualistic character, one that competed with the Marxists'
notions of opposition to the bourgeoisie's social and economic order. Anarchists
used the word *association* to denote group action. It had a more nebulous, less
rigid, and, consequently, to anarchist ears, less sinister connotation than the
word *organization.*

Other anarchists, however, stressed the more individualistic themes of
the movement and, while not necessarily ignoring the class struggle and other
social issues, emphasized personal human rights. They claimed that the era's
most pressing needs were the full establishment of individual liberty and civil
rights. Consequently, they stressed that these issues were the most pressing
ones for anarchists to address.

Perhaps no issue brought out this aspect of French anarchism as did the
Dreyfus Affair of the 1890s. At the same time, no other issue of the time
divided the anarchists—or indeed most sectors of French society—so greatly.
While most revolutionary anarchists sympathized with the Jewish captain
unjustly sent to Devil's Island on charges of treason and viewed him as a victim
of unfair judgment, their conflicts over the meaning and nature of anarchism
caused their diverging in interpretations of the meaning of the affair. Consequently, they advocated different courses of action regarding publicization of
the case before their compagnons.

Connected with this cause was the question of how anarchists could
defend an officer of the military who came from an apparently prosperous
family. Would a pro-Dreyfus stand dilute the essence of class hostility so vital
to the anarchist movement?[30] In using his base within the movement to defend
Dreyfus, Sébastien Faure made himself vulnerable to the charge that he was not
acting like an anarchist but instead was standing up for the wealthy.

As we have seen, Faure was the anarchist most closely associated with the
Dreyfusard cause. He had become convinced of Dreyfus's innocence through
the persuasion of his Zionist friend, Bernard Lazare—himself attracted to
anarchist ideology. Beginning in July, 1898, Faure devoted an increasing
number of articles in *Le Libertaire* (the Libertarian) to the Dreyfus case—
following the courageous lead of Emile Zola's polemic, *J'accuse.* In February
of the next year, Faure began a daily newspaper entitled *Le Journal du Peuple*
(the People's Daily) and focused nearly all of its reporting on the Dreyfus case.
Of course, he also tried to link the affair to social questions pertinent to
anarchism and insisted that this cause would ultimately create a more revolu-

tionary climate.[31] He expressed satisfaction at seeing bourgeois division ensuing from the question and hoped that this internal unsettlement would aid revolutionaries in their quest for power. Yet he also stated that he was willing to ally his anarchist sentiments with those of the bourgeoisie in defending Dreyfus, thus expressing his commitment to individual liberty and freedom from unjust persecution.[32] Faure expanded upon this case in anarchist meetings in Paris and eventually organized a series of meetings and conferences exclusively devoted to the Dreyfus cause.

Faure attacked the anti-Dreyfusard, anti-Semitic press run by Edouard Drumont and Henri Rochefort. He singled out Rochefort for especially bitter criticism, pointing out that this anti-Dreyfusard had originally been a Communard in 1871 but had been swept along by the wave of chauvinistic nationalism and reaction directed by the military and the Catholic Church.[33] Rochefort was also undeniably anti-Semitic, and he combined this bias with extreme nationalism and devotion to the Third Republic to claim that Jews were working together with Germany to plan a future military invasion of France. This assertion revealed how monarchism was not the only reactionary force then conceivable. Even republicanism could create a xenophobic reactionary tendency. As part of the entrenched status quo, republicans, thus disposed, could focus attention upon both non-Christians and the Germans as the enemies of France.

Rochefort's ideas from his Communard involvement through the Dreyfus Affair display continuity in his central concern for the national interest. In fact, like Drumont, he was reflecting the new form of anti-Semitism that addressed mass audiences by appealing to feelings both of economic anxiety and national chauvinism. Such a phenomenon was then in vogue not only in Paris but also in Vienna and other centers.[34] Nevertheless, Rochefort was not averse to using traditional anti-Semitic language within his broad, sweeping vision. Faure was dismayed to hear Rochefort defend the Third Republic under the banner of anti-Semitism, to attack Dreyfus as an "odious Iscariot," and to proclaim that the Dreyfusard Terror had replaced the White Terror—the infamous period of blood-letting during the French Revolution primarily directed against Jacobins.[35] Some traditional church views were thus combined with a defense of the republic (supposedly instituted on behalf of the people) and an attack upon the Thermidoreans who had overthrown Robespierre over a century earlier and cut down the Jacobins. Anarchists like the poet Adolphe Retté believed that the new rise of militarism and clericalism was almost solely attributable to the writings of Rochefort and the right-wing aesthete Maurice Barrès.[36] Whatever the vantage point of observers, it was clear in studying the Dreyfus Affair that the right wing in France was no longer the exclusive domain of monarchists and Bonapartists; it now had a mass base and even was attached to republicanism.

Faure felt that anti-Semitism was an ideology that disguised the forces of the military, clerics, and royalists.[37] Zo d'Axa believed that Drumont's paper *Le Libre Parole* (the Free Word) was "simply nationalist . . . traditional and royalist."[38] D'Axa was also puzzled by Rochefort's own "conversion" to anti-Semitism, which, he claimed, represented a renunciation of his former revolutionary stance. Both nationalism and anti-Semitism were clearly at odds with anarchist ideology as it had been developed up to this point, and it was not easy for one adhering to it to mesh a Communard past with participation in the anti-Dreyfusard movement. D'Axa could only mock Rochefort and publish a fake obituary proclaiming the latter formally dead as a revolutionary.[39] Nevertheless, as we can see, Faure and d'Axa both underestimated the strength of the new right-wing forces as they transcended the limitations of past conservative movements and learned the extreme rhetoric so easily embraced collectively by the masses. Anti-Dreyfusards were not simply resurrecting traditional forces in French history (though they did so partly) but expanding their emotional terrain into mass society and its wide expanse of phobias and paranoia. From our perspective we can, thus, understand how D'Axa and Faure were easily bewildered by the puzzling political evolution of someone like Rochefort.

Certainly anarchists' commitment to the Dreyfusard camp partially reflected their opposition to the reactionary anti-Semitic press operated by former leftists with backgrounds similar to their own. Grave expressed dismay over the fervor with which Drumont and Rochefort directed their attacks on Dreyfus and Jews and, in doing so, profited both politically and financially—an attack he also levelled against Faure.[40]

Nevertheless, anarchists were unable to offer a uniform judgment upon the Dreyfus Affair nor, given their political predispositions, to arrive at a complete assessment of it. Not all anarchists supported Dreyfus, not even (as noted above) Louise Michel. She was not overtly anti-Semitic but refused to write or speak on behalf of Dreyfus because of her work with Rochefort's newspaper and dependence upon his financial support.[41] It was not until 1899 that Grave endorsed Faure's Dreyfusard efforts. In doing so, he lowered the level of criticism he had earlier directed at Faure for overemphasizing individual liberty at the expense of social goals.[42] Faure's response to Grave's previous attacks had been to remind him that liberty and revolution were intertwined. One of Faure's friends, Georges Renard, believed that Grave's attacks had been motivated by a secret, underlying sympathy for Rochefort's racism. What such a series of positions and accusations reveals, however, is uncertainty and awkwardness arising from a largely ambiguous political terrain just being confronted by anarchists in unprecedented circumstances.[43] Clearly defined instances of injustice were obvious to the viewer, but working out their connection to revolutionary ideology was not. At anarchist conferences and meetings, questions arose as to whether or not such short-term involvements as the Dreyfus Case were sacrificing vital and real revolutionary goals.[44] Faure's cooperation with Jean Jaurès and socialists (willing under Alexandre Millerand in 1899 to enter the government coalition) also provoked other anarchists to label him an "anarchiste de gouvernement," an unacceptable oxymoron.[45] Other members of the movement also held that even if Dreyfus were innocent of the specific charges against him, he was guilty in the larger sense of involvement in the military—an institution falling under the broad, sweeping, hostile anarchist glare of condemnation.[46]

Perhaps the most difficult prejudice to combat was the association of Jews with capital and money. Even in those reviews that refrained from the vicious anti-Semitism of Drumont and Rochefort, there were references to "King Rothschild".[47]

Grave received a letter from Captain Gustave Nercy, who claimed to be a libertarian but who feared France's vulnerability to foreign and domestic enemies. Nercy issued a blanket condemnation of capitalism but stated that Jewish capitalists stole more money than did Catholics. His conclusion was that Dreyfus was a traitor because he was a Jew.[48] Faure viewed such anarchist or socialist attacks as examples of racial prejudice directed against particular individuals, but also depicted them as naive and pointless diversions from the movement's real purpose—to combat clerical and military power.[49] If many anarchists most emphasized the struggle against capitalists, Faure focused upon clerics and generals as the chief enemies of progress.

Other anarchists were indifferent to the Dreyfus Affair and disavowed both anti-Semitism and Faure's libertarianism. Some, like Grave, hesitated because they saw no immediate connection between the controversy and the movement. Emile Pouget emphasized in workers' terminology that both Christian and Jewish capitalists existed in abundance but that "un capitalo est un capitalo."[50] He concluded that since the Affair concerned only the bourgeoisie, it was up to that class to settle it.[51] While mocking Rochefort's anti-Semitic stands, Zo d'Axa felt no real enthusiasm for the Dreyfusards, emphasizing only the anti-Dreyfusards' evil and hypocrisy as they cast blame upon Jews for every conceivable wrong in the world.[52]

Such anarchists saw no relation between the affair and their struggle against government, social inequality, and militarism. Their hesitation in making any fixed commitment was more revealing of indifference than of racism—though they may have unconsciously promoted the latter tendency. Looming largest for them was determination of the limits of anarchists' proper concern, and they concluded that defending the liberties of military officers lay outside those limits. Anyone who defied such boundaries could only damage the movement's original revolutionary basis.

Faure attempted to create a public sense of just such a relationship between the affair and anarchists' goals. He believed that anti-Semitism was merely a disguised facade behind which reactionaries sought to impose a monarchy or military dictatorship upon the people. Therefore, the only way possible to prepare for an anarchist future was by defending the republic from its many enemies. Despite acknowledging the republic's many faults, Faure believed it to be essentially a positive force—especially when compared to previous regimes. Its overthrow was to be dreaded and contested at all costs. Life under republican government, it was concluded, was certainly preferable to subjection to monarchs or dictators—always distinct possibilities in France and obvious to anyone studying its history. In this light, the struggle on behalf of Dreyfus was crucial to the republic's continued safety.

The Dreyfus Affair cannot really be isolated from the divergent views of the republic held by anarchists. If one viewed the Third Republic as the outcome of past revolutionary triumphs over monarchical and clerical forces, then it was acceptable to compromise and to cooperate with moderates and socialists in defending Dreyfus. It did not mean that Faure viewed the republic as perfect and in no need of revision. Indeed, Dreyfusard anarchists continued to attack the system and to endorse further revolutionary action. The real question involved the necessary tactics to be employed when the republic was still fragile.

On the other hand, those who attacked the Third Republic as merely another government felt that it made no sense for anarchists to work within its system. Such action could even be counter-productive. As such a divisive issue, however, the Dreyfus Affair posed a dilemma for Parisian anarchists, who were forced to confront guiding principles inspired by Peter Kropotkin, Elisée Reclus, and Grave during the 1880s. The affair certainly forced them into complicated justifications of their ideology by including the defense of a victim of injustice alongside such goals as the elimination of authority, the abolition of the military, and the destruction of capitalism. It also brought forward human and emotional issues, which had not been confronted by their ideological founders but now needed to be addressed due to transformations in the Parisian social and political climate. In doing so, anarchists like Faure would give their movement a more human face.

## SYNDICALISM

Syndicalism offered an altogether different approach to anarchism and thereby posed novel problems for the movement's coherence. Grave and Faure both endorsed political action and propagandizing in the form of local clubs and newspapers. Anarcho-syndicalists, in contrast, felt that the most effective means of organizing a social revolution was through the unionization of workers. As they organized strikes against factories and workshops, they also could endeavor to bring down the system economically. Among such anarchists, Fernand Pelloutier and Paul Delesalle also vigorously pointed to the great contrasts evident between their structures and British trade unions. They viewed syndicates as inevitably revolutionary in nature, and their goal was not simply to improve working conditions and wages but to instigate revolution. If other compagnons on the left castigated unions as only seeking short-term changes in the labor environment and avoiding a direct confrontation with social conditions and the class structure, Paul Delesalle stated, "The general strike . . . is in reality nothing more than a new form of revolution suitable to modern industrial society."[53] Syndicalism was to be central to the construction of such a newly conceived revolutionary view.

Delesalle and Pelloutier were both young activists within the syndicalist movement. In the 1890s, both were in their twenties, but with different backgrounds. Delesalle was born in 1870 in Issy to working-class parents, his father being a metal worker and his mother a dressmaker. Delesalle became apprenticed in his father's shop at age thirteen.[54] By 1888, he was working in advanced industrial design and chronophotographics. After arriving in Paris, Delesalle became attracted to the anarchist ideas circulated in Grave's *La Révolte* and in student meetings. By 1891, he was publicly an anarchist and wrote for Grave's review. His greatest concern in that role was to infuse anarchist beliefs into revolutionary workers' organizations. Delesalle's articles increasingly stressed the need for anarchists to direct their message to organized workers, and he complemented his writing with participation in workers' congresses held in Amiens and London. He published the proceedings of these meetings in Grave's review but provoked the disapproval of his journalistic mentor, who believed that anarchism should not be immersed in organizations devoted primarily to the workers' needs. Grave felt more attention needed to be devoted to issues that were larger and more central to political society.

Pelloutier had been born in Paris in 1867. His ancestors, however, had come from Piedmont.[55] His father was a functionary at Saint Nazaire who sent his son to a religious school. Fernand's brother was married and worked at the

Préfécture de la Seine.[56] After an attempt at escape, Fernand received a bachelor's degree from St. Nazaire in 1885, at which time, however, he also began writing an anticlerical novel indicating great hostility to his assigned religious education and tension with his father. Soon thereafter, he became a journalist on *A la Democratie de l'Ouest* (On Western Democracy), where he came to know the future politician, Aristide Briand. At this time, his political ideas also began to take clearer shape.

Pelloutier's first political affiliation came as a socialist with Jules Guesde's *Parti ouvrier français* (French Workers' Party) in 1892. Nevertheless, it was immediately evident that Pelloutier's version of socialism was more focused on the issue of the general strike and clashed with the ideas of Guesde and Millerand, which stressed traditional formal political organization and vote-gathering.[57] Pelloutier was dissatisfied with the more moderate approach adopted by these figures and stressed revolutionary socialism. As anarchism had more of a radical aura about it at this time than did socialism, he became attracted to the anarchist program. Pelloutier, however, was critical of its lack of emphasis upon organization and sought to transcend this weakness through syndicalism.

Pelloutier's inclination toward socialism remained with him as an anarchist. While favoring the anarchists' call for direct, spontaneous action, he pushed for greater organization. He found a solution to the dilemma in syndicalism, in which small units were coordinated within a field of large, simultaneous action exemplified by the general strike. He thus hoped to create a movement that was unified and large in scope but drew its energy and inspiration from the small club.

The growth of the *Fédération des bourses du travail* (Federation of Workers' Groups) during the 1890s cleared the way for such a merging of anarchist groups with workers' organizational structures maintained by intimate association. Pelloutier was the organization's general secretary and Delesalle his closest associate. He continued to write and relied upon Emile Pouget's strong support in contesting Grave's objections to syndicalism. In Pelloutier's words:

> unions today are in the process of listening to, studying, and receiving libertarian doctrines; on the other hand, anarchists have nothing to fear in taking part in the corporative movement; they will not be obligated to abdicate their independence. The former are ready to admit the latter who could strengthen an organization resulting from free accord; who follows the word of Grave will have neither laws, statutes, nor rules to which he will have to submit under penalty of a punishment.[58]

The Bourses du travail was later enlarged into the Confédération générale du travail (CGT), which included both the "Bourse" and the rival Federation nationale des syndicats.[59] The CGT would develop into a powerful force and along with the Confederación Nacional del Trabajo (CNT) in Barcelona represent a novel cross-national challenge to capitalism. Nonetheless, many anarchists remained suspicious of such large organizations, which seemed to threaten their local spheres of action.

Pelloutier was eventually enfeebled by tuberculosis, which began to afflict him in 1888 and caused his early death in 1901. He was attracted to anarchism's call for a universal popular uprising and drew the support of those who were unhappy with the impositions and confining restrictions of organized socialism. Pelloutier's rebellion against formal institutions began early with his dislike of religious education, and his break from socialism must have followed a similar underlying pattern in that he never saw one way leading to an end but many ways leading to many ends.

Delesalle ended up following a different revolutionary path. After participating in the Dreyfusard cause, he turned away from syndicalism by 1907 and devoted his time to writing. He later joined the Communist Party although he disagreed with its authoritarian bent and in the 1930s left it to return to anarchism.[60]

Pelloutier and Delesalle felt that they could revitalize unions by infusing them with the anarchist spirit of independence and rebellion. They also believed, however, that anarchism, as it then existed, lacked the necessary cohesion and organization that allowed it to be effective. So many diverse viewpoints necessitated a dogma or strategy to serve as a bridge.[61] Pelloutier hoped that the "Bourses" would function as the bridge and integrate workers seeking social and economic revolution into an organizational structure. In this way, they would learn the lessons of cooperation in a "free and voluntary" manner.[62] He furthermore wished to reassure anarchists that "the emancipation of the people should be the work of people themselves" and not the directive of an impersonal leadership.[63] During a time when the anarchist method was felt to be too vaguely drawn and in need of a new cohesive element, Pelloutier, Pouget, and Delesalle presented syndicalism as the most challenging anarchist form. It could also, they believed, reassure compagnons of their sense of individual freedom of action.[64]

In order to convince anarchists that syndicalist leaders would not pursue exclusively economic goals, Pelloutier reiterated their revolutionary dedication. As he stated: "We are . . . rebels at all hours, men really without God, without a master, and without country, irreconcilable enemies of all despotism."[65] It was a matter of directing the anarchists' revolutionary fervor into the unions and the political struggle into the factories and workshops upon which the French economy was partially dependent. Since France was still primarily agricultural, the struggle needed to be extended into the countryside; this also was in keeping with anarchist doctrine upholding the importance of the traditional peasant sector. The hopes for extensive widespread change in both cities and the provinces still were powerful. French anarchists also focused their attention upon Spain, where a strong libertarian force revealed a parallel situation albeit within the context of a less developed society. Pelloutier and Delesalle felt that anarchist activity within larger networks would give it greater effectiveness than it could have in continual confinement within small coteries.

While some anarchists were enthusiastic about the possibilities of syndicalist engagement, others were more skeptical. Despite Pelloutier's reassurances, these libertarians felt their freedom of action threatened and contrasted anarchism of the ancien manière to syndicalism, which, they felt, admitted too many rules and governing authorities into the movement. Emile Janvion condemned any group "which does not endorse violent revolution and propaganda by the deed"—suggesting that syndicalists were excessively patient and needed to adopt more radical measures.[66] At a meeting of the *Groupe Parisien de Propagande Anarchiste* (Parisian Group of Anarchist Propaganda) in Montmartre in 1892, another compagnon, Jacques Prolo, "rebuked the principle of unions, since the anarchists do not want to consider anything which results from laws, law bringing about slavery."[67] Such statements highlight the deep suspicion held by anarchists against all forms of organization extending beyond their local territory. As seen above, they tended to distrust all notions of law or abstract standards. Like the sans-culottes they suspected Parisian-wide networks and esteemed, in contrast, the club meeting in their quarter. Evidently, many compagnons agreed with Emile Gauthier's contention that an anarchist meeting was only an occasion for friends to discuss informally matters that interested them.[68] They felt a deep reluctance to submit to an organization that would coordinate the various Parisian groups, even if this entailed greater effectiveness in spreading their message. The tradition of loyalty to the local group or club was simply too strong to overcome and reflected deep resistance to any centralizing tendencies, which they especially attributed to Marxism. Anarchists designated any force that even slightly curtailed one's individual voice as authoritarian. As noted already, Grave himself questioned the validity of Pelloutier's ideas, which he previously had allowed to be expressed in his reviews.[69]

Syndicalists, in contrast, believed that the ancien manière had not fulfilled the hopes placed in it. They departed from the idea of anarchism as a movement composed only of freely acting individuals and replaced it with anarcho-syndicalism, which was intended to instill greater revolutionary cohesion in the workplace. Emile Pouget, prominent among such anarchists, supported the syndicalists—who envisioned the union as the "initial and essential group" that developed independently of theory in protecting group interests. Pouget evoked historical remembrance, finding lessons in the experience of the 1791 Le Chapelier laws. In doing so, he drew upon many anarchistic aspirations and ideals in support of traditional workers' groups, which Marx deemed reactionary and obsolete. As forward looking measures of a regime during the French Revolution dedicated to the removal of medieval corporate life and of all feudal vestiges, the Le Chapelier measures forbade workers' associations—most notably the guilds and compagnonnages. Although advocates of such measures justified them in the names of progress and economic liberalization, Pouget believed that the measures also initiated the undoing and reversal of the Revolution. This was evident in the disappearance of enthusiasm and fervor for the Revolution that also, coincidentally or not, was derived from the archaic classes. These remnants of medieval life had been most engaged in the great events of the Revolution (such as the seizure of the Bastille and the Tuileries) and fought to prevent tyrants' subversion of their cause. Such obsolete workers could offer another social and political dimension to the struggle and counteract the leaders' tendencies toward abstract revolutionary strategies without roots in the daily concerns of the people. In abolishing the workers' associations, these bourgeois leaders were able to deny laborers the promise of meeting their economic goals and confine the Revolution to political change convenient only for bourgeois domestic hegemony.[70]

Pouget hoped that by raising social and economic questions that were important to late nineteenth-century French society, unions could provide other avenues for transcending politics as usual in the Third Republic. His support for syndicalism was based upon a belief that it would not only improve working conditions but also expand the scope of anarchists' confrontations with capitalist society. Other anarchists chose to remain steadfast in their devotion to an older, more familiar form of protest. The debate witnessed in the last two points of view was but further evidence that during the last decade of the nineteenth century anarchists confronted unfamiliar terrain in their plan of action. Although the devotees of the ancien manière were uncomfortable with syndicalism, the new phenomenon would prove instrumental in transforming the urban history of Paris, Milan, and Barcelona among other European cities during the twentieth century.

## NATURE AND CIVILIZATION

The issues just discussed all centered around social, economic, and political concerns critical to anarchists and framed within a distinct historical setting. Continual references to the French Revolution reflected a strong awareness of historical tradition. The social problems of the Third Republic were seen as having been shaped by the past. In order to attempt to solve contemporary problems it was, thus, necessary to come to grips with French social and economic realities.

Other anarchists, however, coming forward during the late 1890s (although not in accordance with Voltaire's concluding words in *Candide*) expressed a desire to escape society altogether and to "cultivate their gardens" by retreating from the conventional world. Their escape could be found either in the natural world or in the cultivation of the ego. These currents reflected a growing disillusionment with politics, intellectual and cultural institutions, and class structures—a condition found throughout Europe at the time. Anarchists sharing this reaction emphasized either the establishment of agrarian utopias beyond the boundaries of the civilized world or the cultivation of a strong, independent self in order to achieve individual detachment from society. Both preferences were based upon an "organic" perception of reality and the minimization of history as a means of understanding and appreciating the present.

Jean Grave emphasized the use of both machinery and theory in his program of action.[71] His enthusiastic view was attacked by anarchists from Montmartre known as the Naturiens as part of their general condemnation of mechanization and call for a return to nature and the simple life. They went further and scorned the entire notion of civilization itself. The Naturiens defined anarchism as free and natural living in defiance of the conventional social constraints imposed upon individual behavior and, in this vein, supported free love and rejected marriage.[72] Their notion of freedom differed markedly from Faure's in that they were more concerned with the establishment of utopian communities along the lines of those proposed by Charles Fourier earlier in the century. Such societies would serve as buffers against ordinary moral constraints and ensure that members could follow their own needs. Faure, in contrast, envisioned liberty within the parameters of a just society. As his defense of Dreyfus demonstrated, freedom entailed the assurance of civil liberties and protection from governmental harassment—neither of which the persecuted Captain Dreyfus could enjoy. The Naturiens dismissed such matters as trivialities compared to industrial society's horrors. In their opinion, liberty was only found in the state of nature as it existed before civilization (especially in its modern form) had imposed its tyrannical patterns of artifice.

The Naturiens most esteemed the natural life, which they restricted to dependence upon the earth and its products. At the same time, they rejected the artificial life created by human reason and knowledge. Their mistrust extended to all artificial devices and things not directly provided by nature. There were no improvements, in other words, that people could make upon nature. Cities were rejected in favor of the rustic life, which, in many instances, was depicted in as primitive a light as possible. The founders of the group, Henri Zisly and Emile Gravelle, felt that all human needs could be satisfied by distributing to each person a certain amount of land on which all food could be grown and cultivated.[73] Grave's own version of communal anarchism was supplanted here by a firm belief in the self-sufficiency of individuals—provided each possessed land. Nevertheless, it is worth noting the contradiction between the stress upon complete self-sufficiency and yet the apparent need for some social enclave to foster this way of life.

The Naturiens had definite ideas on the kinds of foods to be consumed by those who lived on such strips of land. Gravelle, for instance, believed that people should cultivate their land and only eat vegetables and fruits grown on it. Meats were to be avoided because of their alleged unhealthfulness and contribution to emotional instability. He extended this attack upon the "artificial life" to include scientific medicine, electricity, clocks, and fuels—all of which distracted people from living in accordance with their instinctual inclinations and wisdom. The Naturiens also felt that herbal medicines were more effective than pharmaceuticals in combating disease.

Obviously, the Naturiens made some gross simplifications here since fuels are products of nature and electricity is a natural phenomenon; both are harnessed, not created, by people. Zisly and Gravelle, in fact, failed to explain sufficiently the points at which human interference with nature began and ended. Only products grown wildly and spontaneously, they believed, could be used. However, agriculture itself could not possibly be described as operating in this way. So much obsession with the particular way in which material life was conducted underlines the fact that of utmost concern to the Naturiens was the revival of an emotional and organic relationship with nature in somewhat Rousseauean terms and the removal of human interference in the unfolding of natural processes.[74] Only in such a manner would life itself be finally enriched.

This vision, stated within the rhetorical bounds of anarchism, shocked other libertarians because of its apparent reversal of the idea of progress and its acceptance of senseless suffering. Anarchists like Grave believed enough in progress and civilized life to recognize that human artifice and technology had helped restrict and alleviate misery.

Zisly and Gravelle, nonetheless, considered themselves anarchists and criticized Grave for monopolizing the term "anarchist." Zisly believed that land redistribution was the most important issue, which, once accomplished, would enhance human security and comfort according to nature's guidelines.[75] The Naturiens also were at times drawn to the communal aspects of Grave's anarchism. As previously noted, however, they placed greater stress upon the need for individuals to escape civilization's constraints and condemned Kropotkin's and Grave's communistic ideals as threats to individual liberty.[76]

Zisly did not stop at criticizing industrial society alone—as many others with a variety of political and moral views were doing. He attacked the very notion of civilization itself. This radical view endeared him to few other anarchists since an esteem for community and civilization was implicit in their ideology. Despite their often-stated Romantic dispositions, libertarians like Bakunin, Kropotkin, Grave, and Michel did not consider a complete rejection of civilization, only a metamorphosis of it. The Naturiens, however, drew on Fourier's and Rousseau's idealizations of passion and nature to extend their rejection of established society. They even held banquets commemorating the unconventional ideas of the two writers.[77] As Fourier and Rousseau were already considered eccentric, such banquets only served to underline the Naturiens' obsession with goals not relevant to anarchist ends. It was also problematic that despite many anarchists' admiration for Rousseau and Fourier, there were authoritarian implications in the ideas of both. This was especially true of the nebulous nature of Rousseau's call for a general will that would "force people to be free." Excessive reference to Rousseauean ideas was a double-edged sword.

Anarchists, in fact, generally distanced themselves from Zisly and his circle. Grave considered the Naturiens ridiculous, and Zisly an "imbecile."[78] Responding, Zisly reminded Grave of his enthusiasm for the anarchistic spirit of revolt evident in *La Révolte* and *Les Temps Nouveaux*. He also, however, emphatically condemned mechanization and reiterated that it was on that point that the two parted company. Machines, Zisly felt, led to authoritarianism in a new form and disrupted the harmony and freedom found in nature. Machines and authority (now linked in his mental glossary) were stark contrasts to nature and anarchism, and within this bipolar context, Grave opted for the wrong choice. In this manner, the journalist of rue Mouffetard was betraying the very movement he allegedly championed. This argument is clearly semantic, and Zisly was forcing *anarchism* to fit into his own conception. He and the Naturiens believed that the movement emanated from nature because only within its domain was total freedom possible. Artifice led to tyranny. He further wrote to Grave:

> Permit me to thank you for calling me an imbecile. Without bragging of myself, I judge myself otherwise and so do other comrades. In any case, between an imbecile and an authoritarian there is a difference because an imbecile can become intelligent, but an authoritarian cannot help but be a bigot.[79]

In his instinctual resort to the word *authoritarian,* Zisly pinned on Grave the one label that attracted immediate anarchist attention. His contention that it was possible for an imbecile to become intelligent reflects his confusion of natural wisdom with lack of education. As noted above, however, while they expressed their eccentric vision in a particular manner, the Naturiens were but one European group among several condemning refined, urban fin-de-siècle society and offering instead a retreat into an alternative world. At the same time, irrational and mystical movements proliferated throughout the continent. As H. Stuart Hughes has written, a "revolt against positivism" marked the intellectual world of the 1890s and indicated a sense of ennui with the scientific and empirical approaches of the time. In different circles, theosophical societies conducted seances (or influenced such proceedings in the Cafe du Néant) to communicate with the dead, and German youth expressed their disdain for modern *gesellschaft* (artificial society) by yearning for treks into forests, mountains, or other rugged natural settings. Historical attention has been focused on the intellectual expression given to such trends as in Ferdinand Tönnies's proclivity for *gemeinschaft* (natural community) and antagonism to artificial society. Once taken up by Georges Sorel, such currents would later provide intellectual food for extreme chauvinists, irredentists, and fascists.[80] However, the Naturiens were more arcadian in their aspirations and less concerned with national or ethnic questions. They did not seek the reinstitution of *volkish* (folk) values but the creation of an Eden-like utopia divorced from the pressures of modern cities. At the heart of their concerns was a flight or escape from the fast pace of contemporary society—a sentiment that resembles aspects of the 1960s' and 1970s' American counterculture seen particularly in university towns of the time. From their habitat in Montmartre, the Naturiens may have felt removed from the urban frenzy of Paris, but they still were immersed in its anarchist dialogue. In this setting, the Naturiens justified their obsessions in anarchist terms but never succeeded in alleviating the fears and suspicious discomfort that their opposing compagnons felt toward them.

## NONCONFORMITY AND THE EGO

Many anarchist ideals defined by Grave, Michel, Faure, Pouget, and even Zisly had a group or communal foundation. Other anarchists went further and resisted such affiliations, relished their indefinable status, and extolled the virtues of complete expressive individualism. Zo d'Axa emphasized that the essential nature of anarchists revolved around their ambiguous character and their nonconformity to convention—even to the "conformity" of the movement inspiring them. He believed that it was necessary for anarchists to eliminate this paradox and reject all absolutes, believing that:

> We are individuals, without any saving faith which binds us. Society disgusts us, it does not engender in us deep convictions. We fight for the joy of battle and without dreams of a better future.[81]

This type of anarchism involved living entirely for the present and detaching oneself from plans for ideal societies to be constructed in the future. D'Axa had no illusions about final ends and believed it meaningless to live for goals that were not necessarily achievable. Only the present mattered. In his use of the term "anarchist," he emphasized individuals who were unbound to any groups or doctrines. An anarchist was always to remain skeptical about ideologies and religions and concerned only with the immediate "battle." The struggle itself was never drawn in the same terms but varied according to the enemies situated before one. Zo d'Axa held a unique place in the anarchist movement, and his stance hid a complex of assorted concerns as his pseudonym disguised a previous identity assumed in other circles. His wanderings and dedication to new ventures would continue after his anarchist period.

D'Axa was born Alphonse Galland in Paris in May, 1864. His father was a successful engineer descended from the navigator La Pérouse.[82] Until 1882, the young Galland studied at Chaptal and then became a royalist Catholic. He also developed a fascination with the military and, after joining the army, was sent to Algeria for service.[83] The experience did not meet his expectations, and he deserted after running off with his captain's wife. From that point, Galland was an antimilitarist, although for some time, he dedicated himself entirely to hunting in Africa—a fact indicating that hatred of weapons was not at the center of his disillusionment with the army. Eventually, he left for Brussels where he worked as a reporter for *Les Nouvelles du Jour* (the Daily News). By 1889, he had been given amnesty in France for his desertion and promptly returned.

Emerging as an anarchist, Galland began publishing the journal *L'Endehors* in May, 1891 under the pseudonym Zo d'Axa. As the name of the review indicated, he was now a social outsider and observer. This anarchist review was brought into being through the collaboration of a wide variety of militant anarchists, including the terrorist Emile Henry. During the trial of the thirty, when the paper was formally suppressed, D'Axa left France only to return in 1896 to publish a new review—*La Feuille* (the Leaf).

D'Axa's purpose was not to state views necessarily consistent with those of the anarchist movement as a whole but to raise his voice and attack as many institutions as possible. He was an anarchist who could not commit himself to any party or group—not even to one centered around the libertarian ethic.[84] In this venture, he used irony to a degree that dismayed other anarchists, and it was apparent that his devotion to ironic cynicism was stronger than his feeling for moral issues and justice. He could castigate the working classes as much as he ridiculed capitalists and poked fun both at Dreyfusards and anti-Dreyfusards. His ambiguous viewpoint threw other anarchists off balance. Adolphe Retté, for one, described D'Axa in this way: "a bizarre man, content just to be himself, without any party etiquette, without political acquaintances, this anarchist cannot be tolerated very long."[85] D'Axa's opinion was that an anarchist merely had to scorn bourgeois mentality and live in accord with the self's true instincts.

Understandably, the working classes having access to his review did not find d'Axa endearing. This "outsider" seemed elitist and aristocratic not so much in brandishing a family name or tradition but in excessive self-cultivation and scorn for convention. Mainstream anarchists felt that their movement was being robbed of its revolutionary ardor as d'Axa inserted too many irrational and individualistic strands into it. His inclination was that the revolution would depend not upon social action but upon the development of strong individuals. As he explained:

> We live beyond all laws, rules, and theories—even those of the anarchists; it is from the moment . . . that we want to give expression to our pities, our anger, our gentleness, our rage, our instincts, as we are proud of being ourselves. Nothing . . . reveals to us the radiant beyond. Nothing gives us the constant criterium. The panorama of life ceaselessly changes.[86]

Not only were all philosophical systems to be rejected, but all political goals were considered irrelevant when compared to life's existential joys and despairs. D'Axa felt that anarchists essentially had faith in nothing and needed to scorn all conventions and doctrines. They expressed revolt only through intense living. This vision is not too removed in many respects from Nietzsche's ideas in *Also Sprach Zarathustra* (Thus Spoke Zarathustra) and was also later expressed in the mid-twentieth century by Nikos Kazantzakis through the teachings of Alexis Zorba.[87] In fact, this vision was already bound to a strong rejection of conventional life, and its expression in certain anarchist circles was to be expected.

D'Axa was hunted by authorities throughout the 1890s and forced to abandon his publishing ventures. He finally decided to devote himself entirely to travel.[88] Since he had become an anarchist for the sole pleasure of fighting, he gave up the struggle when it appeared too sterile and believed that individuals needed to free themselves and not await their emancipation from above. His quest (in a similar, but slower, manner to that adopted by Jack Kerouac in America during the 1950s) was to ride by bicycle along the roads, rivers, and canals of Europe and to continue his devotion to skepticism and irony, which he believed he inherited from the Voltairean culture so engrained in France.[89] The road offered the best hope for attaining this goal. If d'Axa had become an anarchist it was only in an effort to distance himself from institutions and accepted values. His love for travel, thus, reinforced his rebellion against discipline as it implied a self-willed pattern of wanderings intended to foster irony and detachment from conventional life found in the many places he visited. This experience reflected the same desire for nonconformity and individual expression that first brought him to the anarchist movement.

Much of the strength of this strand of anarchist thought derives from the influence of Nietzsche's and Max Stirner's ideas. Earlier in the century Stirner had stressed the need for the ego to be satisfied as much as possible. During the late nineteenth century, a number of anarchist intellectuals chose to contest the movement's communal orientation because of their adherence to Stirner's dictum that the self achieve gratification even at the expense of social concerns.

The fin de siècle also saw the increasing influence of Nietzsche's thought upon French intellectual and artistic circles.[90] The flourishing number of articles about Nietzsche in anarchist and avant-garde reviews revealed the extent of such influence during the 1890s. Both currents were marked by a common immersion in the strong individualism and elitism dominating the non-systematic, but powerful, tide of his reflections. Anarchists and avant-garde thinkers alike admired Nietzsche's scorn for conventional morality, his admonition that "man" should create values from confrontation with an absurd, meaningless world, and his ardent individualism. Some, like Camille Mauclair, placed more emphasis upon the creative side of Nietzsche's thought, which expressed the need for Apollonian transcendence of the Dionysian abyss.[91]

These anarchists mocked not only the military, the church, and the state but also all ideas and social standards of conventional ethics. In this sense, they linked even Kropotkin's notion of mutual aid to other oppressive morals. Consequently, their interest in cultivating the self precluded any discussion of social and economic issues and made the movement even more incoherent than it already was.

Manuel Devaldès was the most vocal of the individualists. The founder of *Revue rouge* (Red Review) called himself an "egoist" and said that once people had rejected social prejudices, they would be masters of themselves as individuals.[92] In fact, Devaldès felt that the root of all government lay in the conscience and morality. If one wished to become a true anarchist, it was necessary to rid the ego of all constraints and give it sole expression of the self's voice. Such action would overturn the debilitating effects of social, political, and moral dictates, which, until then, had deprived most individuals of freedom and the ability to live uninhibitedly. Ironically, Devaldès included anarchist morality in this indictment. He contrasted the egoists' disregard for conventional standards with other anarchists' meaningless standards of communal ethics that continued to oppress individuals in search of self-satisfaction. It needs to be stated that Devaldès did not explain which factors or acts most contributed to human aspirations and bliss. He gave psychological freedom itself a rather ambiguous, but strong, determining position in this regard—with its corresponding blanks to be filled in freely by each individual.

The social consequences of this "liberation" were never clearly explained as such considerations were irrelevant to the egoists' cause. In true Nietzschean fashion there was little discussion of such effects, and it was supposed that evolutionary development would reveal the eventual result. The point was that social ills already existed and egoism could hardly worsen matters if adopted on a mass scale.[93] Devaldès ridiculed altruism and anarchist and socialist attempts to impose social equality. While completely rejecting Chrisitian morality, Devaldès conceded lukewarm praise for it as he pointed to its foundations upon firmly drawn principles and a definite notion of the absolute. The collapse of religious absolutes, however, was followed by secular altruism that only could be upheld by state power. Therefore, he drew a long historical line of dependence upon state authority beginning with Robespierre and the Committee of Public Safety and culminating in socialism. Devaldès also expressed fears that Jaures's "religion of humanity" could result in a society finally controlled by an all-embracing state. Pitying, altruistic sentiments only disguised sinister authoritarianism, and communal anarchism held the same dangers.[94]

Such an anarchistic vision strongly resembles many anti-governmental stands now readily adopted in 1990s American libertarian circles. It also was directed against all extra-ego powers—including educational institutions, religions, and movements based on all-embracing social theories. Unlike today's libertarian theories, the stress was not on the right to accumulate property, possess firearms, or defy environmental regulations, but to mark out a free psychological space. The ego needed room to grow in an unlimited manner. While Stirner and Nietzsche were significant influences upon this anarchist intellectual current, it also had a pre-Freudian tone. The ego and the conscience, which Freud would call the super-ego, were placed in a hostile standoff, and one could only grow at the other's expense. Devaldès believed that the world was reduced to a philosophical and psychological struggle for fulfillment, and in the end one force had to give way—the ego or the conscience.

Camille Mauclair tried to reconcile the two aspects of this struggle by emphasizing the synthetic powers of art and creativity. The self was not to follow its own momentary whims; its energy was to be utilized in artistic or intellectual catharsis. Still, he too was mostly concerned with the self's struggle for fulfillment and was more attuned to Devaldès's egoism than to Grave's social concerns. Such anarchist thinkers saw the movement as furthering rebellion against social morality and convention and defending individualism from society's dictates. They viewed the fundamental threat emanating from social anarchism, in fact, as lying in the creation of a new society with an alternative array of ethics and conventions. Thus, they felt little need to discuss the range of questions with which such libertarians were concerned.


## EDUCATION


In his novel, *L'Abbé Jules,* Octave Mirbeau attacked the educational system operated by religious orders and explained the defects inflicted upon human character by such schools and others:

> they have warped the functions of my intelligence as well as those of my body, and in the place of natural, instinctual man, filled with life, they have substituted an artificial puppet, the mechanical plaything of civilization filled with ideas . . . the ideals from which are born bankers, priests, swindlers, debaucherers, murderers, and the miserable.[95]

It has been seen how Pelloutier, among other anarchists, rebelled against religious schools and involved himself in revolutionary socialism. Mirbeau, like Fénéon, dreaded the ability of dehumanizing forces to displace organic intelligence in people, although in this situation he singled out the church, rather than Marxism, as the principal villain. Mirbeau attacked education, however, in a more general sense. Education held a key position in anarchists' conceptions of revolutionary development and of the political and social order to follow.

This concern was not new to political theorists.[96] The ideal society Rousseau envisioned in the *Social Contract* also depended upon a properly educated community, without which majority rule would be impossible. In the same way, some anarchists believed that in order for their movement to gain strength and cohesion, it was necessary for compagnons to overcome their prejudices and biases through education.

In addition to propaganda and mobilization efforts, anarchist reviews and conferences also were intended to educate the public in the movement's perspectives. Of course, as we have seen, each group's intrinsic goals, methods, and beliefs varied, and their respective intentions and educational aims reflected such contrasts. The various conceptions of education depended on the particular anarchists and the audience they wished to reach. Emile Pouget and his associates at *Père Peinard Almanach* were interested in addressing the popular classes and used slang to do so. At the same time, they did not hesitate to include in their issues Nostradamus's prophetic statements, revealing their belief that working-class rhetoric did not exclude superstition. This approach was combined with the use of the French Revolutionary calendar initiated by the First Republic in 1792. *Père Peinard's* editors obviously relied upon both devices in attempting to manipulate popular taste for political purposes.[97] As Mirbeau believed that traditional education had "warped" people's natural instincts, so anarchists attempted to reverse the process and utilize their educational form to mold popular opinion. Accordingly, they believed that, in reversing the system's innate hierarchical authoritarianism through indoctrination, they naturally pointed the way in a more positive direction. Of course, it now seems clear that the lines drawn between education and propaganda were very thin indeed.

The Naturiens rejected established education, reasoning, and institutions altogether. Like Rousseau, they believed that knowledge was best gained from the direct experience of nature. The establishment of schools was futile and counterproductive, leading only to alienation from nature. In their Romantic vision, theory did not matter as much as experience itself. Therefore, it was essential to give learning a practical basis.

Jean Grave considered the task of education to be vital to the anarchist cause:

> It is in our minds that we must first make the revolution; we must erase prejudices from our habits and acts. We must help the indidividual to transform himself in his conceptions and in his acts. We hope to inspire as many minds as possible to will self-transformation; once done, this will be a further step to the revolution.[98]

The people, it was thought, were correct in detesting the system, but they first had to effect the revolutionary process mentally before proceeding to destroy the capitalist system and the state. Since anarchists believed that the revolution and their envisioned community could only emerge from the spontaneous, sincere, and self-willed actions of individuals, education was most important in mobilizing the future agents of change. Grave believed that he was not fooling or beguiling people into becoming anarchists. Rather, they were convinced to do so by the powers of reason and persuasion, which led them to esteem individualism and liberty. This is why he so frequently used the expression "by themselves" to refer to the anarchists' volitional engagement, logically consequent upon mastery of reason and theory. Grave also consistently spoke of instilling the movement's guidelines in the peasantry and reversing the counterrevolutionary roles they had played in the past. Peasants now had to be educated to discriminate between those who fought for their liberation and those who would exploit them.[99] It is doubtful, however, that his paternalistic attitudes actually transformed peasant aspirations and judgments.

Grave viewed his publications as best suited to educate the public in a social and anarchistic awareness. *Le Révolté*, *La Révolte*, and *Les Temps Nouveaux* featured not only polemical stories directed against the government, but also highly technical political and economic articles not accessible to the public at large. This type of approach already presumed the existence of an educated or literate public able to comprehend the complexities of anarchist thought. Consequently, while Grave criticized contemporary education and stressed the need for critical thinking among the masses, he remained within the bounds of journalistic persuasion. In the same way that he conceived of bourgeois education as an accomplice of capitalism and authoritarian government, Grave forecast the inauguration of anarchist society from the efforts of rational, independently minded people.[100] Nevertheless, he merely urged the ignorant to learn theory, without suggesting the means by which they could do so. Such dictates earned him the previously-noted epithet of "the pope of rue Mouffetard."

There were attempts, however, to educate youth through different types of schools. Grave, Kropotkin, Reclus, and Michel were among those belonging to the *Ligue d'enseignement libertaire* (the League of Libertarian Education), which sought to establish schools without authority-figures and focused around the guiding theme of anarchy.[101] Sébastien Faure founded a school called *La Ruche* (the Beehive) with a similar orientation in 1904.[102] Faure differed from Grave in de-emphasizing revolutionary doctrine and fostering students' completely free development. He believed that "a society of concord and abundance" would result from such a system of education since a necessary connection between proper schooling and the anarchistic future existed.[103] The anarchist school would encourage people to follow their own urges rather than ideological dictates. Such a situation, in turn, would spontaneously create the foundations for the society libertarians envisioned. A community of free individuals would be more valuable to anarchist ends than all the calculations and maneuvers conducted by the movement's leaders.

Louise Michel, who had always been interested in the political possibilities of education, spoke at meetings of the need to encourage free thinking and skepticism toward conventional standards among youth. She lamented the bourgeois domination of nineteenth-century education as such pedagogical hegemony helped mold future thinking—thus ensuring the economic, social, and political position of that class. Only a new educational system established with much difficulty and effort would reverse the situation.[104] Of course, much of the speculation over the issue was vague and idealistic, and assumptions of direct connections to social transformation were not entirely clear. Nevertheless, anarchists clearly comprehended the central position of education in intellectual and cultural awareness and realized, thus, its political relevance to their aspirations.

In addition to advocating libertarian education, anarchists also discussed the need for practical and experimental teaching. In a manner somewhat resembling John Dewey's, they underlined the importance of complementing abstract thought with "doing." Practice and experiment encouraged the development of individuality and differed starkly from the "metaphysical conceptions," that had controlled and guided learning for too long. This idea was derived from Rousseau's *Emile,* in which experience was described as a prerequisite for learning. The hope was that such an approach would heighten the individual's natural alertness, curiosity, and critical thinking since knowledge and work were considered to be so closely connected in stimulating self-development.[105]

Anarchists optimistically predicted that if such educational changes occurred on a massive scale, the social ramifications would be irreversible and revolutionary. The last two decades of the nineteenth century witnessed several attempts in France to liberate learning from the control of the Catholic Church and other powerful traditional forces. The most famous of these were the Ferry Laws put in place by Jules Ferry by 1886 to create free and mandatory public elementary schools. Such efforts were expanded to other levels as well and eventually included women. Generally, they demonstrated an effort on the part of Third Republic leaders to counter church influence and create a secular basis to education. Anarchist opinions on education only reflected the great concern given to the subject at the time. Anarchists contrasted their notions of correct education (oriented around students' freedom) with the authoritarian approach of French academic institutions and concluded that they pointed to something essential. Nevertheless, anarchists were also troubled by one other problem intrinsic both to education and revolutionary strategy—language. Discussion of this issue revealed a surprisingly troubling problem that dramatized both the underlying vitality and the weakness of the movement.

## LANGUAGE

The problem of language was manifest in two ways. To begin, there were differences in the ways anarchists used language to evoke various reactions among their audience. These differences were most obvious in the contrasting styles of language used by Pouget and Grave. As Eugen Weber has explained, until very modern times France was not linguistically homogeneous, being marked by provincial dialects, which were cast by Parisian observers as different languages. The railroad and other developments only began to erode such linguistic differences during the later nineteenth century. Nevertheless, dialect remained a fact of French life for some time.[106] George Steiner, in another context, also has noted that language simultaneously communicates ideas, expresses emotions, and reinforces differences.[107] As has already become evident, Pouget and Grave both unconsciously took part in demonstrating this point; the former used street-talk and slang to reinforce irreverent anti-employer attitudes among workers and the latter relied upon highly technical and restrained language to express his rational, scientific anarchism.[108] Such differences also extended to other reviews. For instance, Zo d'Axa and Sébastien Faure stressed different styles to convey contrasting anarchist visions—in this case, sarcasm and moral indignation respectively.

A second issue was the manner in which the variety of national dialects seemed to limit the geographic scope of the movement. Since anarchists sought revolution on an international scale, they recognized the problems posed to their movement by so many divergent cultures, dialects, and languages—however ironic this may seem when considering anarchism's general celebration of diversity. They were caught in a tactical web of political contradiction.

Anarchists viewed the uniting of their cause under a common language as a tactical advantage, since the future world order depended on the disappearance of cultural differences and the emergence of a unified international culture. Louise Michel in 1887 wrote that:

> everything leads to the common ocean, solicited by the needs of renewal, by means unknown until now and whose inevitable development nothing

can stop. The human species which since the beginning of ages had ascended from the family of the tribe, to the horde, to the nation, ascends again and forever, and the family becomes an entire race.[109]

The nation-state, created as the result of historical development, would itself be transcended in the future revolution by global identity. In her exile in New Caledonia, Michel was struck by the similarities in culture and rebellious disposition between the natives and Europeans. She expressed an interest in the development of contemporary anthropology and sought to relate it to the revolutionary movement in which she participated. In her utopian opinion, revolution would cause people to unite under one language and culture. These differences had helped prevent social revolution from occurring on the scale she envisioned.

> Languages, which have developed according to human vicissitudes, adopt for their new needs similar words, because all people feel the same need: Revolution. And the revolutions in science, in the arts, as in industry, render more and more necessary this universal language which results from it and which will be a corollary of the great hatching.[110]

Such a sweeping statement, unifying transformations in various disciplines with revolutionary ideals, reflected the nineteenth century belief in progress and social perfection—most dramatized by the utopian socialists. Auguste Comte's "Religion of Humanity," one example of this intellectual current, continued to fascinate thinkers from a variety of political perspectives at the fin de siècle. Michel not only castigated the contemporary establishment as exploitative and authoritarian, but also expressed a grievance with the multitude of languages and cultures that made possible the illusion that people from different regions really were different. She believed that social, economic, and technological changes were rendering this view false and bringing about the emergence of a universal language and culture.

Michel dreamed of the day when human unity would become a reality in the linguistic as well as in the social sense. Since the truth was universal and not relative to particular cultures, then it was possible to construct a universal language corresponding to the truth. This conclusion was paradoxical for an anarchist—who might be expected to emphasize the freedom of small communities from the burdensome demands of large oppressive forces. Michel's internal dialectic between her respect for the particular and her esteem for the unifying bridge resembles Isaiah Berlin's analysis in "The Hedgehog and the Fox," based on fable but astutely applied to two great Russian novelists.[111] The

legend depicts foxes as knowing many small things and hedgehogs as understanding one large truth in their respective struggles to survive. Referring to this
metaphor, Berlin envisions Leo Tolstoy as a fox and Fyodor Dostoyevsky as a
hedgehog; in particular, Tolstoy is cast as one who delighted in variety and
Dostoyevsky as a zealot who focused his ardor upon the *grand truth* of Russian
Orthodoxy. It appears that Michel herself was caught between the two opposite
poles of this dialectic. However, although her vision of a universal culture could
seem contradictory to her anarchist esteem for small things, it also was in
keeping with her adherence to Internationalist politics. Perhaps an all-
embracing language, overcoming the chaos of Babel, did not seem as menacing
as an omnipresent state. In any case, some anarchists believed both in the
desirability and the feasibility of ending linguistic differences and in the parallel
creation of an international language.

The various anarchist papers and reviews reflected the movement's linguistic international basis. Translation offered possibilities already and was
critical in making foreign anarchist works available to French compagnons.
Bakunin's and Kropotkin's works and those of other anarchists were already
available in a number of European languages. Mutual translations of Russian,
Spanish, Italian, and French texts were especially common since these languages
reflected those societies where European anarchism most flourished. Grave's
publications included translated articles, and foreigners like Errico Malatesta
wrote for several of the anarchist reviews. In this way, journalists sought to
spread anarchist writings, emanating from widely separated places, across
national boundaries.

Charles Malato was another libertarian who was highly conscious of the
problems posed to the movement by racial and linguistic barriers. Police noted
Malato's fluency in Spanish and English in addition to his native tongues
originating in a cross-Alpine youth—Italian and French.[112] They also observed
how Malato's knowledge of several languages facilitated his ability to maintain
close relations with comrades abroad—most notably in Britain, Spain, and Italy.
Malato's periods of exile during the 1890s reinforced such international connections. In turn, exile aroused a sense of humor as evident in *Les joyeusetés de
l'exil* (the Joys of Exile), written as a guide for compagnons seeking political
refuge abroad and needing to understand important features of life in their
newly adopted homelands.

Malato's favorite foreign asylum was England, and he wrote favorably of
its tolerant and liberal traditions. Such features had been previously esteemed
by the philosophes of the Enlightenment, and such a legendary character as
Voltaire had written of England as an ideal society for those fleeing political

persecution. Malato also praised the secure place of dissent and unionization within English society. In finding points of criticism, he did not go much further than warning French readers of the dangers of English cuisine. Of course, Malato's praise needs to be placed in perspective. British society was not necessarily revolutionarily disposed nor conducive to anarchist ideals. Authority was used just as much to maintain the political and class system and law and order as on the continent. British tolerance was also tested in the highly publicized trial of Oscar Wilde revolving around the writer's homosexuality. The difference was that, relatively speaking, a degree of tolerance was present. Therefore, anarchists like Malato, Michel, and Kropotkin found London to be a safe refuge and a good city for organizing other anarchists.

In addition to introducing his audience to London's streets and neighborhoods, Malato provided the reader with a brief appendix that included a key to important words and phrases. This glossary would provide the dissident "tourist" with as complete a guide to the texture of London's life as was necessary. Some of these phrases (with Malato's own over-literal translations) indicate both the style of exile Malato had in mind and matters he was used to hearing discussed:

| | |
|---|---|
| cochon | pig |
| fermez ça | shut up |
| Je vous une bonne pile | I'll give you a good thrashing. |
| Sacre étranger | Bloody foreigner! |
| Sacre homme | Bloody man! |
| Sacre femme | Bloody woman! |
| Voyou! | Ruffian! |
| Donnez moi un shilling. | Give me a bob. |
| Je vous tirerai le nez. | I will pull your nose. |
| Je vous mettrai mon pied dans le derrière. | I will put my foot on your bottom. |
| Dites moi quels sont les journaux liberaux? | Tell me which are the liberal papers? |
| C'est comme chez M. Peyrouton qui demandait autrefois la destruction de la propriété et qui reclame maintenant la guillotine pour les enemies de l'ordre social. | It is quite as in our country with M. Peyrouton, who once advocated the destruction of property and demands now the guillotine for the enemies of the social order. |
| A Hyde Park, le soir pour moins d'un shilling. | In Hyde Park, at night, for less than a shilling.[113] |

Such expressions were meant to assist potential exiles in surviving the conditions of life in London and to guide them through the labyrinth of activities there. Insults and threats, food, sex, political orientation, and colorful allusions to national history were at the center of the refugee's concerns, indicating that comfort and satisfaction of bodily functions were at least as important as political contacts in making one's way through London's hidden corners. Malato gave the reader a succinct introduction to the slang and political phrases of the city in order to make life in exile as comfortable as possible.

Malato was well suited for translation because he was well-versed in several languages, had traveled extensively, and was familiar with foreign cultures. During this time, anarchists spent much time traveling and crossing national borders in and out of exile. Consequently, they were keenly aware of the anarchist situation throughout Europe and carried their vision wherever they went. Travel, thus, played an important role in sustaining the movement's international character. While they were aware of national differences among their comrades, anarchists hoped that they soon would belong to a federated revolutionary movement sweeping across Europe.

In confronting the reality of different languages, the anarchists witnessed a difficulty that also symbolized the movement's inherent divisions and fragmentation. Thus, they sought solutions to this problem with either extensive translations or the adoption of an international language. Like syndicalism, such methods were designed to give anarchism greater cohesion and success in uniting its component parts.

Michel's call for an international language was taken up by anarchists who wanted to find a practical means of creating it. A group was devoted to teaching and learning Esperanto—a language that had been created earlier to accommodate all Romance-language peoples. Esperanto was conceived for the purpose of utilizing the simplest structure and vocabulary possible in order to facilitate its learning. Esperanto thus would form a bridge among all the Romance languages and render a state of more effective communication first within Europe, then perhaps throughout the world. Since many Europeans spoke Germanic, Slavic, and other non-Romance languages, certain lingua-centric presumptions were already being made. An offshoot of French, Spanish, Italian, or Portuguese would dominate the new form of communication.

Originally, linguists, fearing the deeply entrenched nationalism of the European states, espoused Esperanto. From their viewpoint, the reality of numerous languages aggravated tensions among nations, and the use of Esperanto would help counteract this situation. Anarchists were also drawn to this potentiality and further saw it as a means of molding their own movement into a truly international one—united in both goals and language.

In 1907, Emile Chapelier and Gassy Marin wrote a pamphlet on the possibilities offered to anarchists by Esperanto. In presenting their argument, they also emphasized their perceptions of the movement's fundamental problems. They argued that all anarchist organizational and ideological problems were, in fact, consequences of the multitude of languages through which comrades had to communicate. If such were the case, then the future success of the movement would hinge upon the resolution of linguistic and cultural differences within Europe. Consequently, they urged their fellows to utilize Esperanto as a linguistic means to cultural, social, and political unity.

The envisioned adoption of Esperanto as an international language would achieve several goals essential to anarchism. In the first place, it would overcome the barriers imposed by nationalism upon socialists and anarchists in their attempts to launch an international social revolution ending class divisions. Nation-states were not only divisive entities; they also directed the masses' attention toward chauvinism and postponed the inevitable social crisis. As cultural nationalism revolved around language, linguistic differences caused and deepened national misunderstandings that, in turn, made meaningful communication among peoples troubled, if not impossible. It was ironic that in the modern world technologically advanced means of transportation and communication exacerbated linguistic differences by making them more apparent. Modern transport could only do so much because, as Chapelier and Marin wrote:

> In a few hours we travel from Brussels to Berlin, but the language difference makes it impossible for us to fraternize with our Berlin brothers . . . And if we suppose the absurdity that each of us can learn a dozen languages, won't the fact remain that our planet will still remain a Tower of Babel?[114]

The only way this "Tower of Babel" could be transcended was through the creation and adoption of a language that could bring all peoples together and enable them to have instant and direct communication with one another.[115] It was not surprising that this issue should have evoked religious imagery since it was universal and its solution would fulfill so many ideals. The bridging of centuries-old traditions of misunderstanding involves aspirations with a religious and millenarian basis—even for a secular movement like anarchism.[116] Unlike right-wing nationalists who adored their distinct languages, socialists and anarchists were more likely to search for a universal language. They thought that progress and world unity would not depend so much upon technology as upon education and language. In this situation, it was imperative for new symbols to be learned and absorbed. Translation was not the key to this purpose. Esperanto was.

A second consideration involved anarchist tactics and strategy. If anarchism was best suited to collective action emanating from the individual, free will of each comrade, then it was necessary to remove any grounds for misunderstandings among them. A common language for libertarians throughout the continent would go far in coordinating their purpose. Anarchist strategy would operate most efficiently within a common, international language that also would eliminate the time-consuming work of translation. An international newspaper written in Esperanto would help harmonize the tactics of different anarchist groups and mobilize them into a worldwide movement instead of one broken into national fragments. Such visionaries ignored the unique aesthetic qualities of different languages, considering them only as obstacles to mutual understanding. Communication, in their opinion, mattered more than aesthetic considerations, and Esperanto would hasten its progress.

As already noted, anarchists valued the existence of the many small groups composing their movement. They resorted to words like *mutualistic, associative,* and *federated* to describe concepts of cooperative group action. Still, this very notion of small and intimate groups posed its own problems. What would be the consequences, for instance, if some groups pushed their own concerns at the expense of those of other groups and made association impossible? Some anarchists feared such ensuing chaos and devised strategies by which these difficulties would be overcome. Others remained suspicious, as was also seen in the syndicalist issue.

"Linguistic" anarchists criticized the self-centeredness among groups that encouraged the construction of walls.[117] It was suggested that a unifying language would break down such walls and facilitate the libertarian pursuit of a common, rational purpose. If one could change the words, then one could also affect the ideas themselves. This process then would result in a common language and rhetoric.

The most successful form of anarchism, then, would be one combining radical ideology with linguistics, sociology, and logic.[118] Chapelier and Marin thought:

> that we are united not only by the community of ideas, and sentiments, and aspirations but also by a common language; the Libertarian International must not be arrested in its progressive march by the horrifying obstacle of the multiplicity of languages; those who want to be useful to the organizational solidarity, must study, use, and spread Esperanto;

future International Congresses must be convened in an international language.[119]

Chapelier and Marin also believed Esperanto to be a rich language that would help enliven political debate. They criticized sociological language as overly monotonous, technical, and dull. As terms peculiar to it infiltrated common language and rhetoric, communication was becoming increasingly less of an organic phenomenon. Although they viewed sociology itself as a valuable field of learning, they also felt that the abstraction in terminology it engendered was divorcing language from the common people and deepening the divide between the learned and the ignorant—an underlying criticism of Grave's reviews. These anarchists believed that Esperanto was simple enough for all to learn and, thus, would create an immediate leveling effect by forcing everyone to communicate on the same plane. In the process, language and political debate would both be revitalized, and the world repoliticized from an entirely different direction.

One can detect in such ideas a Romantic disposition. Like the Naturiens, the "linguists" believed that it was important for people to reconnect themselves to nature—even at the expense of relinquishing their original language. Language needed to regain its earlier organic qualities. They did not realize, however, that in the process they were creating an artificial language that had not evolved through time but reflected the excessively artificial and abstract culture they condemned. Nevertheless, they devoted their attention to the criticism of cultural artificiality and highlighted their perception that language was losing its vitality and importance to the masses. Their hope was that anarchism would regain its communal relevance through the implementation of a new language and that the political and organizational problems of the movement would be resolved through Esperanto.

## CONCLUDING REMARKS

In these debates, a few further points are worth remarking. To begin, the problem of resolving the tension between the individualistic and libertarian side of anarchism and its social and collective aspects was an intrinsic part of anarchist ideology as it developed throughout the nineteenth century. It was a question that came to the forefront not only during the Dreyfus Affair but also during the wave of terrorist bombings during the 1890s. At stake were the questions: To what extent could anarchists act on their own without consulting the group? Could one person decide what was best for all? Furthermore, how much attention could be addressed to the needs of individuals? Would so much concern neglect the problems of the entire society that superceded the plight of the lone person?

Some believed that terrorism represented the authentic voice of the individual and, thus, was the most sincere form of direct action. Others were critical of "propaganda by the deed" and urged patient group action. As noted above, Grave believed that true collective action could occur only when a sufficient level of education had raised mass consciousness. Grave kept to the collectivist side of anarchist theory, expressing the belief that revolution could only begin when society was ready for it. It was, therefore, necessary to restrain individual actions and to help shape a real movement. Along these lines, the syndicalists attempted to persuade anarchists that the collective movement could only be enhanced through better organization, as they offered in unions. They viewed the movement's problems as deriving from the lack of a cohesive organization and the eternal splintering within it. Against them stood the anarchists of the ancien manière who vehemently defended the tradition of local clubs dating in origin to the French Revolution.

At the same time, anarchism was affected by a variety of cultural forces that were strongly evident during the 1890s. As one such force, the Naturiens reflected a Romantic retreat from modern society in seeking to reshape the world through a utopian, natural community. Their rejection of technology and science and endorsement of extreme individualism underscored a vision that was completely at odds with "mutual aid." Grave's collectivist vision could not have been further absent from their aspiration toward a utopia where individuals lived in a state of nature and cared only for themselves. The Naturiens declared themselves anarchists largely because of their great hatred for contemporary society and their esteem for individualism. In this regard, they shared with the egoists a more self-directed lifestyle based upon momentary, spontaneous instincts. They also espoused nonconformity and the precedence of culture over politics. In essence, both of these "movements" reflected the flourishing atmosphere of irrationalism flourishing during the 1890s.

Perhaps the "linguists" were the only group that grasped the problems posed by so many divergent tendencies and tried to bridge them by uniting culture with politics. Such anarchists saw linguistic change as a redress both of the cultural splintering already evident and of the disparate centrifugal forces threatening to destroy the anarchist political vision. In their approach, they touched on all the problems dividing the movement—education, culture, and organization. Nevertheless, they composed such a small enclave that they ended by not having very much effective influence at all.

# Art and Anarchy

In addition to contentious dialogues dividing Parisian anarchism on the previously discussed questions, contrasting views of artists and other activists regarding the purpose of artistic images also affected the movement. This issue arose at a time when avant-garde artists emphasized stylistic concerns and growing indifference to traditional subject matter. Anarchist leaders, on the other hand, were primarily interested in the use of art for propagandistic purposes and envisioned the depiction of particular subjects in as realistic and direct a manner as possible in order to draw the attention of a sympathetic audience. Journalists like Jean Grave and Emile Pouget sought to persuade readers through the immediacy of visual images and frequently included drawings and etchings as complements to their verbal arguments in the reviews and brochures they published. Such anarchists expressed an interest in the plight of modern artists, but their intention, quite obviously, was to convey anarchistic ideals and protests through the powerful weapon of art. They ran into the reality, however, that many artists joining the movement also had another concern—to remain dedicated to their aesthetic pursuit and creativity.

Artists and aesthetic critics were highly conscious of the radical nature of anarchism as a dissenting ideology and often were eager to further its goals in their work. Like other anarchists, they saw themselves as common participants engaged in a struggle leading to the revolutionary demolition of the capitalist order. Nevertheless, by 1890 such artists and aesthetes also were aware of their position within an artistic revolution, which they perceived as a liberation from the rigid, oppressive forces of traditional standards. They hoped that this revolt would enable them to find a free and expressive voice. Beginning in the nineteenth century, avant-garde artists created works that satisfied their needs but found little reception from a hostile public. Avant-garde artists creating works for political purposes, then, were already sensitive to the pressures for acceptable forms and subject matter imposed upon them by taste or revolutionary needs.

The Romantic artists, Théodore Géricault, Eugène Delacroix, and Jean-Auguste-Dominique Ingres had earlier departed from academic standards in creating works that shocked the public. Géricault's studies of the mad and Ingres's depictions of harems were examples of such works. Nevertheless, Romantics generally continued to use heroic and mythological subjects and iconography to which the French Salon audience was accustomed. As Gustave Courbet and Jean-Francois Millet endeavored to study common scenes of ordinary life, the artistic implications of their works were even more radical. In ignoring myth and heroism, they suggested that even the lives of peasants and workers merited an artist's concern. Of course, Courbet and Millet were redefining new myths and forms of heroism—as attached to popular life. There was, however, no attempt to disguise the nature of the subject or to embellish it. Critics perceived this effort as banal and offensive.[1] From this realistic focus grew the Impressionists' desire to emphasize the "true" nature of light and color in landscapes and places of leisure. While many such subjects departed from the realist ethos and represented bourgeois life, continuity in intent was still evident.[2] On the one hand, there was a shift from the presentation of monumental subjects and motifs to those involving people and situations familiar within the contemporary setting. Coinciding with this, however, was a radical change in form and style. Impressionist paintings were presented with a view to scientific laws of light and color, but such laws seemed abstract. The erosion of three-dimensional space and the blur of color and light forced the viewer to stare very intently in order to comprehend the setting and the subject.[3]

While these works seemed obscure according to the perceptions of the general public and tradition-bound critics, they also endowed to such artists the status of belonging to a superior caste. At the center of this caste's existence was devotion to art in a nearly religious manner. In the process, despite their many differences, these artists mutually socialized and acquired a self-conscious group identity. They jointly exhibited their works and became known as the "avant-garde." Eventually, this inclination to exhibit independently divided the avant-garde itself into different camps. This chapter will not examine the technical aspects of artistic style but the relationship between art and politics during a time when artists increasingly felt their works to be innately revolutionary. Within this context, particular emphasis will be given to the perspectives offered by anarchist artists on the subject of art as engagement.

## ANARCHISM AND THE PURPOSE OF ART

Artists and journalists expressed contrasting opinions about the manner in which art furthered the anarchist cause. This clash was heightened by the avant-garde's self-conscious aim to transcend conventional taste. Francis Haskell has stated that much of the harshest criticism of the avant-garde came from left-wing critics who depicted such transcendent and exclusively aesthetic concerns as reactionary and antisocial.[4] Leftist critics as Albert Wolff felt that artists should use a form and subject accessible to all. Even Emile Zola, not an anarchist but definitely a social critic, only slowly came to the defense of the Impressionists after accepting the avant-garde nature of all great artists.[5] While some of these critics favored academic styles, libertarian leaders tended to choose realism as the most appropriate artistic style because its form was easily understood by a mass audience—an essential revolutionary goal. In holding this view, they self-consciously kept to the tradition of social depictions evident in the works of Honoré Daumier, Courbet, and Millet. Haskell has also pointed to the avant-garde's delight in evading the general public's scope of comprehension and in accepting their exile from the official artistic salons and academies. Their exhibitions in small galleries only highlighted a larger struggle against the establishment. Furthermore, their self-righteous belief in the validity of their cause brought to their side critics who snobbishly identified with them as members of the avant-garde.[6]

The paradox was that the avant-garde artist was opposed both by the academies and the Salons and by leftist critics espousing a social purpose to art. As during the early years of the Soviet Union, a serious problem existed in reconciling social revolution with aesthetic innovation. Revolutionaries favoring only the realistic style failed to consider the fact that artists initially adopting it did so for aesthetic as well as political reasons; in doing so they had alienated the public. Realism was not necessarily easily understood. Those wishing to reduce it to a formula for political communication, thus, antagonized artists who felt that their aesthetic creativity partook of the same rebellious spirit that earlier had inspired realists like Courbet. At the same time, the avant-garde's self-assured, arrogant stance could cause complications and breakdowns in communications.

In fact, the avant-garde was not a monolithic body with a particular, firmly defined, and consistent world view. As T. J. Clark has written of the avant-garde of 1848:

> the aim of the avant-garde was to snatch a transitory and essentially false
> identity from the unity of the Parisian artistic world . . . . The more we look

at the artistic world in Paris, the more its schools and dogmas seem an artifice; what really mattered was the ease of transition from attitude to attitude, style to style, posture to imposture . . . . It was a kind of initiation rite . . . . It was a finishing school, an unabashed form of social climbing.[7]

There were, of course, artists with sincere artistic convictions. Nevertheless, the avant-garde did acquire a unique social identity and included artists with a questionable devotion. In addition to dedicated artists, there were also poseurs wanting to belong to this advanced elite. Furthermore, a multitude of social and political convictions were found among the great avant-garde artists. While Courbet and Camille Pissarro were on the left, Auguste Renoir and Edgar Degas were conservatives. There was little in the way of a united political stance at work here. Such realities made the avant-garde seem as varied and complex a group as the anarchists. The avant-garde was a fluctuating group whose aim was to work for artistic innovation and to further artists' freedom from external constraints. Such artists became involved in social movements, but their participation was subject to the limits imposed by their whims. Some were more serious than others. This discussion, thus, involves two diverse groups that often interacted and cooperated for a common purpose. They could just as easily, however, go their separate ways.

At one point, Peter Kropotkin had called for artists to lend their talents to the anarchist movement and to engage their work in a more socially constructive direction. As he stated in *Paroles d'un révolté* (Memoirs of a Revolutionary):

> You poets, painters, sculptors, musicians, if you have understood your true mission and the interest of art itself, come then, put your pen, brush, burin in the service of the revolution. The arts have a mission to accomplish for the achievement of the future society . . . . Depict for us in your vivid style or in your fervent paintings the titanic struggle of the people against their oppressors; inflame young hearts with the beautiful breath of revolution which inspired our anarchism . . . . Show the people the ugliness of contemporary life and make us touch with the finger the cause of this ugliness.[8]

The emphasis upon "vivid style" could be interpreted in a number of ways, and the avant-garde could find a sustaining hope there. "Fervent" could also denote individual expression. Still, it is apparent that Kropotkin, while sympathizing with artists, was preaching social realism as a guiding principle for their work. Content was most important. Style itself was only significant insofar as it could direct the audience's attention to the injustice, exploitation, and ugliness inherent in the capitalist system. No scene could be considered too banal for this goal—in keeping with the precedent set by Courbet.[9] Kropotkin hoped that artists could continue to evoke revolutionary messages and called upon them to adopt particular styles and themes with the intent of inflaming people with the spirit of revolt. In some ways, his plea was similar to Tolstoy's *What Is Art?* in which the famous Russian author of *War and Peace* made the plea for simple and purposeful art—scornfully contrasted to the "obscurity" found in contemporary art. Like many anarchists, Tolstoy felt that subjects involving peasant life evoked the greatest and most significant artistic depiction, but he did not call for explicit political messages in works of art, maintaining a belief in an independent artistic sphere.[10]

Kropotkin believed, in fact, that artists had a unique power to reach popular moral and emotional layers otherwise inaccessible to verbal rhetoric. Due to its emotional impact, art was more effective than theoretical and technical arguments in attracting the attention of a mass audience. Nevertheless, Kropotkin discouraged anarchist artists from exaggerating the extent of their role. They would not govern the people nor inculcate in them independently conceived values. Their purpose was simply to translate underlying popular values and aspirations into artistic images that would inspire people with the anarchist message.[11] Aesthetic expression did not rank as high a need as communication of the cause's themes.

How far could artists and critics go in following this particular advice? The role and meaning of artists within the anarchist movement was, indeed, highly problematic. Strangely enough, from his organizing position within syndicalism, Fernand Pelloutier also discussed the subject. In 1896, he spoke on the subject of "L'art et la révolte" to *Le Club de l'Art Social* (The Social Art Club), which Adolphe Tabarant regularly convened to enable artists and writers to discuss the revolutionary possibilities of art. Socialists and anarchists began meeting in 1889, and among those participating in discussions were Camille Pissarro, Auguste Rodin, Jean Grave, and Emile Pouget.[12] In his talk, Pelloutier emphasized the need for a social purpose in art and scorned the work of the avant-garde oriented exclusively around aesthetic ends. As he, too, believed that artists should identify with popular needs, he accepted Kropotkin's artistic ideas. Artists, in addition to struggling against the establishments dominating their craft, should share in:

> the sufferings and sentiments of the community by an equal desire for revolt against inequality and by aspiring towards a society where each person would be independent and find the satisfaction of his own needs

in the satisfaction of the needs of his fellows. We do not separate art from socialism, and oppose those who refuse to write for the masses, considering them to be incapable of intellectual perception. We want to add communism of artistic pleasure to the communism of bread.[13]

The equation between aesthetics and bread obviously entailed a popular, material basis to art, and the passage betrays an underlying suspicion of the avant-garde's motives. Pelloutier believed that art had always been a reserve of the elites, intensifying the people's sense of inferiority. After all, peasants and workers rarely felt that their lives were deemed worthy of an artist's attention. On the other hand, artists did portray the aristocracy and the bourgeoisie, and, in doing so, reinforced their class dominance; whether it be classical or Romantic in inspiration, such art was largely a frivolous ornament of the powerful.

Pelloutier cast equally harsh criticism at mystical and erotic trends then current because they focused more attention upon introspection and privacy than upon social conditions. Art would only be considered democratic, he believed, when the masses were able to appreciate paintings and poems. This circumstance would only occur, however, when their material needs had been satisfied. Pelloutier clearly did not consider the reality of oral epics that had traditionally flourished in popular circles. He was interested, however, in popular access to "high art." Pelloutier felt that it was necessary for revolutionaries to encourage a leveling conformity of taste that would liberate art from the snobbish circles then dominating it. An infusion of popular feeling, following the revolution, would metamorphose the character of art forever. That same revolution, envisioned as transforming material conditions and shattering class distinctions, would also improve education, and encourage the growth of popular taste, appreciation, and a critical attitude to society.

Pelloutier saw the most promise for future art and literature in Emile Zola's naturalistic novels, praising them for their scientific observation, material analysis, and representation of people's lives. He also admired Zola's understanding of the ways in which popular attitudes and habits were connected to historical and social factors. Zola's works represented "sane" art because they stimulated anger and revolt, although this was not necessarily the author's principal concern.[14] Pelloutier viewed pure aestheticism, in contrast, as a stimulus to social indifference and private satisfaction not extending beyond the immediate pleasure gained from hearing certain rhythms or seeing particular tones of color.[15]

It is worth asking whether Pelloutier would have been equally enthralled with artistically mediocre realism. What is of the greatest concern here, however, is the fact that a labor organizer like Pelloutier should have found it necessary to speak on the subject of art. It is clear enough that both he and Kropotkin perceived art to have a revolutionary potential. For this reason, they called for certain formulas and propagandistic themes to serve as artistic guidelines. Eventually, this preference became known as social realism and during the early twentieth century in such places as Weimar Germany and the Soviet Union was regarded as an obstacle to artists' creative efforts. Pelloutier and Kropotkin sensed that the artistic transformation evident in their time was taking on a direction of its own and sought to restrain it in mobilizing it for their purpose. There were others at this time, however, who still envisioned creative possibilities in the infusion of popular themes into art.

This line of reasoning also was taken up by the critic E. Museaux, who believed that artists were altering the direction of poetry, painting, and music and creating a truly socialist art—the singularly most significant development of the nineteenth century. He also believed that the final restructuring of society would bring even greater artistic change and an ultimate standard of taste.[16] Museaux wrote that the finest artistic themes were evident in the observation of popular lives, enabling audiences to share in their struggles. As he phrased it, the "human ocean" was greater than the egoist.[17] Eugene Châtelain complained in a poem that "art for art is an Olympus where the gods imprison the artists."[18] Implicit in such opinions were: an attack upon the notion of art as an isolated activity removed from the political, economic, and social realities burdening the people; and the belief that art could serve as an agent for change.

These writers were socialists, but as already noted, similar ideas were found in the writings of Kropotkin and Pelloutier. "Aesthetic socialism" was current in both socialism and anarchism. Nevertheless, anarchists also had to be more sensitive to the libertarian aspects of their ideology that, in fact, attracted artists in the first place. Anarchist artists were highly conscious of this fact and wanted to have creative freedom when approaching their work. This attitude entailed potentially deep suspicions on their part of any prescriptions offered by political leaders.

For this reason, artists wishing to become politically active were often more drawn to anarchism than to mainstream socialism, feeling that socialist leaders were less sympathetic to their creative needs and more willing to impose uniform standards. This brought to mind the collective opposition to such uniformity by Impressionist artists during their rebellion against the salons, when they emphasized the necessity of freedom to their calling. For this reason some Impressionists and other avant-garde artists viewed anarchism as an ideology that vindicated both their struggle against Salon dictates and standards and their aspirations for social justice.

Anarchist journalists tended to present this situation in more hesitant terms. While stressing their preference for certain styles and themes, they continued to uphold the artist's freedom from external restrictions, pointing to traditional bourgeois suffocation of such freedom. There was obvious tension within this perspective. Jean Grave glossed over it by stating that drawings created for his brochures should be inspired by an "idea" but that the exact choice of subject and method could be left to the artist's discretion.[19] The idea, of course, was anarchy, but the way in which it was rendered was kept open to artistic choice—one that could seemingly be as endless and vast in possibilities as the very concept itself. Grave's rhetoric offered one way of reconciling the differences between the needs of propaganda and those of aesthetic freedom.

Emile Verhaeren was a renowned Belgian symbolist poet of the fin de siècle, who also wrote art criticism and was drawn to anarchism. His aesthetic thinking went through a series of transformations that reflected the complexity of interconnected ideas circulating among artistic and political circles. Increasingly, he distanced himself from the movement of art for art's sake and called for artistic works that partially satisfied Pelloutier's criteria. Verhaeren esteemed the paintings and drawings of the anarchist Maximilien Luce because they seemed to offer some of the most advanced examples of social, revolutionary art. Luce's works were already considered "violent, harsh, brutal," expressing "the bloody soul of the people, the life of crowds anguished and exasperated by suffering and rancors, divided in two by the social curse."[20] Critics admiring Luce, in fact, focused on the social aspects of his art instead of its aesthetic merit. Verhaeren praised Luce's reluctance to distance himself from the people's plight, expressed in a complete identification with the lives of those he portrayed. As he wrote of Luce:

> He loves the worker passionately. He follows him in his terrible and suffocated life to the ends of the earth; he embraces his angers and rages; he understands and supports his revolts. His drawings demand justice and pity. They are harsh and unpolished. They are always improvised and exhibit the effects of haste . . . . Luce tries to convey the true aspects of modern labor in its real milieu. The worker hardly appears to him to be isolated. He only shows him as a part, a figure within the whole; he helps to put together the groups, the ensemble, which themselves are based on nature. Landscape painter above all, the painter has remained faithful to the tendency to dissolve great human effort in nature. That which surrounds man determines his existence and his history.[21]

Such opinions approach Pelloutier's admiring tone for Zola's naturalism. Luce's work, Verhaeren believed, gave credence to the potential for innovative art to express political engagement and transcend socially the separate aesthetic realm occupied by dandies and Bohemians. The consequence of Bohemian aesthetic attitudes was to surround art with a stultifying, lifeless atmosphere. Verhaeren felt that artists should strive not for detachment from oppressed workers but for identification with them. In so doing, they needed to depict unabashedly the reality of suffering and to give greater visible expression to social anger. Like Pelloutier, Verhaeren believed that the artist's only purpose was in being a revolutionary.

Nevertheless, Verhaeran's stand was more complicated than it initially seems. As a symbolist poet himself, Verhaeran supported the avant-garde's break from convention. He considered its innovations to be revolutionary in its evocations of new social visions that would assist in the shattering of the old order.[22] Despite the confusion and disorientation initially attached to the public's experience of such poems or canvases, it would only be reactionary to seek comforts in previous standards and forms. Verhaeren stressed that there was a:

> true tradition of the century: that which came from Delacroix, continued with Jongland and Corot and ended with Manet, Renoir, Pissarro and finally Seurat. This tradition, the only living and original one, has given our age a painting of its own. The others only try to rejuvenate the past. They can interest, produce masters of first rank, dazzle us by precious qualities, redo superb facades of art, damaged by time—they are not authentic and profound life—like ours.[23]

Like Félix Fénéon and Octave Mirbeau, Verhaeren attacked the Ecole des Beaux-Arts and the various salons and academies and criticized decadent and symbolist artists for creating new schools that were as restrictive as previous ones. This attack also was directed against an offshoot of the avant-garde that tended toward obscuranticism, but Verhaeren wished to underline the imperative for artists to contest and overcome such norms through their emotional inspiration. Along these lines, he believed that the Neo-Impressionists had superceded the Impressionists and that Georges Seurat's scientific colorism would inaugurate a new age. There was no standing still or adhering to a permanent norm where art was concerned.

Verhaeren's perception of a new avant-garde was not atypical of the time. The poet Paul Adam wrote that a new generation of writers and artists had emerged to replace the "old guard" during the 1890s. Thus, Maurice Barrès and Andre Gide were taking the place of Emile Zola and Joris Huysmans, among others, as the literary standard-bearers of the age. Such pronouncements, of course, were not necessarily correct, but they reflected the ways in which Verhaeren and Adam emphasized youth and generational succession as factors in the ongoing avant-garde revolt. They were not the only critics to state this case. With the search for ever-newer forms, artists could no longer rest content with their past accomplishments. The need for continual innovation also caused younger avant-garde artists to seek justification through anarchism. As Roger Shattuck has stated:

> Anarchism served not only to unsettle the political smugness of the Third Republic, but also to challenge any formulated aesthetic. The dynamism of pre-war artistic activity ran a close parallel to anarchism; post-war Dada and surrealism look like its artistic parodies. By acting on their ideas, the anarchist "martyrs" inspired artists to demonstrate as boldly.[24]

Verhaeren envisioned the synthesis of aesthetics with social criticism and pointed to the deeply held anarchistic attitudes of Paul Signac and Camille Pissarro as reflections of the fusion of innovative art and politics. These pointillists had included industrial landscapes and the life of the popular classes within their field of observation, thus contesting the creation of art solely for art's sake.[25] Close observation reveals a similar trend in the works of Impressionists whose coloristic concerns were complemented by portrayals of popular life.[26] Verhaeren felt it possible for artists to create socially reflective works that were not stale and lifeless. Social art did not necessarily entail a blind following of formulas prescribed by political leaders; it could be creative and inspired, following the path carved out by the avant-garde.

Two sides of the artistic question concerned anarchism. On the one hand, artists wished to indict the injustices and exploitation intrinsic to capitalistic society and to assist in its overthrow. When raising this question, artists expressed a momentary absorption in politics and addressed a problem lying outside of their usual boundaries. On the other hand, artists were also interested in determining their position in anarchist society. They wondered whether their aesthetic development would be allowed further expression. This question was paramount for them since the anarchist promise of individual freedom had induced their initial involvement in the movement. Luce was convinced that under anarchism the artist's position would be enhanced, since it was an especially vocal social movement seeking to correct abuses from which artists also suffered.[27] Such artists assumed that, as part of the oppressed masses, they would benefit from an anarchist revolution. In reaching this conclusion, they generalized somewhat and did not consider the highly successful and prosperous position of painters like Edgar Degas who were quite content with the status quo. Still, an undeniable poverty and misery afflicted many others. Anarchism, thus, would help free such struggling artists from poverty and the dictates of bourgeois taste. Camille Pissarro expressed this opinion in a letter that discussed Luce's apparent request for help in composing an article about the role of the artist in anarchist society. Pissarro explained that Luce was:

> indicating how artists could work with absolute freedom once rid of the terrible constraints of Messrs. capitalist-collector-speculators and dealers. How the idea of art would be further developed, the love of beauty and purity of sensation.[28]

Artists certainly were aware of financial impositions that constantly intruded upon their work. The artist was a unique social being living in the context of an oppressive system and faced with the same injustices afflicting others. Paul Signac also emphasized this matter in his articles and his diary. He, too, was very eager to create works conveying political statements and saw no conflict between this concern and those of the avant-garde. In fact, he interpreted the history of art in a political manner and pointed to the maltreatment of great artists of the past. As he emphasized, these artists had been vindicated by the appreciation of later generations but, in their own lifetimes, suffered from injustice, persecution, authoritarian oppression, and "ill-advised" taste.[29] Signac simultaneously emphasized the need for political change and the need for artistic freedom and saw anarchism as offering the most solid support for both. Regarding artistic engagement, Signac explained that it was up to each individual artist to decide how best to serve the movement. As he wrote:

> The anarchist painter is not the one who will create anarchist pictures, but he who, without concern for wealth, without desire for recompense, will fight with all his individuality against official bourgeois conventions by means of a personal contribution.[30]

The vague nature of the proper "personal contribution," however, was an issue that troubled artists. We can see this reflected in the life, ideas, and work of Camille Pissarro—one of the fathers of Impressionism and an adherent to anarchism.

Pissarro's entry onto the French artistic and political scene was by no means a determined fact. He was born on July 10, 1830 on the Caribbean island of St. Thomas in the Virgin Islands to Jewish parents. His father was a French Jew of Portuguese descent who had settled in St. Thomas in 1824, while his mother was a French Jew and originally her husband's aunt—a fact causing no small local scandal. Nevertheless, they eventually overcame the uproar and built a comfortable existence through a business involving hardware, shipping equipment, and general merchandise.[31]

In 1847, they sent their son, Camille, to be educated in Paris. At that time, he visited the studios of several painters and became interested in their work. After returning to the Caribbean, he took several trips to Venezuela with an artist named Fritz Melbye who urged him to paint natural scenes. By the mid-1850s, Pissarro again decided to leave for Paris to become an artist. At that time, the famous landscape painter Camille Corot became Pissarro's mentor and reinforced his tendency to receive direct inspiration from nature.[32]

Between the years 1860 and 1880, Pissarro emerged as one of the foremost French artists and together with Claude Monet, Alfred Sisley, and Auguste Renoir helped found the Impressionist school. Initially, these artists were ridiculed and failed to find Salon acceptance. They decided, therefore, to exhibit their assembled works outside the mainstream galleries in what they designated as "Salons des Refusés" where they were appreciated by a small audience. Pissarro was especially inspiring as an artistic rebel, having a pronounced impact upon Paul Cézanne. Not only was he Cézanne's artistic mentor for some time, but his friendship proved to be critical in comforting the Provençal artist during personal crises. The Impressionists' existence was marked by poverty and instability, but by the 1880s they had become somewhat more accepted, successful, and prosperous. At this time, they also began to exhibit their canvases separately and to develop in different artistic directions.

During the later 1880s, Pissarro became acquainted with Paul Signac and Maximilien Luce, who influenced both his painting and his political stands.[33] Following the lead of the younger artists, Pissarro adopted the pointillist style (begun earlier by Georges Seurat) and became known as a Neo-Impressionist. In addition, he became an anarchist. The connections between the ideology and painting were not only evident in the examples of Signac, Luce, and other artists but also in those of Fénéon and Mirbeau—the most vocal critics defending and inspiring them.

It is noteworthy that Pissarro accepted the influence of youthful movements as he approached his sixties. His stylistic change, however, brought mixed artistic success, occurring at the time when mainstream Impressionism found more public acceptance. While Monet and Renoir increasingly prospered, Pissarro continued to struggle, and anarchistic engagement added a further element of revolutionary estrangement from the French political and social establishment.

Several factors contributed to Pissarro's espousal of the movement. To begin, when he had first visited France in 1847, the country was beset by the hardship and poverty of the lower classes and on the verge of the 1848 revolution.[34] After witnessing slave revolts in St. Croix the same year, he developed a further sense of social outrage. His political consciousness grew to the point that by 1871 he supported the Paris Communards.

Such experiences would not alone have necessarily evoked an attraction to the anarchist creed. Pissarro's support for the movement grew from the observations he had made of peasant life. Such daily contact was provided by homes he established in areas like Louveciennes, Pontoise, and Eragny where peasants were found in abundance. Pissarro accordingly focused many of his Impressionist and pointillist works on this aspect of local life, finding much reflection of his concerns in Kropotkin's mystique of peasants.[35]

Pissarro's beliefs also were motivated by his reactions to some artistic trends of the 1880s and 1890s. His friend Paul Gauguin and other artists were breaking from the Impressionist principle that art must accurately reflect the natural world. Instead, they used colors and forms to express symbols or underlying ideas. Pissarro viewed this as a form of blasphemy and reaction that clashed with the realism of Camille Corot and Daumier. He accepted such realism wholeheartedly and remembered Corot's sustaining personal words: "The muse is in the woods." Corot and Pissarro both continued to feel that artistic obliviousness to nature was, in fact, tantamount to an inclination for the religious. Therefore, any departure from this advice was implicitly religious and regressive, reflecting the increasing mysticism of the times. In describing Gauguin's *Jacob Wrestling with the Angel* of 1891, Pissarro wrote:

> I do not criticize Gauguin for having painted a rose background nor do I object to the two struggling fighters and the Breton peasants in the foreground, what I dislike is that he copied these elements from the Japanese, the Byzantine painters and others. I criticize him for not applying his synthesis to our modern philosophy which is absolutely social, anti-authoritarian, and anti-mystical. There is where the problem becomes serious. This is a step backwards; Gauguin is not a seer, he is a schemer who has sensed that the bourgeoisie are moving to the right, recoiling before the great idea of solidarity which sprouts among the people—an instinctive idea, but fecund, the only idea that is permissible.[36]

Written by a Portuguese-French-Jewish artist born in the Caribbean, these words exhibit a particular Eurocentric sensitivity but not a racist mentality. His critical reference to Japanese and Byzantine style reflects the European bias viewing "orientalizing" (emanating from the Near East or Asia) as medieval or backward. Similar perspectives had been expressed during the Enlightenment about French Romanesque and Gothic architecture.

Pissarro's statement does reflect the prevailing nineteenth century inclination toward realism, science, and empiricism—an inclination that was then coming into question from irrationalist currents. When combined with a sense of social commitment, Pissarro's stance was defensive and combative and joined class struggle with the struggle against reactionary mysticism. He thought that progress could only occur when previous tendencies blocking true human awareness had been rejected. As one of the founders of Impressionism, Pissarro felt that the movement had supported progress in its continued adherence to rationalism, science, and empiricism. Nevertheless, he perceived rebellions against his beliefs to be finding increasing and threatening strength in fin-de-siècle Europe. Gauguin's abstract and mystical style exhibited this irrationalist current, and Pissarro was quick to attack the manner in which Gauguin and other newcomers on the artistic scene gave nature only an indirect and oblique depiction. Consequently, anarchism reinforced Pissarro's social and artistic opinions through its fierce rejection of what he believed to be the Catholic Church's superstitious teachings.

Nevertheless, Pissarro felt his world view to be increasingly on the defensive in the modern world. As he wrote in a melancholic tone:

> Perhaps I am out of date, or my art may conflict and not be concilable with the general trend which seems to have gone mystical. It must be that only another generation, free from all religious, mystical, unclear conceptions, a generation of the most modern ideas, could have the qualities necessary to admire this approach. I firmly believe that something of our ideas, born as they are of the anarchist philosophy, passes into our works which are thus antipathetic to the current trend.[37]

Pissarro's use of the word "modern" again presupposes a mentality that is receptive to science and rationalism. During his time, however, that same word was given new meaning through the understanding of irrational forces in a variety of areas. What Pissarro desired was a revival of "modern" as it was understood in the Enlightenment to suggest common sense, empiricism, positivism, and all other methods that were useful in the struggle against such traditional institutions as the church and monarchy. He believed that Seurat and Signac through Neo-Impressionism were revitalizing art and preserving the realistic and social concerns of his own earlier work. He had always felt a familial cohesion with the Impressionists, having been like a father to Cézanne. This same need was now met in his association with the younger pointillists. During the late 1880s, Pissarro became both an anarchist and a Neo-Impressionist— following Fénéon's lead in attaching a sense of mission and mutual connection to the two movements. Anarchism and Neo-Impressionsm were woven into a unified vision in which art and social consciousness belonged to the same struggle against the establishment. Nevertheless, Pissarro's commitment to both also made his stands as an anarchist artist internally troubling. While agreeing to produce a separate book of anarchist prints for Grave and to contribute drawings to his reviews, Pissarro felt ambivalent about the prescriptions for form and subject espoused by Grave and other anarchist leaders.

Pissarro believed fervently in the anarchist ideal, having written about Kropotkin's vision:

> One must admit that if it is utopian, in every way it is a beautiful dream, and as we often have had examples of beautiful dreams become realities, nothing prevents us from believing that it will be possible one day, unless man fails and returns to complete barbarism.[38]

It would turn out that the plunge into barbarism would prove more likely than the achievement of utopia. Still, his enthusiasm for anarchism is evident in this passage. Anarchism sustained him in reinforcing his urge for artistic freedom. Pissarro was optimistic about the potential role for anarchism to play in liberating the arts. He was more ambiguous about the extent to which artists should adapt their styles and concerns to propaganda needs. Regarding Kropotkin's belief that artists should strive to identify with the subjects they depicted, Pissarro wrote:

> A propos of art, there would be many things to find fault with. Kropotkin believes that one must live as a peasant in order to understand them. It seems to me that one must be wrapped up in his subject to render it well, but is it necessary to be a peasant? Let us be artists first and we will have the ability to feel everything even a landscape, without being a peasant.[39]

In fact, artists were attracted to anarchism because, more so than other social movements, it seemed to allow people the possibility of maintaining their individual identities while fulfilling a revolutionary role. The anarchists' espousal of libertarianism encouraged artists to believe that they could serve the movement and remain free of social regimentation and aesthetic controls. Some artists were surprised and dismayed to discover that the issue of aesthetic independence was unresolved. Anarchist compagnons could see Pissarro's point of view as elitist and distant from the cause. Accordingly, aesthetically-minded anarchists resisted the demands that anarchist journalists made upon their revolutionary work.

Artists had their own ideas about the essence of anarchist expression. These ideas did not always coincide with those of editors who wanted ideological statements translated directly into artistic images. It was for this reason, as noted above, that they endorsed social realism.

Pissarro was convinced that all of his works gave expression to anarchism. Even paintings that apparently were apolitical conveyed the spirit of the idea.[40] He felt that works of art could be anarchist even when not directly treating obvious political subjects like poverty, oppression, and injustice. They need not consist solely of propagandizing drawings and prints nor be commissioned by politically active editors. One could be an anarchist simply by challenging bourgeois convention and presenting an unfamiliar perspective of nature and society to the public. Anarchism could be implicitly present in each daring work hanging on a gallery wall before a baffled audience, and all strong individuals were anarchists by the force of their personalities, and so were their works.

Pissarro's son, Lucien, expressed a similar sentiment and differed with Grave's call for "social" art. As an aspiring artist living in London he stated that no differences divided art for art's sake from social art because:

> every production which is truly a work of art is social (whether or not the creator wishes it) because he who has produced it makes his fellow men share the most passionate and purest emotion which he has felt before the sights of nature.[41]

The two Pissarros assumed that only through the depiction of natural scenes were artists able to arouse both individual and communal emotions. Nevertheless, they also believed in the necessity of stylistic experimentation and in the potential of innovative canvases to both expand the public's appreciation for natural beauty and shape social sentiments in as pronounced a manner as the realistic prescriptions demanded by Kropotkin. (As will be evident below, the elder Pissarro used social realism when occasion arose but with a degree of uneasiness.) In other words, free expression was itself revolutionary.

Camille Pissarro felt that new ways of perception and expression fostered rebellious individualism and rejection of the establishment. His anarchist aspirations also were reflected in the hope that all people would one day be able to comprehend and perceive beauty completely.[42] Therefore, he did not reorient his art to fit Kropotkin's "anarchist mold" because "all arts are anarchist when they are beautiful and good."[43] Such an attempt at evading conformity and prescribed stylistic formulas also helped redefine anarchism during the time when the word was taking on countless implications.

There is an elusive quality to the entire understanding of anarchist art. Kropotkin and Pelloutier were eager to call for themes and subjects best suited to social realism. However, most avant-garde artists were reluctant to accept such requests, believing that they infringed upon their rebellion from the Salons that initially had evoked their fascination for the anarchist movement. As intellectuals and artists were very aware of the Vatican Index of forbidden books, they feared that all political aesthetic standards could easily be converted into new forms of censorship. Avant-garde artists felt that their struggle against Parisian artistic institutions in itself reflected a truly anarchistic stand and greatly furthered the movement's progress.[44] While the question was not as urgent in fin-de-siècle Paris (given the relative absence of governmental proscriptions) as it would be in the Soviet Union of the 1920s, artists were, nonetheless, very sensitive to it and suspected any ideological calls for "correct" art.

The avant-garde and anarchists both felt that they participated in constant revolt—in one form or another. By 1890, Signac, Seurat, Pissarro, and Luce formed their own exhibiting society. The Société des Artistes Indépendants they had helped create in 1884 was already attracting rebellious artists unable to find galleries in which to exhibit their work. This society, which would continue its work for over a century, gave new meaning to the pursuit for artistic freedom and creativity beyond the confines of Salon taste and the audience catering to it. Henri Rousseau commemorated the organization's significance in a later painting depicting its twenty-second organized exhibition. Rousseau gave mythological and allegorical expression to two revolutions. "Liberty," representing the revolutions of 1789, 1793, 1830, 1848, and 1871, flies above the gathering group of aesthetic rebels and blows her horn to inaugurate the exhibition. She is the usual bare-breasted Marianne made famous by Delacroix during the Romantic period. Nearby, a lion lies alongside the plaque dedicated to the society's first artists. Among the names on the plaque, one can decipher those of Signac, Luce, and Pissarro. In this way, the artistic and political revolutions demarcating recent French history are combined as "liberty" accompanies the avant-garde in its path of rebellious creativity.[45]

Nevertheless, the avant-garde was fragmented into groups with differing concerns. Some artists like Paul Gauguin created increasingly unconventional works that elicited abstract, symbolic, even mystical interpretations. Vincent Van Gogh's paintings reflected subjective concerns that later influenced the course of expressionist art. Arthur Rimbaud and Stéphane Mallarmé created poetry focusing upon the musical and symbolic qualities of their verse and departing from all convention.

The wing of the avant-garde including Signac, Seurat, and Pissarro, in contrast, adhered to the earlier principle guiding realistic tradition. Although experimenting in new styles like pointillism that mystified the public, they continued to believe in the tenets of realism and defended their Neo-Impressionist works by basing them upon Eugène Chevreul's scientific theories of color and light. As seen in Pissarro's criticism of Gauguin's "religious and symbolic" works, they openly extolled the guidelines of science and nature as the most appropriate for artists to follow. Despite their persistent call for artistic freedom, the pointillists did not contradict the anarchists' general opinion of realistic art as being the most accessible to the people.[46] Adherence to the very flexible anarchist ideology also furthered resistance to excessively stringent demands made upon their choice of style and subject. Neo-Impressionists maintained all along that their work, even when seeming obscure and baffling to general audiences, was, in fact, relevant to ordinary life.

The art critics Félix Fénéon and Octave Mirbeau took active roles in connecting Parisian anarchism and Neo-Impressionism. While actively espousing the anarchist creed, they also linked their verbal attacks upon artistic centers to caustic assaults upon political institutions.

Fénéon's nature as an anarchist art critic has already been noted. Octave Mirbeau occupied an equally prominent position in the literary dissemination of anarchist ideas. He was born in Trevières (in Calvados) in February, 1848, attended a Jesuit school in Vannes from 1858 to 1863, and then unsuccessfully studied law in Paris from 1866 to 1868. During the Franco-Prussian War, Mirbeau became a lieutenant in the Garde Mobile de l'Orne and was wounded in action. His first strong political inclinations (reflecting the ongoing attraction especially exerted by one contemporary French political force) were in the direction of Bonapartism, and he was among the few supporters of a return to imperial rule after the French defeat. Until 1877, Mirbeau opposed the Third Republic from such a perspective and gained his initial journalistic experience on Bonapartist newspapers.

Until 1882, he worked at a variety of jobs including "chef de cabinet" to the prefect of Ariege and a position with the Paris Stock Exchange.[47] Throughout this period, he wrote as a journalist and art critic for the monarchist papers, *Le Gaulois,* and *Le Figaro.* Though no longer a Bonapartist, Mirbeau remained on the right of the political spectrum, and his views became more extreme as seen in the militaristic and anti-Semitic articles he wrote for the paper he founded in 1883, *Les Grimaces.* In an attempt to create more harmonious relations with new leftist colleagues, Mirbeau later attributed his early anti-Semitism to a grievance he had had with the Jewish editor of *Le Gaulois* and tried to diminish the significance of his earlier statements.[48] The notoriety of his previous positions, however, continued to cause him embarrassment among French leftists.

Amidst the uncertain French political climate of the time, Mirbeau shifted his position in 1886 and renounced his former beliefs. At this time, he also began serious work as a novelist and playwright while continuing to write art criticism. Like Fénéon, he promoted the avant-garde's efforts and especially defended the pointillists. His novels, *L'Abbé Jules* and *Sébastien Roche,* analyzed the Catholic Church's adverse effects on peoples' lives and revealed in the process both a distaste for institutions and sympathy for individuals. Also brought into focus was his strong hatred of the church—originating, no doubt, from his Jesuit experience.

According to the historian Reg Carr, Mirbeau's shift to the left was only the final formalization of his true viewpoint and should not surprise us by its abrupt nature. Mirbeau had always been a rebel and individualist unable to find a place in society. Unfortunately, he had directed his ire at the wrong targets. The episode with the editor of *Le Gaulois* served only to justify his disenchantment with the right. Mirbeau did, in fact, use much of the paper's right-wing vocabulary ("corrupt," "decadent," etc.) to vilify the various objects of his wrath. Doing so, he reflected much of the contemporary perspectives of decline influencing the mentality of both conservatives and revolutionaries. In searching for a compatible leftist ideology, Mirbeau viewed anarchism as most satisfying his undeniable individualism and as the force most capable of reversing the downward spiral of French society. After his "conversion," Mirbeau overcame embarrassment of his former views and became one of the chief critics of the virulent, mass-oriented anti-Semitism propagated by Edouard Drumont and Henri Rochefort.[49] (In contrast, his fellow art critic, Camille Mauclair, moved from an ardent Dreyfusard stand during the 1890s to an extremely chauvinistic and anti-Semitic position during the turbulent 1930s.)

As an art critic, Mirbeau favored the advancement of individual creativity and, like Fénéon, denounced the Salons' and the Academies' stifling of innovation:

> beyond the Academies, the juries, and the Salons, there is a movement which grows every day and which will go further. The leaders and recruits of this artistic "confession" . . . have for the Salons in general and for administrative constraints in particular the indifference which they merit.[50]

Mirbeau transferred the fervor of military "recruits" and religious "confession" to the avant-garde's mission in art. He also very vocally blamed bourgeois taste for the mediocre nature of mass commercial art, stating that the "merchants of canvases" corrupted art while the Salons encouraged "prostitution of taste and the suicide of talent." True creativity, Mirbeau felt, was most visible when removed from the domain of artistic institutions, which only deserved artistic, critical, and public indifference.[51]

By 1892, Mirbeau was an avowed anarchist and endorsed violence as a means of bringing down the capitalist order. In his open support of Ravachol's terrorist bombing, he viewed terror as necessary retaliation against the brutality carried out by states and felt that:

> do what they may to deliver themselves to the reactions of fear, governments will not prevent the inevitable. We are at a decisive moment in human history. The old world collapses under the weight of its own crimes. It is that world itself which lights the bomb which will destroy it.[52]

While admiring Kropotkin's vision of anarchistic communes, Mirbeau especially stressed the struggles carried out by individuals against governmental and institutional "straightjackets." He worked with Faure (sharing with him a Jesuit background, a dislike of the church and the military, and his conversion to anarchism) on behalf of Dreyfus. Mirbeau's perspective, however, was derived from his focus as an artist and his strong position defending individual creativity from conventional standards. Accordingly, he was not one to back the call for social realism as the solely appropriate art form for anarchist artists. (The different expectations of anarchist expression can be seen personified in the stances of a Mirbeau and a Faure. One desired expressive freedom as an end in itself; the other sought its use for social and political ends.)

Fénéon was the most important and outspoken of the critical supporters of the pointillists, and in promoting their work, he did not avoid castigating artistic institutions. His regard for exhibitions held at the Luxembourg Museum has already been noted.[53] He increased the violent tenor of his rhetoric in an article for *Père Peinard* where he expressed his anarchistic distrust of institutions. Fénéon damned the Ecole des Beaux-Arts and all the "tottering machinery" of the Academies, which he regarded as puppets both of the government and of bourgeois taste. Great art was created by individuals standing alone. For innovative works to have a larger life-renewing and art-enhancing effect, it was necessary to rid the world of all institutions and governments.[54] The liberation of artists had to be tied to political revolt.

In his vociferous defense of Seurat and Signac, Fénéon placed his support behind the young painters who opposed what he perceived to be the decadent art of the past. In fact, he suggested that youth furthered the spontaneity and freshness inherent in the creative work of art.[55] Fénéon believed this to be true even for Pissarro's adoption of pointillism in his late fifities. While Pissarro's later readoption of "pure" Impressionism received praise, Fénéon felt that the style was by then outmoded and part of the past. Therefore, Neo-Impressionism could only give Pissarro a burst of youthful energy.

Such contrasts of old and new can also be extended to the perceptions of artistic meeting places. Signac admired the Bohemian tradition of artistic cafes and contrasted the invigorating discussions conducted there to the "pontificating" witnessed in artistic banquets, reviews, and soirées. In expanding the physical dimension of their artistic revolt, the avant-garde used cafes to replace the Salon as their center of social life.[56] This was another way by which they continued to "épater les bourgeois" (scorn the bourgeoisie).

There were no strict, universal rules regarding the factors motivating avant-garde involvement in anarchism. Some avant- garde artists were attracted to anarchism because they saw a direct correlation between their artistic concerns and the social and economic problems highlighted by the movement's leaders. Their most vocal grievance, however, was held against the Salons. In other cases, the situation was more ambiguous. It has been said of Pissarro that he had no special theories about anarchism but only an emotional sympathy for it emanating from his artistic nature.[57] It is clear that artists tended to avoid the kind of theorizing indulged in by Kropotkin or Pelloutier. Other motivations involving moral instincts were critical to anarchist engagement. One had to be passionate about issues such as justice and hatred of the state. Artists were not immune from having such feelings, but they directed their wrath against both governmental and cultural authorities. While some artists were clear in expressing social discontent, others were more ambiguous and attempted to create a special role for themselves.

Part of the problem revolved around the insulated atmosphere in which members of the avant-garde lived and worked. By the 1890s, symbolist art encouraged the formation of cults as was later paralleled in Germany in the youthful adoration of Stefan Georg's poetry. Poetry and paintings were infused with mystical meanings that were increasingly difficult for the public to decipher. Success in breaking such codes enabled one to gain entry into a special circle, an exclusive sect. Followers perceived Mallarmé's poetry and Odilon Redon's paintings as virtual scriptures that were inaccessible and exuded airs of mystery and religious awe to those wishing to follow an artistic path to salvation. Even if neither high priest consciously sought such a position or a religion of art, followers and admirers could draw other conclusions and endow the artists with near sainthood.

Symbolism, indeed, frequently became tied to and equated with the anarchist movement and, thus, was an important point of contact between aesthetics and politics. Several symbolist poets and critics became anarchists, and some observers saw a close connection between the new artistic movements and anarchism. Fénéon believed that Neo-Impressionism, symbolism, and anarchism were the most stimulating and creative movements at the fin de siècle.[58] He himself served as a link among the three and was responsible for bringing artists to anarchism.[59] Fénéon saw the three movements united in a struggle pitting cultural and political revolutionaries against institutions and established traditions. If the new order were to flourish, all restraints upon human expression and creative freedom would need to be removed. Symbolists and anarchists were one in underlining the need for complete individualism and spontaneity and if some figures within each movement were not in accord on some questions, they still found common ground on this point.

Many symbolists published works in reviews that were either overtly anarchist or frequently included articles written with a strong inclination in that direction. Among such reviews were: *Entretiens Politiques et Littéraires, La Plume* (the Pen), and *La Revue Independante*. The poet, Francis Vielé-Griffin, launched *Entretiens* in an effort intended to publish not only works of symbolist poets but also socially and politically critical essays with an anarchist tilt.

Adolphe Retté, one of the Symbolist-anarchists, wrote "L'art et l'anarchie" for *La Plume* in 1893. Retté was a tempestuous figure whose anarchist engagement wavered according to the fluctuation of his moods.[60] Eventually, he renewed his religious conviction and converted to Catholicism—in exact contrast to Faure's and Mirbeau's rejections of the same faith. In all honesty, "conversions" in both directions at the time were common among artists. Nevertheless, during the 1890s, he was involved with both the avant-garde and anarchism. His writing offered clear evidence of the tension between the contrasting facets of politically conscious aesthetic thought. In "L'art et l'anarchie," he castigated the advocates of social art for practicing "sociological dilettantism."[61] In addition, he did not offer hope of an eventual compromise between art and anarchy because:

> one is either a sincere anarchist whose duty it is to give himself entirely to doctrines and to put them in practice . . . and whose writings would be writings of struggle destined for people speaking the same language; . . . thus he is a sociological militant, not an artist. Or one is an artist whose sole duty is to pledge his life to the defense and glorification of art.[62]

Retté criticized Zola and other naturalists, scorning the excessive social and economic descriptions found in their work. Such an approach demonstrated a confusion of art and sociology. Readers were, thus, bombarded with empirically based details that detracted from pure aesthetic contemplation. This Platonic idea belonged to a traditional view of artists as mystically endowed, spiritually focused transcenders of earthly affairs. Expanding on this point, Retté posed an antithesis between democracy and "Beauty" and bestowed upon artists an aristocratic stature. Developing his own political perspective, Retté condemned the French Revolution both for destroying the aristocratic tradition in art and for bringing into prominence "the malign beast of the bourgeoisie" and the people, described here as a "massive brute."[63] Retté's opinions on such points clearly represented a rejection of Pelloutier's call for social art. In keeping to Stirner's and Devaldès's anarchistic current, Retté urged anarchist artists to devote themselves not only to aesthetics but also to egoism and aristocratic hauteur. He equated proletarian society with a barbarian invasion bringing about the destruction of civilization. Only the deification of art would provide refuge, sanctuary, and salvation from the chaos and confusion ensuing from excessive democratization. Retté was undoubtedly espousing here a hierarchical role for art—even within the anarchist domain.

Retté believed that sincere artists were opposed to the modern world's leveling tendencies and that only an elite few could contemplate and express Beauty. Democracy only encouraged conformity and homogeneity and a parallel hostility to the great artist's individual vision. Although Retté found much to admire in anarchism's esteem for the individual ego, he objected to its egalitarian impulses. Retté, like Devaldès, reflected the transformed intellectual world of the 1890s characterized by recognition of Nietzsche as the principal cultural critic—even in his debilitated condition in madness. The era also saw followers of Nietzsche take his more ambiguous ideas out of context and distort them. The "cult de moi" and detachment from social conditions were among the consequences. Retté himself eventually modified his views and spoke more favorably about the need to find democratic solutions to social and political problems.[64] As he continued to insist, however, on the need for his poetry to ignore political themes, Retté provided a constant source of tension within the Parisian artistic anarchist community.

In a letter to *La plume,* Retté defended his unique application of art to anarchy. He was especially addressing himself to Maurice Barrès, who had recently questioned the consistency of his views. Retté maintained his opinion that Beauty was an absolute found in "an eternal law of rhythm" but added that it was contingent upon freedom of expression.[65] True beauty could not be appreciated through exclusively political notions of social art. Anarchists' esteem of individual liberty was significant in underlining the crucial role that the individual artist's voice played in the discovery of absolute form. In glossing over the contradictions found in wavering between ardent individualism and adherence to absolute aesthetic laws, Retté could only reiterate that such standards of beauty were not defined by traditional formulas but by free artists struggling against convention. Therefore, symbolism and anarchism were united in a common striving for creative harmony reached through expressive freedom.[66] As the anarchists desired to construct a society involving the free, uncoerced volition of individuals, so symbolists envisaged an artistic harmony ensuing from the artist's uninhibited voice. Retté felt, consequently, that artists needed to reject social art as an aesthetic norm in order to further their creation of satisfying works.

By 1894, Retté was less hostile to social art and more frequently resorted to political themes within his works. This followed a growing disenchantment with Mallarmé's antinaturalistic style and a renewed interest in politics. As noted already, the Parisian art world at the time was divided on the relevance of symbolism, Decadence, and other increasingly esoteric styles.[67] Retté himself began to turn away from symbolist ambiguities by adopting naturalism.[68] Both in poems and in polemical articles, Retté addressed political and social issues and called for revolution, being especially stirred by the Greek uprising against Turkish rule in Crete.[69] He offered his unqualified support, and, like Lord Byron earlier in the century, found an impulse to political engagement emanating from his concern for the Greeks—so central to the creation of democracy and idealized classical style in the ancient world.

Nevertheless, Retté hesitated to give his work too political a tone and followed his conversion to anarchism with another to Catholicism. As his biographer, William Cornell, explained, anarchy, symbolism, and pantheism were only a few of many escapes taken by Retté, whose central concern was devotion to aesthetic style.[70] In this light, the poet perceived anarchism as an aesthetic form, comparable to a poem. In the same way that Pissarro considered all arts to be anarchistic, so Retté viewed anarchism itself as another artistic dimension. Within this pattern of thought, Retté reiterated that rebelling artists should prevent their craft from becoming subject to standardization intended exclusively to further political aims.

While Neo-Impressionists relied upon scientific laws and symbolists upon mystical clairvoyance, both were convinced of an absolute standard of beauty—Seurat and Signac justifying their aesthetic works upon Chevreul's laws of color, the symbolists more so on introspection and music. It is a significant paradox that such absolutes were based upon the transient phenomena of colors and sounds changing and passing with the elapse of time, but that did not diminish the resolution with which such beliefs were held. In seeking sources of support, symbolist and Neo-Impressionist artists sometimes turned to anarchism as an ideology that could enhance their own revolt against traditional schools of art. As seen in the case of Pissarro, it was no coincidence that leading Neo-Impressionists and some symbolists were inspired by anarchism to some degree or another. Their involvement was complicated, however, by a parallel dedication to aesthetics and detachment from political movements. Believing that art required complete devotion, they were deeply suspicious of politics and reluctant to diminish their artistic efforts by over-indulging in this mundane area of activity. Accordingly, at best, they approached politics in an impartial manner and with an eye always cast in the other direction. In such a manner, they refused to view their artistic works as passive expressions of political ideas and were determined to define by their own volition the terms and goals of their art.

The publisher and poet Rémy de Gourmant had his own views on the subject. He felt both that art should be more subjective in endeavoring to "touch" the eternal and that truth only existed through comprehension of its momentary forms. Gourmant equated symbolism with liberty and anarchy and stated that the artist's freedom was critical to the creation of harmonious form. The artist's sense of the eternal, in other words, was linked to freedom from external constraints.[71] Like Retté, Gourmant revealed a mystical and Platonic inclination in defining the artist's mission. Beautiful forms existed absolutely, but poets and painters had to work without expressive restriction in order to enhance the creative process. This view approximates Michelangelo's own Platonic vision of the artistic struggle involved in liberation of the already existing form. The great sculptor assumed that the final form already existed, hidden in the depths of marble, but the artist was confronted with the task of removing excess stone to free it. Anarchism was a strong force in supporting and furthering such aesthetic freedom. If, however, the movement made too many burdensome demands upon the artists, it could cause mutual estrangement.

Among anarchist journalists, Manuel Devaldès was most vocal in defending the artist's resistance against demands for conformity. In fact, he took Retté's arguments to an extreme when writing that:

> art in its manifestations should essentially be egoist; the artist should work for his own pleasure and not that of the audience . . . the artist should be a sort of god, with a pure soul, capable of creating beautiful works which are useful by their beauty and without the intellectual help of any layman.[72]

Devaldès supported the creation of art for art's sake centered around this "egoist" approach. He scorned those who called for an altruistic and social bent to art or a method dictated by revolutionary demands. This was a call not only for uninhibited individualistic expression, but also for artistic disdain of the audience's needs. This obliviousness to the public echoed the sentiments of Max Stirner who had earlier written:

But not only for your sake, not even for truth's sake either do I speak out what I think. . . . I sing because—I am a singer. But I *use* you for it because I—need ears.[73]

Devaldès was antisocial even to the point where he had no need of such "ears." Communication was irrelevant, and creation was less an act of reaching an audience than of expressing the ego. Such an outlook both supported the avant-garde's quest for innovation and encouraged its insulation from the outside world.

Other anarchist journalists found their dealings with artists unexpectedly complicated and troublesome. Money, that most uncomfortable of subjects for anarchists, itself became a meddlesome factor. Jean Grave encountered conflicts when publishing excerpts from artists' works without compensation. Consequently, he was confronted by the Société des Gens des Lettres—headed by the famous photographer and balloonist Félix Nadar and espousing the protection of artists' rights, including those involving money. Nadar was in an awkward position because he was both an anarchist and a friend of Grave's. Nevertheless, he was very assertive about challenging Grave's right to quote without permission—anarchy and money not being, it was reasoned, necessarily incompatible. In a letter to Nadar, Grave would complain that the society was not simply protecting artists' rights but making literature into a business and financial matter.[74]

While Grave's concerns about the potential state of art may have been vindicated by the eventual appearance of the twentieth-century supermarket novel (placed directly next to tabloids with bright red headlines), his primary worry here no doubt was artistic intrusion into his publishing freedom.[75] Grave cast such artists as selfish ingrates unwilling to make the necessary sacrifices for a movement struggling on behalf of their rights. Nonetheless, he also overlooked the question concerning the right of artists to be paid for their work—whatever their political inclinations. Grave's liberal use of Zola's work in issues of *La Révolte* or *Les Temps Nouveaux* was a dramatic illustration of this attitude. Nadar felt that questions of monetary compensation did not necessarily negate the social relevance conveyed by quotations from *Germinal* or other works. Grave conveyed an opposing viewpoint, but he also explained how precariously close to ruination anarchist publications would be if their managers were forced to pay the authors of all included works. What the volatile nature of the debate over this question most reinforces, however, is the reality that anarchism depended not only upon actively engaged compagnons for communication of its ideology but also upon the critical views and observations of writers and artists, who lived on the margins of the movement perhaps but were more prominently in the public eye. Zola and Tolstoy were not anarchists, but passages from their work could support the message in Grave's publications and so were of great value.

Despite the complex nature of the debate, artists did produce works for the anarchist reviews. This was especially true of the visual arts. While their work was part of a propaganda effort and usually not related to their most creative work, such artists took their engagement seriously and felt that, as artists, they were contributing to the furthering of the anarchist cause. The next section of this chapter will, thus, examine the nature of some of the visual images they produced.

## ANARCHIST IMAGES

While a variety of views were expressed concerning the role of art as a propaganda tool, artists did create works in which they focused their attention upon social and political themes. In raising the "volume" and tone of their art to a social pitch, they consequently addressed particular social ills and suggested revolutionary solutions. Artistic engagement in anarchism was especially expressed through visual images produced either independently or within the pages of anarchist papers and reviews. Artists like Pissarro and Signac tried to reach a popular audience in their propaganda efforts—in contrast to the narrow one, which was more appreciative of their innovative works. They attempted to convey a message as seen in the themes and subjects discussed in the next section.

### Rancor and Violence

Anarchist journalists and artists expressed their hatred and contempt for the capitalist order by emphasizing the violence that workers would one day carry out against the wealthy. Furthermore, they tried to capture the essence of the capitalist by means of melodramatic and exaggerated caricatures. Most images in this vein tend to resemble that modern phenomenon so inextricably linked to the mass media—the cartoon—in their communication of messages intended to stir the workers' emotions. It is necessary to note as well the importance of political caricature in the years just before and during the French Revolution—a tradition about which anarchist journalists were certainly aware.

Not surprisingly, Pouget's reviews, which had led the way in the use of slang, were also most noteworthy in the printing of such volatile images.

Maximilien Luce produced two such works for the covers of *Almanach du Père Peinard*. In one, from 1898, we see a worker kicking a bourgeois capitalist to the floor and viewing the latter's many coins spill out from bulging pockets. The cover for 1899 reveals an equally vivid example of vengeance and violence. We see a shoemaker, in the process of repairing a shoe, using a bourgeois man's head as a rest for absorbing the impacts of the hammer's blows. (See figures 1 and 2.) This is artisanal revenge in its most basic form, and one can imagine the delight experienced by sympathetic readers as they observed the physical pain and humiliation of the capitalist who is literally at the worker's feet. Roles have been reversed with the worker now on top and the bourgeois forced into a kneeling position easily transformed into prayer. The imagined plea for mercy from a person accustomed to a supreme position strikes the viewer forcefully. Both worker and bourgeois are identified by their clothing—the latter distinguished by his black coat and the former by his cap and apron. The tools of the shop also indicate an artisanal setting—a fact that reinforces the anarchists' esteem for individual shopkeepers. In all, this image serves to depict a satisfying act of social justice, which Pouget expressed in order to reach the hidden layers of anger of the popular classes.

Images of capitalists and other authorities complemented such physically evocative works of vengeance and were intended to create sustaining stereotypes. Anger, after all, was felt so deeply because of the perception of class oppression. Theophile Steinlen's drawing for *La feuille* in 1898 is an example (see figure 3). An old man and woman bow before a priest who recites Scripture to them. Behind a priest hides a huge bourgeois appreciating the contents of his pockets and a cigar. The priest (also rather huge) completely hides the bourgeois's presence but does not protect the poor in turn. The scene occurs before a doorway with a neoclassical pediment and columns—an apparent reference to a bank or the Bourse. In the background stands a soldier ensuring that nothing disturbs the scene. Keeping with anarchists' views of the guilty forces supporting the capitalist edifice, Steinlen brings together the financial, religious, and military spheres.

Anarchist artists also utilized certain mythological and stereotypical images of capitalist conduct. Camille Pissarro's book of drawings in support of anarchism, *Turpitudes Sociales,* included several such characterizations. The capitalist is first shown standing on a pedestal, clutching his bag of "capital" and displaying it before the desperate masses. In the *Temple of the Golden Calf* (or *The New Idolators*) (see figure 4), capitalists parade a golden calf in Old Testament style before the people in an attempt to dazzle and intimidate them. As Pissarro has used a biblical theme to portray the open, hedonistic, and pagan display of capitalist wealth and power, one would expect a modern Moses to

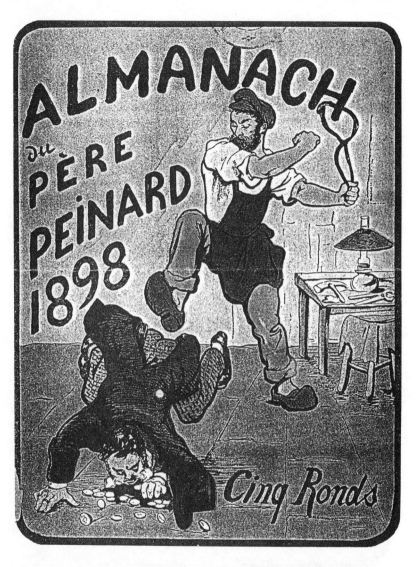

**Figure 1.** Cover illustration for "Père Peinard Almanach" 1898, by Maximilien Luce. Reproduced by permission of C.E.D.I.A.S. (Musée Social), Paris.

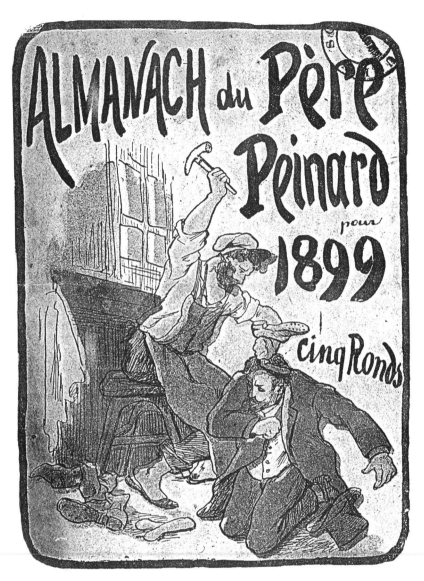

**Figure 2.** Cover illustrations for "Père Peinard Almanach" 1899, by Maximilian Luce. Reproduced by permission of C.E.D.I.A.S. (Musée Social), Paris. (The editor for the almanach was Emile Pouget.)

emerge and condemn this brashly defiant act. It is assumed that anarchism fulfills such a religious, millenarian task.

Images along these lines create a deep sense of contrast and dichotomy between the classes and reinforce the anger and resentment that the poor feel toward the wealthy. They also serve to vindicate violence carried out in the name of social justice and recall certain underlying impulses motivating the Reign of Terror of the French Revolution. Both classes, however, are depicted in the most direct, simple terms possible—such as would negate any attempts at reconciliation and reform. These artists depict the poor in familiar settings and the workers either as artisans or shopkeepers, thereby adhering to traditional mores and iconography as seen in the works of Britain's great eighteenth-century portrayer of popular life in London, William Hogarth. In this particular case, we witness melodrama intended to present sharp political extremes where moderation in the pursuit of change is not possible.

### The Dispossessed

The theme of dispossession is evoked in two forms. First, some images concentrate upon the laboring poor and the homeless, both of whom suffer in inherited social and economic situations. Such perceptions and depictions are in accord with Zola's naturalistic emphasis. Secondly, dispossession also results from the suppression of liberty and from state-imposed incarceration. This dual-edged view is, of course, in keeping with anarchists' attacks upon capitalism and the state.

Historians and art historians have focused attention on the ways in which Pissarro, Luce, and other politically oriented avant-garde artists employed social and political themes in certain works.[76] Luce portrayed the plight of industrial workers in *The City of Woe,* which was printed in the *Almanach du Père Peinard* of 1897. He represented the grueling, dangerous labor that people performed in ugly, polluted settings. While placing these workers in heroic poses, he also emphasized their despair and helplessness as they stood or sagged before the gigantic factories around them. They possessed nothing but their manual labor and, as such, were exploited and exhausted by the capitalist. Such powerful images had an especially prominent role in drawing support for Pouget's syndicalism. Luce used a similar theme in an earlier engraving printed in *La Plume* in 1893 entitled *The Shackled Worker.* The worker is shown here exhausted, deprived of all energy and spirit, his head bent in defeat. He also is chained to a weight upon which is written "Capital" and "Etat." In the background, the Paris Bourse rises with a huge statue of an enthroned pig before it—a mocking reference to the official

**Figure 3.** Illustration for "La Feuille," No. 22, December 21, 1898 by Théophile Steinlen. Reproduced by permission of the Bibliothèque de l'Arsenal, Paris (Bibliothèque Nationale de France). (The editor of "La Feuille" was Zo d'Axa.)

architecture and sculpture of the time. The pig, in any case, represents the capitalist in a primitive, beastly, and devouring state. The workers' misery, it is insinuated, cannot be understood without considering the central role of capital and the stock exchange.

Anarchist artists found other essential subjects for political image-making in the ranks of the unemployed and others condemned to aimless wandering and tramping. Henri Cross's drawing of 1896, *L'Errant* (the Wanderer) is a study of the poverty and loneliness of the homeless in which the central figure is completely isolated from those around him. One can picture the sadness and difficulty constantly accompanying him. Pissarro also studied vagabondage and uprootedness in his lithograph *The Homeless* (1896), in which an entire family is shown wandering in rags with their few possessions packed in one bag and searching for work and a place they can call home. The road on which they are forced to drift is surrounded by desolation and vast distance. Their fate is uncertain and can only vaguely be surmised.

Steinlen further studied this theme for the cover of an issue of *La feuille* in 1898 in which he represented a completely poor and dejected urban dweller standing against the ugly backdrop of an industrial city. Protruding smokestacks belch out black smoke. In his hands is a newspaper, which he apparently has been browsing looking for work. His facial expression indicates a lack of success in that pursuit. Is he an artisan or shopkeeper who has been made obsolete by industrialization? Can his way of life persist in the future? (See figure 5.) Anarchists were concerned with the plight of such marginal and outcast figures who were losing their place and unable to fit into modern industrial society, and such images portray the consequences of the social and economic dislocation throwing formerly proud and productive people into the ranks of the drifting homeless.

Pissarro also depicted the effects of social inequity upon individuals and families and related their subsequent drunkenness, familial quarrels, and suicides to the reality of helplessness and exploitation inflicted by factory owners and other capitalists. In the *Little Scene from Married Life* in *Turpitudes Sociales,* a horrible family quarrel erupts with the man displaying ruthless animalistic violence, dragging his wife by her hair along the floor. All she can do is scream in pain. Pissarro's view is that the couple has been brought to such a state by the poverty, ignorance, and degradation dominating their existence. This anarchist view of family problems keeps to the spirit of Zola's naturalistic representations in *Germinal* and other works. In the *Suicide of the Forsaken,* a young, helpless woman jumps from a Parisian bridge after being abandoned by a man on whom she has depended. *Le Pendu* (the Hanged One) represents a man hanging from a city lamp post. As the inscription explains, poverty

**Figure 4.** From "Turpitudes Sociales," "The New Idolators" by Camille Pissarro. © Denver Art Museum. Reproduced by permission of the Denver Art Museum, Denver, Colorado.

forced his suicide while, ironically, millionaires continue to live with no social conscience and complete devotion only to calculations and increased profits. In these three scenes, tragedies are inconceivable without the existence of capitalism and social injustice. Anarchism proposes to eliminate such evils and outrages. Thus, the view of the man hanging limply is intended to provoke among viewers enough anger and rebellion as to end the injustice. Nevertheless, within the context of *Turpitudes Sociales,* these images represent the misery of people in universal conditions found throughout the eons. They are intended as studies of social conditions that will bring to readers an understanding of the reasons behind personal tragedies.

Félix Valloton in *L'Anarchiste* (1892) drew another, more abstract perspective of governmental persecution. This work depicts a lone figure being seized by police as black-frocked bourgeois stand outside of a wine shop regarding the scene temporarily before going within to purchase wine, champagne, or Armagnac. The young man is angry and reaching for a bomb from his coat. While the scene focuses upon an anarchist as terrorist, the faces and attitudes of the police and the bourgeois convey brutality and selfishness. The audience is, thus, affected by a more ambiguous stand on "propaganda by the deed." Valloton depicts the police as evil perpetrators of state oppression and the instrument of bourgeois dominance. Equally noteworthy in the painting, however, is Valloton's preference for an updated decadent style (strongly resembling that of the British artist Aubrey Beardsley) over social realism in order to express the sinister nature of police and to keep to the character of avant-garde art—always a step or two ahead of conventional taste.

Other vivid expressions of governmental authority and repression are found in prisons. Their walls remove inmates from the society in which they would otherwise live, and confinement within their enclosed space is an ultimate restriction of freedom. Luce created two lithographs depicting Félix Fénéon's confinement in the prison of Mazas during the persecution of anarchists in 1894; the famous critic was tried for participation in the bombings then terrorizing Parisians. In one scene, Fénéon is shown with his head hanging in dejection, claustrophobically enclosed by the walls as in a sarcophagus. The same narrow space, however, is still present in the other work showing Fénéon walking outdoors in a very narrow courtyard, a human being greatly diminished by the receding walls that restrict all human freedom by their very linearity and inhumanity. Such a diminution and fragmentation of life was a ripe theme for the anarchist critique of society, and its power is evident here in the prison. Dispossession, then, involves not only poverty, homelessness, and exploitation. It also extends to the subject of liberty since to be deprived of free will is an

**Figure 5.** Illustration from "La Feuille," No. 24, 15 February, 1899 by Théophile Steinlen. Reproduced by permission of the Bibliothèque de l'Arsenal, Paris (Bibliothèque Nationale de France).

especially striking loss of freedom and dignity. Dispossession is a condition taking on many forms—all deplored by anarchists.

## Labor

Anarchists represented labor not only as a source of human misery and exploitation, but also as a potentially rich activity when allowed to take on its true, essential character beyond capitalistic confines. Pissarro was enthusiastic about labor and commerce and in his later years focused much of his attention upon city boulevard and market scenes. Such scenes of Paris and Rouen are among his greatest works. The vitality of the scene he witnessed while painting *The Great Bridge, Rouen* in 1896 is evident in his letters describing the excitement, noise, and clamor of the great city of Normandy:

> I have effects of fog and mist, of rain, of the setting sun and of grey weather, motifs of bridges seen from every angle, quays with boats; but what interests me especially is a motif of the iron bridge in the wet, with much traffic, carriages, pedestrians, workers on the quays, boats, smoke, mist in the distance, the whole scene fraught with animation and life . . . . Just conceive for yourself: the whole of old Rouen seen from above the roofs, with the Cathedral, St. Ouen's Church, and the fantastic roofs, really amazing turrets . . . . It is extraordinary.[77]

The Impressionist fascination with changing natural kaleidoscopes of color and light combines with a social interest in cities, commerce, and chaos.

As noted already, Pissarro was attracted both to peasant life and labor and rural landscapes. He was particularly influenced by Millet's and Courbet's paintings of peasant labor and associated the representation of hard labor and "peasant sadness" with the radical critique of capitalism.[78] In so doing, he assumed that such studies of rural life evoked empathy for peasants and that, in turn, more people would be moved to work for social change. At the same time, unlike socialists, Pissarro did not believe that peasants were essentially conservative. Consequently, when representing peasants at work in the fields, he believed that he was making a revolutionary statement. This belief, however, conflicted with others—as when, for instance, he distanced himself from the formulas that Kropotkin prescribed for revolutionary art.

Pissarro concluded that such messages could be delivered even by those who scorned the popular classes. This was evident in Millet himself, who was contemptuous of peasants but expended an enormous amount of artistic energy representing them on canvas. Pissarro believed that Millet was "another one of those blind men, leaders or followers, who unconscious of the march of modern ideas, defend the idea without knowing it, despite themselves!"[79] The sweep of ideas was, then, larger than individual artists' particular perspectives, and their brush strokes represented the larger revolutionary movement whether or not they consciously desired this effect. Pissarro's own views of peasant labor are felt in many of his works, and such depictions coincide as well with the artist's anarchist beliefs and with the Kropotkinesque mystique of village life.

While Pissarro generally chose to portray peasant life (especially in scenes of fields and markets), Signac and Luce looked to other types of labor-related subjects for inspiration although they continued to study a variety of appropriate artistic subjects. Signac viewed demolition workers in the same light surrounding the shoemakers in Luce's drawings for *Père Peinard*. Such laborers were not directly involved in industrial work, and their outdoor work united them with the peasants depicted by Pissarro in open-air scenes. Whatever heroism was present among such workers ensued from their interaction with nature.

Luce drew several scenes of miners at work in which he represented the struggle with natural elements—embodied in the miners' labor within the very recesses of the earth to extract coal, iron, or other resources. The natural, heroic, muscular, and near-Michangeloesque character of work here contrasts to the intrinsic dehumanization and alienation of urban industrial life as depicted in other works of social protest. Signac and Luce chose bare-chested, muscular men performing work through the vigorous, rugged actions of their bodies. They were presented on an epic scale as heroes more than equal to the rigor of their demanding activities. Nevertheless, it was also apparent that, as in other epic works, they would soon be exhausted by their dangerous work and fall to tragic circumstances. The same sympathy and identification felt by Pissarro for his peasants is evident here. In representing the workers' heroic plight, both artists sought to further their revolt through anarchism. These images of labor also reinforced the fact that anarchists wished to mobilize both nonindustrial workers and peasants within their movement and did not (as did socialists) see the industrial proletariat as the main agent for change.

Labor was a double-edged weapon as a theme for anarchist propaganda. On the one hand, it could be portrayed as the area of life in which capitalist exploitation and injustice was most vividly felt—again, not restricted to industrial work alone. The extreme distortion of the human body tortured by excessive work made this obvious. On the other hand, labor could be emphasized as an innately valuable activity that was truly essential to the making of an anarchist society. Anarchism, after all, could only be manifested through the voluntary work of individuals. Social criticism and idealism, thus, converged in the artistic portrayals of human beings at work.

Revolt

Anarchist artists, in addition, represented themes that concerned the nature of revolutionary insurrection. While the images just discussed all implied revolutionary discontent and social criticism, artists generally tended to follow the unique painterly traditions of Daumier, Delacroix, and Courbet in portraying armed popular revolt. Nevertheless, while keeping to such stylistic influences, anarchist artists attempted to pay particular homage to the Parisian tradition of revolt and to the newly relevant place of anarchism within it.

Pissarro's cover for *Turpitudes Sociales* shows an older bearded man with a reaper[80] observing the sun of "anarchie" rising over the distant horizon of Paris—identified by, among other things, the newly constructed Eiffel Tower. The man resembles Pissarro, and the reaper implies his identification with the workers' desire to tear down the old society. In the foreground, an hourglass runs, indicating that time is winding down on the capitalist system represented by the many smokestacks of factories belching forth smoke. As a whole, this image is filled with allegory and symbolism. Not only does the reaper imply a mowing down of the tower and smokestacks, but also the general character of Paris as a home for revolutions and anarchism. (See figure 6).

Pissarro depicted armed revolt in a more tangible form in *The Uprising*. The scene is that of a barricade-centered struggle, iconographically similar to Delacroix's *Liberty Leading the People* with the cluster of dead sprawled in baroque diagonals in the foreground. A Parisian revolutionary scene in the manner of 1789, 1848, or 1871 is depicted in its full horror, and Pissarro, the anarchist, attempts to evoke its legacy and inspiration for members of his movement.

Such an intention is even more striking in Steinlen's work. *Au mur des fédérés* commemorated the rebels killed during the final battle of the Commune in 1871 within the walls of Père Lachaise Cemetery. The many skeletons tearing through the earth or placed on the wall seem to call to past revolutionary martyrs to reawaken and join in the final apocalyptic revolt. This may seem like a bizarre and discordant note of millenarian religion. Nevertheless, the millenarian character of anarchism has already been noted and the emphasis again on allegory and symbol serves to unite the past, the present, and the future.

Crowd composition offered another subject for study. Depictions of anarchist crowds in paintings, in fact, seem to resemble descriptions in past accounts. Steinlen's *18 mars* depicts an 1894 Parisian anarchist crowd demonstrating in support of the "thirty" as mythic and historical elements converge around them. It is historical in that the artist presents an actual contemporary event, but mythic and symbolic elements are also highly visible. A bare-breasted

Figure 6. Cover for "Turpitudes Sociales" by Camille Pissarro. © Éditions d'Art Albert Skira SA, Geneva, Switzerland. Reproduced by permission.

Marianne leads the march. Viewers think not only of Delacroix's portrayal of revolution but also of the inspiration of radical republicanism. The workers are an assorted group. Some wear aprons indicating their status as artisans. Others resemble peasants with reapers or members of the middle class. The many pikes and reapers also evoke memories of events in 1789 and 1792—such as the seizure of the Bastille, the Women's March on Versailles, or the Storming of the Tuileries Palace. We could easily believe that we are looking at a crowd of sans-culottes as the portrayal of crowd action here is directly inspired by such prototypes from the past. If artists sought to underscore revolutionary inevitability, they did so by going beyond the calls for realistic narrative and including allegory and mythic elements in order to connect the present course of action to that of the past.

## CONCLUDING REMARKS

It is evident that the relationship between art and anarchism was complex. Artists were concerned with many social issues during the later nineteenth century and much of their work carried social and political themes.[81] Avant-garde art was not exclusively dominated by stylistic concerns and movements toward abstraction that were largely inaccessible to mass audiences. While modernist artists in Paris and Vienna may have created works with an ahistorical character, others continued to tap into historical and social issues as subjects for propaganda.[82]

Nevertheless, the question is more than just an academic one. Avant-garde artists, expressing social themes in certain works, were also wary of losing sight of their essential aesthetic goals. They perceived themselves as part of an elite that not only advanced the cause of art but also waged a battle for public recognition. The very notion of an avant-garde revolved around the idea of a self-contained group dedicated to a special mission in pursuit of further creativity. Such a quest held even further significance because of the power and prestige of the schools and institutions they contested. Some resented the Salon for withholding recognition of their talents.

This process was supplemented by a historical awareness that the struggle would occur in stages. Thus, Impressionism was a prelude in the conflict and needed to be surpassed. Pointillists believed that they had become the new pathbreakers because of their more specified allegiance to scientific guidance. As was the case with much of nineteenth-century European society, a general belief concerning the inevitability of progress prevailed among artists seeking to pursue their craft free of unnecessary restraints. In the case of artists holding to the anarchist ideology in some form or another, they perceived the central challenge to be both artistic and political in nature. Nevertheless, factions gathered around contrasting views of the proper connections to be established between politics and art. Even where artists sought to keep up with the pace of the avant-garde and create in aesthetically innovative and popular styles, an aesthetic gulf still divided works communicating to a mass audience (usually via the social realistic circuit) from those with a more obscure and subjective intention.

Artists within the anarchist movement always felt that their position was threatened by capitalist society, and they linked their revolt against the Salons with one against bourgeois economic hegemony. From this followed an attack upon bourgeois artistic taste, which, they felt, was hostile to their individual vision. This situation held for some time. Nevertheless, the scope of aesthetic questions was limited. Several anarchist artists emphasized their connection to realism and science and distanced themselves from their fellows who were following more abstract, symbolic, and mystical concerns. By the 1890s, however, when some avant-garde artists became fascinated with symbolism and Decadence (to name but two movements), any semblance of a unified stylistic front was shattered. The ensuing division paralleled that between the social and egoistic components of anarchism itself.

Most troubling was the question relating to the particular use of art for revolutionary purposes. Some felt it sufficient to create individually expressive works that cast scorn upon social conformity. As the scholar Roger Shattuck explained, such an identification of expression with anarchy implied that cultural transformations would be as important in reshaping the world as social and political revolutions.[83] Enthusiastic expressions of this sentiment were found in the post–World War I era when Dadaists produced nihilistic and eccentric works intended to confuse and baffle the public and to evoke the desire for an alternative order. Several anarchist avant-garde painters created works thematically centered around social and political subjects and chiefly intended as propaganda for a wide audience. As such, they executed these works in the social realist style, which differed from the more inaccessible styles they used in other works. Artists like Pissarro and Signac clearly were more enthusiastic about the import of the social message communicated here than with stylistic quality. The great poster artist Steinlen distanced himself entirely from such endeavors despite his anarchist convictions, complaining by 1905 that he no longer wanted to create images for "pages comiques."[84]

In his analysis of art during the Weimar period, the writer John Willett wrote about the necessary connections painters, sculptors, playwrights, filmmakers, and other artists keenly felt to politics. Although this sense of engagement was unsystematic and caused difficulty for political parties seeking to give it practical guidance, it was successful in disseminating oppositional attitudes against traditional authoritarian forces in Germany. The vigorous sense of community feeling evident among German avant-garde artists was also due to the unique society in that country that was shaken by the terrible events of the First World War. In defining the unique cultural phenomenon, he wrote: "the arts are very closely interwoven with socio-political influences and ideas, and . . . this is not be regretted but can at times so stimulate the artists concerned as to produce results that from any point of view are highly original." He stated that artistic creativity was "based on . . . involvement with a new society."[85]

At certain times artists really believe that they have the power to reshape public consciousness and to promote a new world order. Such was the case during the Weimar Republic when several devastating developments that simultaneously shook artistic sensitivity intensified the course of departure from past culture and of movement toward a future filled with both artistic and political promise. Unfortunately, the crises of the era also evoked feelings of desperation, and the struggle was pursued that much more fervently.

The aforementioned *Société des Artistes Indépendants* and *Le Club de l'Art Social* had already provided forums in Paris for artistic debate in which anarchists were frequently engaged. Such clubs were later followed by *Les Iconoclastes,* a gathering drawing the vocal presence of artists and anarchists who discussed themes dealing with artistic freedom, anarchist communes, mutual life, and morality, among other points. The combination of political, social, and artistic issues previously noted again stimulated questions, ideals, and visions motivating artistic engagment in the anarchist movement. Because of the deep commitment obviously present in the intense debate, a stimulating atmosphere encouraged infinite avant-garde experimentation and had great effect upon the work of early twentieth-century artists. For example, the art historian Patricia Leighten has noted that Picasso's entry into the Parisian art world in 1904 was effortless due to the imprint made upon that culture both by symbolism and anarchism—currents with which he had already become familiar in Barcelona.[86]

While living during the fin de siècle and before the horrors of the twentieth century, anarchists still sensed the urgency of their mission. Many political, social, and economic changes had transpired,[87] and anarchist ideological convictions also evoked feelings of living on the edge. Within the movement, many political activists experienced to some degree the millenarian sensation of living at the end of one order and the beginning of another—even if later they grew with the times. Anarchist artists also felt this way and believed that their artistic contributions would, in one way or another, hasten the process of change as well. In their writings and works (whether done in a social realist or innovative manner) they expressed their ambivalent stand regarding their dual commitments. Like others to follow, they were confused.

# Conclusion

As may be readily apparent, the word *anarchism* has taken on a host of meanings to suit the purposes of those in particular who wish exploit it. The word, in fact, takes on a form easily adapted to a specific cultural context. One seeking to provide a consistent definition for *anarchism* may run into the problem depicted by Fyodor Dostoyevsky's narrator in *Notes from Underground*. Metaphysicians attempting to analyze *being* into its final components only run into the need for endless dissection and find that the original concept has proven to be more elusive than ever. It, in fact, increasingly recedes from comprehension the more one applies the finest analysis. This frustration meets the historian attempting to make sense of anarchism as a movement with a consistent purpose.

At its most basic level *anarchism* could continue to focus upon hostility to authority and upon the fostering of individual freedom. Through the development, however, of movements and currents that tapped into the reservoir of the word, the concept took on a multifaceted and dissonant nature in which the participants only agreed on issues immediately of concern to them; as a whole, it is a truism that anarchism was more defiant of harmony and unity than socialism.

Nevertheless, the adoption of the concept by people in particular locales reveals the diverse nature of human aspirations as they correspond to specific cultural contexts. The examination of this process displays to us the means by which several groups of such aspirants adopted and transformed the word. In the process, the movement splintered and anarchism itself became more elusive as a clearly defined ideology.

Such a situation was found in Paris in the fin de siècle. A century of revolutionary heritage inspired figures such as Jean Grave to publicize locally in a theoretical manner the ideas of Mikhail Bakunin and especially Peter Kropotkin. By centering his publishing and propaganda activities near the legendary Latin Quarter, Grave attained a prominent public place in the city's political life, albeit one that could never seriously contend for center stage of the Parisian world. This position, however, also enabled rival anarchists to define him in ways that he did not desire—as an intellectual and revolutionary "pope." Others, like Emile Pouget, sought to communicate through popular slang and to express popular, unmitigated anger as directly and violently as possible. The ongoing contrast between subtle rhetoric and popularly based polemics was also found in movement-wide debates concerning terrorism, the Dreyfus Affair, and other matters critical to the Third Republic—including the legitimacy of republicanism itself.

A similar conflict was found in the realm of art, where vigorous views flourished regarding the purpose of artistic engagement. Painters, poets, and playwrights drawn to the movement often responded to calls from leaders urging artistic contributions to the propagation of the anarchist message. Important figures like Camille Pissarro and Paul Signac, who represented Impressionism and other currents, had been initially enthusiastic about the way in which anarchism could defend and enhance individual artists' defiance of the Salons. When confronted by what they considered excessive calls for aesthetic conformity dictating social realism, however, they balked. In fact, they thought that such demands compromised the struggle that had drawn them to anarchism in the first place. Art and politics, thus, came into conflict at this time in a manner that resembled several instances during the early twentieth century in heightened political and artistic circumstances—as seen in Weimar Germany and the Soviet Union. The avant-garde's rejection of anarchism was not a necessary consequence. Far from it! Rather, some in their ranks developed a sense of dual obligations and learned that art and political engagement did not necessarily always connect. Yet the word *anarchist* proved to be irresistible to those who could find no other to describe and encapsulate their struggle. Egoists and Romantic vegetarians were among such cultural rebels. While usually in conflict with the more mainstream libertarians, these outcasts, at odds with conventional society in so many ways, nonetheless embraced that provocative word and described themselves as anarchists.

Confusion was also evident in public consciousness as the urge to equate *anarchists* with *terrorists* often proved overwhelming. From this blurring of the lines emerged a stereotyping of the movement. While anarchists in many circles of Paris attempted to refute this stereotype, it also turned out that some continued to endorse terror as a most applicable modern weapon that conveniently reflected the "glorious terror" of the French Revolution. In this case, anarchists juxtaposed historical contexts as they sought to find a precedent for the terror evident during the late nineteenth century. Despite the many distinctions drawn between terrorism and anarchism, the two continue to seem synonymous to the general public. The case of the Unabomber has certainly reinforced this general image of anarchism as his by-now famous manifesto, centered around a critique of modern technology, was highlighted all the more by his history of social isolation and his famous campaign of terror.

Fin-de-siècle anarchism also reflected the influence of other contemporary intellectual and cultural movements. Most noteworthy perhaps in this regard were the roles of irrationalism, mysticism, and the Romantic worship of nature. Such forces were manifested in the egoism, vegetarianism, and decadence found in various anarchist pockets. One is hard-pressed to find parallels between the efforts of Naturiens in the Butte and those of Jean Grave on the left bank or of Emile Pouget in Montmartre. How can rejection of civilized life be reconciled with a continued emphasis upon progress? Could anarchism have really and effectively met both needs?

The endeavors and beliefs of the various anarchists during the next half-century added further evidence to the complex picture. Many remained as anarchists or opted for anarcho-syndicalism. Some turned to the Communist Party, others became religious or, like Jean Grave, supported the French effort in the Great War of 1914. Others still renounced politics altogether, focusing upon artistic pursuits or, as in the case of Zo d'Axa, turning to the bicycle and aimless wandering in the manner of Charles Chaplin's tramp.

There is also the example of Félix Nadar, the famous photographer. Born Félix Tournachon in 1820 in Paris to a basically royalist bourgeois family, the future rebel attended several schools in Lyons and Paris in preparation for a medical career. His undisciplined nature and intellectual curiosity, however, evoked an interest in literature, and after the collapse of his father's book-selling business, Félix supported himself by writing and taking up the newly created art of photography. He and his brother began their own portrait studio and used some bizarre (often painful) methods to obtain particular grimaces from their subjects. Félix eventually became the more successful of the two and performed his work independently. In doing so, he became one of the famous artistic figures of the Latin Quarter and was well acquainted with Charles Baudelaire, Eugene Delacroix, George Sand, and other artists. His other famous photographs included a series on the renowned mime Pierrot and a series on the Paris sewers and catacombs. During the 1840s, Nadar became friendly with Louis Blanc and actively supported Blanc's frustrated goals during the 1848 Revolution. This early revolutionary bent led him to an interest in the Commune and eventual conversion to anarchism in the 1880s.

In the 1890s, Nadar began work for Grave's *Les Temps Nouveaux* and later for Gustave Hervé's *Guerre Sociale* (the Social War). Yet, as noted earlier, Nadar also headed the Société des Gens des Lettres and opposed Graves's unauthorized quotations from artists' works. His experience as an independent professional is evident in this confrontation with the anarchist leader he supported and reinforces the esteem for individualism so intrinsic to the movement. Like Pissarro and Signac, Nadar defended the need for complete freedom in artistic engagement within political causes. However, Nadar's artistic and political attitudes looked back to the Bohemianism and Romantic republicanism of the generation of Delacroix and Baudelaire—forces that had shaped his own youthful outlook and that continued to move him. At the center of that generation's assumptions was its sustaining belief that idealism and passion were supremely important in expressing artistic and political opposition against the established order, and Nadar continued to maintain the need for sincere emotion and art as an independent realm. This attitude stood out against the increasingly cynical and skeptical tone generally creeping into the French world after the 1840s.

Nadar's insistence on aesthetic freedom was paralleled by a devotion to ballooning, pursued vigorously and providing unexpected vistas for photographs. Ballooning was already a famous pastime in France and had captured the public imagination since the eighteenth century. Prefiguring the aviational pioneers of the twentieth century, balloonists indulged in the eagle's eye view and drifting that Nadar must have linked to the thirst for freedom. Like D'Axa, Nadar was impossible to categorize as an anarchist and chose the traveler's perspective in maintaining an individual stance.

Considering such a myriad of rebels within Parisian anarchism, one can conclude that as a movement it was destined to be divided, inconsistent, and without a single purpose—that it could never be anything but a subculture. Yet the phenomenon continues to resurface—as it did in 1968 with the May riots and demonstrations in Paris that challenged the authoritarian "neomonarchism" of Charles de Gaulle and as it appears to have done in December, 1995 with the massive strikes organized to challenge the new Gaullist president Jacques Chirac. The word itself has become so associated with the French that British Broadcasting Corporation (BBC) commentators in 1984 continued to refer to the labor actions and disruptive tactics of French lorry drivers as emanating from "an anarchistic people."

During the late nineteenth century, the flexible nature of anarchism made it quite adaptable to the political, social, and cultural movements responding to the problems and concerns of the day. As such, anarchists took a very active part in the issues generally troubling the Third Republic, and their debate assumed a significant aspect of the public dialogue—even if they were not destined to decide the outcomes. The language of anarchism, in fact, reveals another side of the culture and mentality of a people accustomed to historical fluctuations between authoritarian rule and disorder. Anarchism was able to find a place within the vocabulary and traditions of the French because it addressed so exactly the emotions of those who either wanted to achieve stability or to continue the process of rebellious questioning.

# ABBREVIATIONS USED IN THE NOTES

| | |
|---|---|
| AN | Archives Nationales |
| APP | Police Préfécture de la Seine |
| BHVP | Bibliothèque Historique de la Ville de Paris |
| BN | Bibliothèque Nationale |
| BNA | Bibliothèque Nationale, Arsenal |
| CRHMSS | Centre de Recherche pour l'Histoire des Mouvements Sociales et du Syndicalisme |
| IFHS | Institut Français de l'Histoire Social |
| JD | Bibliothèque Jacques Douçet, Université de Paris |

# NOTES

## INTRODUCTION

1. See Richard Sonn, *Anarchism and Cultural Politics in Fin de Siècle France* (Lincoln, NE: University of Nebraska Press, 1989).
2. See Richard Sonn, *Anarchism* (New York: Twayne Publishers, 1992).
3. See Temma Kaplan, *Red City, Blue Period: Social Movements in Picasso's Barcelona* (Berkeley, CA: University of California Press, 1992).
4. See John G. Hutton, *Neo-Impressionism and the Search for Solid Ground: Art, Science, and Anarchism in Fin-de-Siècle France* (Baton Rouge, LA: Louisiana State University Press, 1994) and Deborah L. Silverman, *Art Nouveau in Fin-de-Siècle France: Politics, Psychology, and Style* (Berkeley, CA: University of California Press, 1989), 212-14.
5. George Woodcock, "Anarchism," in *Encyclopedia of Philosophy* (New York: Macmillan Company, 1978), 111.
6. Ibid.
7. See Roger Shattuck, *The Banquet Years: The Origins of the Avant-Garde in France, 1885 to World War I* (New York: Random House, 1955).
8. See Sonn, *Anarchism and Cultural Politics*.
9. See Stewart Edwards, *The Paris Commune: 1871* (New York: Quadrangle Books, 1971).
10. See Harvey Mitchell and Peter Stearns, *Workers and Protest: the European Labor Movement, the Working Classes and the Origins of Social Democracy, 1890-1914* (Itasca, IL: F.E. Peacock, 1971), and *Bernard Moss, The Origins of the French Labor Movement, 1830-1914: the Socialism of the Skilled Workers* (Berkeley, CA: University of California Press, 1976).
11. See Robert Darnton, "The High Enlightenment and the Low-Life of Literature in Prerevolutionary France," *Past and Present*, no. 51 (Oxford, May 1971): 81-115.
12. *The Impressionist and the City: Pissarro's Series Paintings*, an exhibition held in 1993 at the Dallas Museum of Art, the Philadelphia Museum of Art, and the Royal Academy of Arts, London. The catalogue is edited by MaryAnne Stevens with articles by Richard R. Brettell and Joachim Pissarro and was produced and distributed by Yale University Press, New Haven, Connecticut.

## CHAPTER 1

1. See Peter Kropotkin, *The Great French Revolution: 1789-1793* (New York: G.P. Putnam's Sons, 1909).

2. One can note the recent commemorations of the five hundredth anniversary of the Columbus sailings as a current parallel.

3. George Woodcock, "Anarchism," in *Encyclopedia of Philosophy* (New York: Macmillan Company, 1978), 274; and David Stafford, *From Anarchism to Reformism: A Study of the Political Activities of Paul Brousse Within the First International and the French Social Movement, 1870-1890* (Toronto: University of Toronto Press, 1971).

4. For more on the destruction of the Bastille see Simon Schama, *Citizens: A Chronicle of the French Revolution* (New York: Random House, 1989), 408-419.

5. Kropotkin, *The Great French Revolution*, 4.

6. See Albert Soboul, *Les Sans-Culottes* (Paris: Editions du Seuil, 1968), and Richard Cobb, *The Police and the People* (New York: Oxford University Press, 1970).

7. Peter Kropotkin, *Fields, Factories, and Workshops, Tomorrow* (New York: Harper & Row, 1899), 142.

8. Peter Kropotkin, *Mutual Aid: A Factor of Evolution* (Boston, MA: Porter Sargent Publishers, Inc., 1902), 298. For a favorable twentieth-century response to Kropotkin's ideas on cities see Lewis Mumford, *The City in History* (New York: Harcourt, Brace, & Jovanovich, 1961).

9. See A.F. Weber, *The Growth of Cities in the Nineteenth Century* (Ithaca, NY: Cornell University Press, 1899).

10. Louis Chevalier, *La formation de la population parisienne au XIXème siècle* (Paris: Presses Universitaires de France, 1950), 80.

11. Ibid., 82.

12. Ibid., 130.

13. Ibid., 138.

14. See David Landes, *The Unbound Prometheus* (New York: Cambridge University Press, 1972), and Tom Kemp, *Economic Forces in French History* (London: Dobson, 1971).

15. Kropotkin, *Fields*, 142; Landes, *Unbound Prometheus*; and Kemp, *Economic Forces*.

16. Alexander Herzen, *My Past and Thoughts* (Berkeley, CA: University of California Press, 1855), 323.

17. See Carl E. Schorske, *Fin-de-Siècle Vienna*, (New York: Alfred A. Knopf, 1980).

18. APP BA/303, report of August 20, 1887.

19. Jean Maitron, *Histoire du mouvement anarchiste en france* (Paris: Francois Maspero, 1951), 113-16; and Theodore Zeldin, *France: 1848-1945, Politics and Anger* (New York: Oxford University Press, 1973), 412.

20. Among the groups were L'Aiguille, les Antipatriotes, les Antipropriétaires, l'Autonomie Individuelle, la Justice Sociale, l'Avant Garde, l'Egalité Social, les Egaux, Group de Levallois, les Insurges, la Ligue Cosmopolite, la Lutte, la Panthère, Terre et Liberté, la Panthéon, la Vengeance, and la Ligue Anti-Clericale.

21. Emile Gauthier quoted in Jean Maitron, *Le mouvement anarchiste en france, 1,* (Paris: Francois Maspero, 1975), *122.*

22. Jean Grave, *Quarante ans de propagande anarchiste* with a preface by Jean Maitron, (Paris: Flammarion, 1973). Also see Louis Patsouras, *Jean Grave and French Anarchism* (Dubuque: Kendall Hunt Publishing Co., 1978).

23. APP BA/1500, report of January 5, 1894.

24. Quoted in Maitron, *Le mouvement,* 145.

25. IFHS, 14 AS 184 (b), Letter from Henri Zisly to Jean Grave, July 19, 1896.

26. Max Nettlau, *Histoire de l'anarchie* (Paris: Editions du Cercle, 1933), 158.

27. See Andre Chadourne, *Le quartier latin* (Paris: 1884).

28. Edouard Crueuel, *Bohemian Paris of Today,* W.C. Morrow, ed. (London: Chatto & Windus, 1899), 16.

29. Kropotkin, *Fields,* 142.

30. Crueuel, *Bohemia,* 16.

31. Ibid., 12.

32. Ibid., 109.

33. Ibid., 145. See also Walter Benjamin's study of the *flâneur* type in "Paris, Capital of the Nineteenth Century" in *Reflections* (New York: Harcourt, Brace, and Jovanovich, 1955).

34. For two contrasting interpretations see T. J. Clark, *The Painting of Modern Life* (New York: Alfred Knopf, 1985), and Jerrold Seigel, *Bohemian Paris: Culture, Politics, and the Boundaries of Bourgeois Life, 1830-1930,* (New York: Viking Penguin, 1986).

35. Among those who subscribed to *La Révolte* were: Anatole France, Emile Zola, Stéphane Mallarmé, J. H. Huysmans, and Rémy de Gourmant. See Maitron, *Le mouvement anarchiste, 1* and AN F7 12506, (1894).

36. Among the groups were: Groupe Anarchiste du Panthéon, Groupe Anarchiste d'Etudes Sociales, la Vengeance, le Leopard du Panthéon, Groupe d'Etudes Economiques et Sociales, and Ancien Groupe Anarchiste des 5me et 13me Arrondissements. See APP BA/1505.

37. Ibid.

38. Ibid.
39. Ibid., report of March 27, 1887.
40. Ibid., reports of 1896.
41. Ibid., report of November 21, 1885.
42. Ibid., reports of 1896.
43. Gerard Jacquement, "Belleville ouvrier à la belle epoque", *Le Mouvement Social,* no. 118 (Paris, January 1982), 61.
44. Ibid., 73.
45. Such changes are observable today in European Mediterranean cities undergoing late-twentieth-century urban and social transformation.
46. See Jacquement, "Belleville," 71-76; and Alexis Martin, *Paris promenades dans les vingt arrondissements: les éstapes d'un touriste en france* (Paris: A. Hennuyer, 1890), 345.
47. Ibid., 345.
48. Ibid.
49. See Edwards, *The Paris Commune.*
50. Meaning "the Black Flag."
51. The police files in APP BA/1497 and BA/1498 are particularly informative on theft and violence.
52. APP BA/1508, report of August 19, 1895.
53. APP BA/1508, report of October 28, 1887.
54. *Paris* (London: Ward & Lock & Co., 1898), 100.
55. Martin, *Paris promenades,* 34.
56. Ibid. See Martin's notes.
57. Ibid.
58. Louis Chevalier, *Montmartre: du plaisir et du crime* (Paris: Editions Robert Laffort, 1980).
59. Ibid.
60. APP BA/1500, report of January 5, 1894.
61. Nettlau, *Histoire de l'anarchie,* 160.
62. Ibid.
63. Félix Dubois, *Le péril anarchiste* (Paris: Flammarion, 1894), 117.
64. APP BA/1500, report of January 5, 1894.
65. Crueuel, *Bohemia,* 99.
66. Ibid., 276.
67. Ibid., 314.
68. See Patricia Leighten, *Re-Ordering the Universe: Picasso and Anarchism, 1897-1914* (Princeton, NJ: Princeton University Press, 1989), for more on the anarchistic influences upon one of the cofounders of Cubism.

69. Joan U. Halperin, *Félix Fénéon and the Language of Art Criticism,* (Ann Arbor, MI: UMI Research Press, 1980), 13.

70. See Joan U. Halperin, *Félix Fénéon: Aesthete and Anarchist in Fin-de-Siècle Paris,* (New Haven, CT: Yale University Press, 1988).

71. See Hutton, *Neo-Impressionism and the Search for Solid Ground.*

72. See John Rewald, "Félix Fénéon," *Gazette des beaux-arts, Tome XXXII,* (Paris, 1948).

73. Halperin, *Félix Fénéon and the Language of Art Criticism.*

74. Quoted in Rewald, "Félix Fénéon," 55.

75. Ibid., 56.

76. See Benjamin, "Paris, Capital of the Nineteenth Century."

77. Rewald, "Félix Fénéon," 60.

78. For information on the German "Volkish" movements see George Mosse, *The Crisis of German Ideology: Intellectual Origins of the Third Reich* (New York: Grosset & Dunlap, 1964).

79. APP BA/1497, report of December 27, 1897.

80. APP BA/894, report of February 20, 1898.

81. See *Celles qu'on oublie les ouvrieres à domicile,* chanson de Xavier Privas, (Paris), Marcel Labbe Editeur. This concludes with the words: "plus de salaire, de misere, imposé par les exploiteurs, il faut qu'une loi salutaire assure un honnête salaire aux travailleurs. Celles qu'on oublie ont faim, celles qu'on oublie ont droit a la vie. Donnez leur du pain?" Surely a call for social justice emanating from the cabaret circles of the Butte.

82. APP BA/894, report of February 20, 1898.

## CHAPTER 2

1. Mikhail Bakunin, *Revolutionary Catechism,* quoted in George Woodcock, *Anarchism: A History of Libertarian Ideas and Movements* (New York: Penguin, 1962), 160.

2. See Louis Bergeron, *France Under Napoleon* (Princeton, NJ: Princeton University Press, 1981), for further information on the nature of French society under Napoleon.

3. Edwards, *The Paris Commune,* 360.

4. Cobb, *The Police and the People,* 211.

5. See Mona Ozouf, *Festivals and the French Revolution* (Cambridge, MA: Harvard University Press, 1988).

6. See Patrick H. Hutton, *The Cult of the Revolutionary Tradition: the Blanquists in French Politics, 1864-1893* (Berkeley, CA: University of California Press, 1981).

7. Cobb, *The Police and the People*.

8. Bakunin quoted in Woodcock, *Anarchism*, 152.

9. APP BA/1497 report of December 19, 1897.

10. Jean Grave, "Enrichissez-vous," *La Révolte*, Paris, December 31, 1887.

11. See "Nos martyrs," in *La Révolte*, October 15, 1887.

12. Grave, "Enrichissez-vous."

13. See "1789-1889," *La Révolté*, January 13, 1889.

14. "Sabre et Révolution," *La Révolté*, April 14, 1888.

15. Georges Etièvant, *Déclarations*, (Paris: La Révolte pub.), 1893, 29.

16. Ibid. 27.

17. See *Père Peinard Almanach, 1894-1899*, Paris.

18. See Maurice Agulhon, *Marianne into Combat: Republican Imagery and Symbolism in France* (New York: Cambridge University Press, 1981).

19. Quoted in AN F7 13052— A. Moreau, *L'anarchisme en france*, Paris, 1897.

20. Ibid.

21. "L'année 1888", *La Révolte*, December 30, 1888.

22. "La regne de la raison," *La Révolte*, October 28, 1888.

23. Peter Kropotkin, *La grande révolution: 1789-1793* (Paris: P. V. Stock, 1909).

24. Woodcock, *Anarchism*, 49.

25. "Sabre et révolution."

26. Ibid.; and see "Le césarisme à nos portes", *La Révolte*, April 21, 1888.

27. Grave, "Enrichissez-vous."

28. See Charles Malato, "Tribune: les muscadins," *Le journal du peuple*, Paris, March 6, 1899.

29. Charles Malato, "Tribune maintenant", *Le Journal du Peuple*, February 7, 1899.

30. Charles Malato, *Philosophie de l'anarchie* (Paris: Tresse & Stock), 1894, 29.

31. Charles Malato, *De la commune à l'anarchie* (Paris: Librairie Tresse and Stock), 1894, 252.

32. Ibid., 252.

33. See Franklin Ford, *Robe and Sword* (New York: Harper and Row, 1953).

34. Charles Malato, *De la commune*, 240.

35. Charles Malato, *Les joyeusetés de l'exil*, (Paris: P. V. Stock), 1897.

36. Malato, "Les muscadins."

37. Grave, "Enrichissez-vous."

38. See Karl Marx, *Class Struggles in France* (New York: International Publishers, 1850).

39. Alexis de Tocqueville, *The Old Regime and the French Revolution* (New York: Doubleday, 1856).

40. Elisée Reclus, "L'anarchie," *Les Temps Nouveaux*, Paris, May 18, 1895.

41. See Karl Marx, *The 18th Brumaire of Louis Bonaparte* (New York: International Publishers, 1852).

42. "1789-1889."

43. "La révolution et le paysan," *Les Temps Nouveaux*, May 27, 1899.

44. Ibid.

45. Ibid.

46. "La propagande dans les campagnes," *La Révolte*, December 17, 1887.

47. Jean Richepin, "La Bastille," *Les Temps Nouveaux*, January 25, 1896.

48. Henri Rochefort, "La patrie française," *L'intransigeant*, Paris, January 7, 1899.

49. "La commune de Paris," *La Révolte*, March 17, 1888.

50. Kropotkin, *The Commune of Paris*, cited in Martin A. Miller, ed., *Selected Writings on Anarchism and Revolution: P. A. Kropotkin*, (Cambridge, MA: MIT Press, 1970), 121.

51. Ibid., 122.

52. Ibid., 125.

53. Lewis Mumford reevoked Kropotkin's urban vision in *The City and History*, 514-15 where he echoed the anarchist's esteem for intimate neighborhoods.

54. Ibid., 126: see also Peter Kropotkin, *Memoirs of a Revolutionist*, (Boston, MA: Houghton Mifflin Co., 1899), 291.

55. Kropotkin, *Commune*, quoted in Miller, *Selected Writings*, 127.

56. Ibid.

57. Ibid., 126.

58. Ibid., 128.

59. Kropotkin, *Memoirs*, 292.

60. The Boulanger Affair involved the threat posed by General Georges Boulanger between 1887 and 1889 when he generated a strong movement in an effort to topple the Third Republic and impose an authoritarian government. Criticism of the republic continued, however, as revelations came forward in 1892 of a financial scandal involving the building of the Panama Canal begun under Ferdinand de Lesseps's creation of the Panama Company. The bankruptcy of the firm ruined a great many investors.

61. Etièvant, *Déclarations*, 29.

62. Charles Malato, *Les travailleurs des villes aux travailleurs des campagnes*, (Paris: Imprimerie Libertaire, 1888), 7.

63. Malato, *De la commune*, 11.

64. Ibid., 1.
65. Ibid., 240.
66. Malato, *Les joyeusetés de l'exil,* 271.
67. AN F7 12505, report of September 23, 1897.
68. See Edith Thomas, *Louise Michel ou la velleda de l'anarchie,* (Paris: Gallimard, 1971).
69. See H. Riviere, *Souvenirs de la nouvelle calédonie: l'insurrection canaque, (Paris: Gallet, 1881).*
70. Louise Michel, "Chants des captifs," from *L'ére nouvelle, pensée dernière: souvenirs de caledonie* (Paris: Librairie Socialiste International, Achille le Roy, 1887). The approximate translation of this poem reads:

> Winter here is not strong/ the woods are always green/ from the sea the fresh breeze breathes on the dreary desert/, and the silence is so deep that from distant shores a sweet song rises/ the poor "caquillages" whisper it to express themselves./ In the forest, the rose laurels, the newly-closed flowers/, quiver from their drunken love for the green./ See the quivering whiteness!/ The fleets are in full sail in the immense deep./ In the night illuminating the planets watch the phosphorescent delusions leave from within./ The captive is hauled up wild and light./ Here he dies in his chains./ Captivity is worse than death./ In our hearts, hope survives,/ and when we return to France it will be again for the sake of struggle./ Regard the universal struggle in the air full of liberty!/ The clamour of the disinherited calls us to battle! . . . / The aurora has chased away the thick shadows/ and the new world stands up to the bloody horizon!

71. Thomas, *Louise Michel,* 179.
72. Michel, "Malfaiteurs et privelèges," *Le Libertaire,* Paris, November 12, 1895.
73. AN F7 12505, report of September 23, 1897.
74. Ibid., report of November 14, 1895—includes clippings of *Le Paris,* November 14, 1895.
75. Bullit Lowry and Elizabeth Ellington Gunter, eds., *The Red Virgin: Memoirs of Louise Michel (Birmingham, AL: The University of Alabama Press, 1981),* 24.
76. Ibid., 65.
77. See Joseph Campbell, *The Hero With a Thousand Faces* (Princeton, NJ: Princeton University Press, 1968).
78. Lowry and Gunter, *Red Virgin.*
79. Ibid.
80. Ibid.

81. See Harriet Applewhite and Darline Levy, eds., *Women and Politics in the Age of the Democratic Revolution* (Ann Arbor, MI: The University of Michigan Press, 1990).
82. See Edwards, *The Paris Commune*, 154.
83. Lowry and Gunter, *Red Virgin*, 67.
84. Ibid., 112.
85. Michel, *L'ere nouvelle*, 5.
86. Elisée Reclus, *L'évolution, la révolution et l'idéal anarchique*, (Paris: P. V. Stock, 1898).

## CHAPTER 3

1. Quoted in Joan U. Halperin, ed., *Félix Fénéon: oeuvres plus que complètes*, (Geneva, Librairie Droz, 1970), 899.
2. See Sonn, *Anarchism and Cultural Politics*.
3. See APP BA/1502, report of January 23, 1882. The poem begins "Gambetta avait promis, Gambetta avait promis, sé faire égorger tout Paris, se faire égorger tout Paris, mais son coup a manque grâce à nos Fédérés on lui coupera la tete. Dansons la Carmagnole, dansons la Carmagnole." Translated, "Gambetta has promised to cut the throat of Paris, but thanks to our 'fédérés' he failed to cut the head. Let's dance the Carmagnole, let's dance the Carmagnole."
4. Emile Gauthier, *Le parlementarisme* (Paris: Derveaux), 76.
5. Malato, *De la commune*, 235.
6. Ibid., 240.
7. Elisée Reclus, "Le droit de suffrage," *La Revue Anarchiste*, Paris, August 15, 1893.
8. APP BA/1498, report of April 8, 1898.
9. APP BA/1498, report of June 9, 1899.
10. *Le libertaire*, Paris, February 18, 1898.
11. See APP BA/1502, report of February 24, 1883.
12. See Emile Zola, *Germinal* (New York: Penguin, 1885).
13. APP BA/1502, report of October 9, 1885.
14. Ibid., report of October 4, 1883.
15. Ibid., report of January 8, 1892.
16. Paul Adam, "Eloge de Ravachol," *Entretiens politiques et littéraires 5, no. 28 (Paris, July 1892)*.
17. APP BA/1498, report of June 12, 1898.
18. AN F7 12504, clippings from *Le Figaro*, Paris, December 21, 1895.
19. AN F7 12506, clippings from *Le Temps*, Paris, April 24, 1892.

20. "Anarchisme et terrorisme," *La Révolte,* Paris, April 16, 1892.
21. "Propagande par le fait," *Le Révolté,* Paris, September 4, 1886.
22. "Le terrorisme," *La Révolte,* Paris, April 23, 1892.
23. See Jean Grave, *La panacée révolution,* (Paris: Les Temps Nouveaux pub., 1898).
24. Jean Grave, "Notre but," *La Révolte,* September 17, 1887.
25. Ibid.
26. "Ravachol," *La Révolte,* May 7, 1892.
27. See *Le Matin,* Paris, March 29, 1894.
28. Camille Mauclair, "Esquisse d'un etat d'esprit," *La revue anarchiste, Paris, October 15, 1893.*
29. "Les anarchistes sont les seuls socialistes," *Les Temps Nouveaux, Paris, September 28, 1895.*
30. Leszek Kolakowski, *Main Currents of Marxism, Vol. 2, The Golden Age* (New York: Oxford University Press, 1978), 21.
31. "Il n'y a pas d'affaire Dreyfus!" *Le Libertaire,* July 7, 1898.
32. "Dreyfus est innocent," *Le Libertaire,* September 4, 1898.
33. See Zeev Sternhell, *La droite révolutionnaire: les origines francaises du fascisme, 1885-1914* (Paris: Editions du Seuil, 1978).
34. See Sternhell, *La droite révolutionnaire.* Hannah Arendt, *The Origins of Totalitarianism* (New York: Harcourt, Brace, Jovanovich, 1951): and Jean Bredin, *The Affair: the Case of Alfred Dreyfus* (New York: George Braziller, 1983), for further discussion of the Dreyfus Affair and its implications.
35. See *L'intransigeant,* Paris, September 7, 1898 and May 21, 1899.
36. "La tribune," *Le journal du peuple,* Paris, February 8, 1899.
37. APP BA/1498, clipping of "Les anarchistes et l'affaire Dreyfus," *Le libertaire,* February 18, 1898.
38. "Drumont et vacher," *La Feuille,* Paris, November 3, 1898.
39. "Rochefort se meurt," *La Feuille,* June 16, 1898.
40. "Journalisme et journalistes," *Les Temps Nouveaux,* July 29, 1899.
41. AN F7 12505, report of June 1, 1898 and APP BA/1497, report of January 15, 1898.
42. APP BA/1497, report of January 23, 1898.
43. Ibid.
44. APP BA/1498, report of November 16, 1898.
45. APP BA/1498, report of October 23, 1898.
46. See *Les Temps Nouveaux,* January 29, 1898.
47. See *Almanach du Père Peinard,* Paris, 1899.
48. IFHS, 14 AS 184 (b), letter from Gustave Nercy to Jean Grave, October 22, 1898.

49. Sébastien Faure, *Les anarchistes et l'affaire Dreyfus*, (Paris: Lafont-Libertaire, 1898), 18.

50. See *Almanach du Père Peinard*, 1899.

51. See *Le Père Peinard*, Paris, November 21, 1897.

52. See *La Feuille*, November 3, 1897.

53. Paul Delesalle, *L'action syndicale et les anarchistes*, (Paris: L'Education Libertaire, 1900), 7.

54. See Maitron, *Le mouvement anarchiste*, 125.

55. See Jacques Juillard, *Pelloutier et les origines du syndicalisme d'action directe* (Paris: Editions du Seuil, 1971).

56. APP BA/1216, report of June 23, 1894.

57. Ibid., report of November 14, 1894.

58. Fernand Pelloutier, "L'anarchisme et les syndicats ouvriers," *Les Temps Nouveaux*, October 21, 1895.

59. Woodcock, *Anarchism*, 300.

60. See Maitron, *Le mouvement anarchiste*.

61. Fernand Pelloutier, *Le congrès générale du parti socialiste français: 3-8 décembre*, (Précédé d'une lettre aux anarchistes), (Paris: P.V. Stock, 1900), 4.

62. Pelloutier, *L'organisation corporative et l'anarchie*, (Paris, L'Art Social pub.) 13.

63. Ibid.

64. Pelloutier, "L'anarchisme et les syndicats ouvriers."

65. Pelloutier, *Le congrès*, 7.

66. APP BA/1498, report of October 16, 1899.

67. APP BA/1502, report of January 8, 1892.

68. Maitron, *Le mouvement anarchiste*, Vol. 1, 122.

69. APP BA/1498, report of June 5, 1900.

70. Emile Pouget, *Les bases du syndicalisme*, undated brochure found in IFHS 14 AS 134.

71. See Jean Grave, *Le machinisme*, (Paris: Les Temps Nouveaux pub., 1898)

72. APP BA/1508, report of April 17, 1895.

73. Emile Gravelle, "La formation de la terre végétale," *La Nouvelle Humanité* (Paris, February 1897).

74. See "Apologie de nature," conference of October 30, 1897, in *La Nouvelle Humanité* (December 1898).

75. Honore Bigot, "De la civilisation," *La Nouvelle Humanité* (October 1895).

76. Henri Zisly, "L'erreur des anarchistes," *La Nouvelle Humanité*, (April 1898).

77. See APP BA/1508, report of December 18, 1895.

78. IFHS 14 AS 184 (b), a letter from Henri Zisly to Jean Grave, July 19, 1896 confirms the insult.

79. Ibid.

80. See H. Stuart Hughes, *Consciousness and Society: The Reorientation of European Social Thought, 1890-1930,* (New York: Random House, 1958): Samuel Hynes, *The Edwardian Turn of Mind,* (Princeton, NJ: Princeton University Press, 1968): George Mosse, *The Crisis of German Ideology.* Fritz Stern, *The Politics of Cultural Despair,* (Berkeley, CA: University of California Press, 1961): and Carl Schorske, *Fin-de-Siècle Vienna.* These works all emphasize the growing hold of irrationalist thought on intellectuals during the latter part of the nineteenth century and the early part of the twentieth. Mosse, Stern, and Schorske all point to the ways in which such currents also caused political fallout, for example in the growing strength of extreme nationalism and racism in Germany and Austria.

81. Zo d'Axa, *Endehors,* (Paris: Chameul, 1896), 124.

82. Zo d'Axa, *Endehors,* Jean-Pierre Courty, ed. (Paris: Editions Champ Libre, 1974), 11.

83. Ibid.

84. See Victor Meric, *A travers la jungle politique et littéraire,* vol. 2, (Paris: Librairie Valois, 1930), 22, and *L'endehors,* Paris, December 27, 1891.

85. Meric, *A travers la jungle,* vol. 2, 17.

86. D'Axa, *Endehors,* 124.

87. Friedrich Nietzsche and Nikos Kazantzakis emphasized the existence of the abyss and the need to overcome it through human self-fulfillment. Zo d'Axa seems to have stressed a similar orientation as he gave up political involvement for travel and drifting, which offered new avenues for life after the anarchist cause ceased to have the same purpose it had formerly. Yet anarchism also seemed to be flexible enough once again to allow for such individual interpretations.

88. Meric *A travers la jungle,* vol. 2, 24.

89. Ibid., 15.

90. See *Le Mercure de france,* Paris, January, 1893 and March, 1894.

91. Mauclair, "Esquisse."

92. "Chronique social," *La Revue Rouge,* Paris, February, 1896.

93. "Ego sum," *La Revue Rouge,* April, 1896.

94. "Chronique social," *La Revue Rouge,* January, 1896.

95. Quoted in "Education," *Les Temps Nouveaux: Supplement Litteraire,* no. 38, 1897, 670.

96. See Theodore Zeldin, *France, 1848-1945: Intellect and Pride* (Oxford: Oxford University Press, 1977) 139-204: and Antoine Prost, *Histoire de l'enseignement en france, 1800-1967,* (Paris: Sirey, 1965), for analysis of French educational development during the nineteenth century.

97. See *Père Peinard Almanach,* 1895-1899.

98. "L'education de la volonté," *Les Temps Nouveaux,* October 24, 1896.

99. "La révolution et le paysan," *Les Temps Nouveaux,* May 27, 1899.

100. Jean Grave, *Enseignement bourgeois et enseignement libertaire* (Paris: Les Temps Nouveaux, pub., 1900), 11.

101. See *Le Libertaire,* May 19, 1897.

102. "Ce que nous voulons," *Le Libertaire,* November 22, 1895.

103. Maitron, *Le mouvement anarchiste.*

104. APP BA/1497, report of September 7, 1897.

105. Paul Robin, *L'éducation intégrale.* Conference, Paris,1900.

106. See Eugen Weber's, *Peasants into Frenchmen,* (Stanford, CA: Stanford University Press, 1976); and *France: Fin-de-Siècle,* (Cambridge, MA: Harvard University Press, 1986).

107. See George Steiner, *After Babel,* (New York: Oxford University Press, 1974). For the analysis of linguistic differences and their implications.

108. See Sonn, *Anarchism and Cultural Politics* for more on Pouget.

109. Michel, *L'ère nouvelle,* 5.

110. Ibid.

111. See Isaiah Berlin, "The Hedgehog and the Fox," in *Russian Thinkers,* (New York: Penguin, 1978).

112. APP BA/894, report of October 8, 1898.

113. Malato, *Les joyeusetés de l'exil,* 316-321.

114. Emile Chapelier and Gassy Marin, *Les anarchistes et la langue internationale "Esperanto"* (Paris: Internacio Asocio paso-Liberico, 1907) 3.

115. Ibid., 1.

116. See Gerald Brenan's discussion of Spanish millenarian anarchism in *The Spanish Labyrinth* (New York: Cambridge University Press, 1943) and Eric Hobsbawm's essays on the same subject in *Primitive Rebels* (New York: Norton, 1959).

117. Chapelier and Marin, *Les anarchistes,* 7.

118. Ibid.

119. Ibid., 10.

## CHAPTER 4

1. Alexander Dumas, the younger, wrote of Courbet in a famous statement:

> From what fabulous crossing of a slug with a peacock, from what genital antitheses, from what sebaceous oozing can have been generated ... this thing called M. Gustave Courbet? Under what gardener's

cloche, with the help of what manure, as a result of what mixture of wine, beer, corrosive mucus and flatulent oedema can have grown this sonorous and hairy pumpkin, this aesthetic belly, this imbecilic and impotent incarnation of the Self? Wouldn't one say he was a force of God, if God—Whom this non-being has wanted to destroy—were capable of playing pranks, and could have mixed Himself up with this?

Quoted in T. J. Clark, *Image of the People,* (London: Thames & Hudson, 1973), 23.

2. See Meyer Schapiro, "Abstract Art," in *Modern Art: Nineteenth and Twentieth Centuries, (New York: George Braziller, 1978), and T. J. Clark, The Painting of Modern Life.*

3. Schapiro, "Abstract Art."

4. Francis Haskell, "Enemies of Modern Art," *The New York* Review of Books, New York, June 30, 1983.

5. See Emile Zola, *Mon salon: Manet, ecrits sur l'art,* (Paris: Garnier-Flammarion, 1970).

6. Ibid.

7. Clark, *Image,* 13-14.

8. Peter Kropotkin, *Paroles d'un révolté* (Paris: Flammarion, 1882), quoted in Ralph Shikes and Paula Harper, *Pissarro: His Life and Work,* (New York: Horizon Press, 1980), 229.

9. See Clark, *Image,* and Linda Nochlin, *Realism* (New York: Penguin, 1971).

10. See Arnold Hauser, *The Social History of Art,* vol. 4, (New York: Random House, 1953), 165.

11. Kropotkin, *Paroles d'un révolté.*

12. Aline Dardel, *Catalogue des dessins et publications illustrées du journal anarchiste "les temps nouveaux":* 1895-1914, (Paris: Université de Paris IV Thèse de Doctorat de Troisième Cycle en Histoire de l'Art, 1980), 36.

13. Fernand Pelloutier, *L'art et la révolte,* Conference, Paris, May 30, 1896, L'Art Social, pub., 5.

14. Ibid., 20.

15. Ibid.

16. E. Museaux, "L'art social," *La plume,* no. 49, Paris, May 1, 1891.

17. E. Museaux, "Mission," *L'art social* (Paris, December 1891).

18. Eugene Chatelain, *L'art social* (December 1891).

19. Letter from Jean Grave to Camille Pissarro, March 25, 1896, quoted in Dardel, *Catalogue,* 99.

20. Georges Darien, "Chromo-luminaristes: Maximilien Luce," *La Plume*, September 1, 1891.

21. Emile Verhaeren, "Petite gazette d'art: exposition Maximilien Luce," *La Revue Blanche, Tome XX,* 1899, 309.

22. Emile Verhaeren, "La libre esthetique," *La Revue Blanche, Tome XV,* 1898.

23. Ibid.

24. Shattuck, *The Banquet Years,* 22.

25. See Hutton, *Neo-Impressionism and the Search for Solid Ground.*

26. See Clark, *The Painting of Modern Life.*

27. Letter from Camille Pissarro to his son Lucien, May 5, 1891. This and all other Pissarro letters are from John Rewald, ed., *Camille Pissarro: Letters to His Son Lucien,* (Santa Barbara: Pèregrine Smith, Inc., 1981) except if otherwise noted. 206-07.

28. Ibid.

29. Paul Signac, "L'éducation de l'oeil," *La Revue Blanche, Tome XVI, 1898, 363.*

30. Signac, quoted in Nochlin, *Realism,* 236.

31. See Shikes and Harper, *Pissarro,* 20.

32. Ibid.

33. Dardel, *Catalogue,* 36; and Hutton, *Neo-Impressionism and the Search for Solid Ground.*

34. Shikes and Harper, *Pissarro,* 22.

35. Ibid, 228.

36. Letter from Camille Pissarro to Lucien, April 20, 1891, 203- 04.

37. Letter from Camille Pissarro to Lucien, April 13, 1891, 200-03.

38. Camille Pissarro to Octave Mirbeau, quoted in Shikes and Harper, *Pissarro,* 241.

39. Letter from Camille Pissarro to Octave Mirbeau, April 21, 1892, quoted in Shikes and Harper, *Pissarro,* 229.

40. See letter from Camille Pissarro to Lucien, April 13, 1891, 200-203.

41. Letter from Lucien Pissarro to Jean Grave, 1895 quoted in Shikes and Harper, *Pissarro,* 237.

42. Letter from Camille Pissarro to Lucien, July 8, 1891, 226- 27.

43. Letter from Camille Pissarro to Octave Mirbeau, September 29, 1892, quoted in Shikes and Harper, *Pissarro,* 241.

44. Ibid.

45. See Agulhon, *Marianne into Combat.*

46. See Nochlin, *Realism.*

47. See Reg Carr, *Anarchism in France: The Case of Octave Mirbeau, (Montreal: McGill - Queen's University Press, 1977.*

48. APP BA/1190, clipping from *L'Aurore,* Paris, November 15, 1898.

49. See Sternhell, *La droite révolutionnaire*, and Arendt, *The Origins of Totalitarianism*.
50. Octave Mirbeau, *La salon de 1885* (Paris: Ludovic Bochet, 1885), 27-28.
51. Ibid.
52. Mirbeau, "Ravachol," *La Révolte*, Paris, May 7, 1892.
53. Quoted in John Rewald, "Félix Fénéon: I," *Gazette des beaux-arts, Tome XXXI*, series 6, Paris, 1947, 56.
54. Félix Fénéon, "Ballade chez des artisses indépendantes," *Père Peinard*, Paris, April 9, 1893, cited in Halperin ed., *Félix Fénéon, oeuvres plus que completes*, vol 1, 233.
55. Félix Fénéon, "L'exposition de Camille Pissarro", *La revue blanche*, May 15, 1896.
56. Quoted in John Rewald, ed., "Extraits du journal inédit de Paul Signac," *Gazette des beaux-arts, Tome XXXVI*, July, 1949: quote is from May 15, 1895, 120-23.
57. Shikes and Harper, *Pissarro*, 241.
58. See Halperin, *Fénéon and the Language of Art Criticism*.
59. Ibid.
60. See William K. Cornell, *Adolphe Retté* (New Haven, CT: Yale University Press, 1942).
61. Adolphe Retté, "L'art et l'anarchie," *La Plume*, February 1, 1893.
62. Ibid.
63. Ibid.
64. See Cornell, *Adolphe Retté* for further details.
65. Letter from Adolphe Retté to Léon Deschamps, *La Plume*, August 1, 1893.
66. Ibid.
67. See Sonn, *Anarchism and Cultural Politics*, and Weber, *France: Fin de Siècle*.
68. Cornell, *Adolphe Retté*, 62-65.
69. As in the lines of "Anniversaire": "O Pauvre, on t'a vole ta force avec la terre, Faut-il, pour t'éveiller, qu'eclate la tonnère?" Quoted in Eugenia Herbert, *The Artist and Social Reform*, (New Haven, CT: Yale University Press, 1961), 18, and also Adolphe. Retté, "Pour Crete," *Les Temps Nouveaux*, Paris, March 20, 1897, wherein Retté condemns Turkish massacres of Greeks in Crete.
70. Cornell, *Adolphe Retté*, 271.
71. Rémy de Gourmant, "Le symbolisme," *La Revue Blanche*, November, 1891, 322-324.
72. Manuel Devaldés, "D'art," *La Revue Rouge*, Paris, January, 1896.
73. Max Stirner, *The Ego and His Own*, (New York: Harper & Row, 1845), 205.
74. Letter from Jean Grave to Félix Nadar, from BN, Fr. Nouv. Acq. 24272.
75. Ibid.

76. See previously noted works of Eugenia Herbert and Ralph Shikes and Paula Harper, as well as Robert Herbert and Eugenia Herbert, "Artists and Anarchism: Unpublished Letters of Pissarro, Signac, and Others," *Burlington Magazine* (November 1960); and Brettell & Pissarro, *The Impressionist and the City* on the artist's anarchism.

77. Letter from Camille Pissarro to Lucien, February 26, 1896, 361-62.

78. Letter from Camille Pissarro to Lucien, May 2, 1887, 370-71.

79. Ibid.

80. This medieval symbol of death is hauntingly visible in Ingmar Bergman's film about the late Middle Ages, *The Seventh Seal,* where the figure is always seen carrying a similar device.

81. See Herbert, *The Artist and Social Reform.*

82. See Schorske, *Fin-de-Siècle Vienna.*

83. Shattuck, *The Banquet Years.*

84. Letter from Steinlen to Henri Barbusse, January 9, 1905, BN Nouv. Acq. 16986. Barbusse was the literary director of Jean Lanquest's socialist journal, *Le Populaire.*

85. John Willett, *Art and Politics in the Weimar Period: the New Sobriety, 1917-1933,* (New York: Pantheon, 1978), 225-27.

86. See Leighten, *Re-Ordering the Universe,* 52.

87. See Weber, *France: Fin de Siècle.*

# BIBLIOGRAPHY

## PRIMARY SOURCES

### Archival Sources

Archives Nationales:$F^7$ 12504, $F^7$ 12505, $F^7$ 12506, $F^7$ 12508, $F^7$, 12842, $F^7$ 13053 (these are various police files pertaining to anarchists sent to the minister of interior).

Bibliothèque Nationale:Fr. Nouv. Acq. 24272, 16986, 16982, 16533 (collections of artists' and anarchists' letters).

Centre de Recherche pour l'Histoire des Mouvements Sociales et du Syndicalisme: Various letters and collections dealing with Parisian anarchists.

Jacques Douçet Art History Library of the University of Paris:Cartons 24, 86, 87 (letters of artists).

Institut Français de l'Histoire Sociale (of the Archives Nationales):14 AS 184 (a & b), 14 AS 24, 14 AS 52, 14 AS 25-26, 14 AS 40, 14 AS 134, 14 AS 136, 14 AS 147 (anarchist letters, pamphlets, artwork).

Musée Social: Extensive collections of contemporary reviews and newspapers.

Archives de la Préfecture de Police:BA/303, BA/894, BA/510, BA/1190, BA/1216, BA/1237, BA/1497, BA/1498, BA/1500, BA/1502, BA/1503, BA/ 1505, BA/1508 (police reports on anarchists in Paris).

### Newspapers and Reviews from Paris, 1880-1900

Anarchist periodicals:*Le Révolté, La Révolte, Les Temps Nouveaux, Le Libertaire, Le Journal du Peuple, L'Endehors, La Feuille, La Nouvelle Humanité, Père Peinard, Père Peinard Almanach, La revue anarchiste, La Revue Blanche, La Revue Rouge.* Other newspapers:*Le Cri du Peuple, L'intransigeant, Le Figaro, Le Matin, Le temps.*

Artistic reviews:*Les Entretiens Politiques et Littéraires, Le Mercure de France, La Plume, La Revue Indépendante.*

### Books and Pamphlets

*L'anarchie en cour d'assises.* Bruxelles: Ensival Pleberen, 1895.

Armand, E. *Qu'est-ce qu'un anarchiste?: thèses et opinions.* Paris: Editions de l'anarchie, 1908.

*Aux affamés.* Paris: L'union de groupes anarchistes de XXème arrondissement, 1887.

Baedeker, Karl. *Paris et ses environs: manuel de voyageur.* Paris: Paul Ollendorff, 1889.

Bakunin, Mikhail. *God and the State.* New York: Dover, 1893.

Becker, George J., and Edith Phillips, eds. *Paris and the Arts: 1851-1896, From the Goncourt Journal.* Ithaca: Cornell University Press, 1971.

Chadourne, Andre. *Le Quartier Latin.* Paris, 1884.

Chapelier, Emile, and Gassy Marin. *Les anarchistes et la langue* internationale "Esperanto." Paris: Internacio Asocio Paso-Liberico, 1907.

Chatelain, Eugene. *L'art social.* Paris, December, 1891.

Crueuel, Edouard. *Bohemian Paris of Today.* Edited by W. C. Morrow. London: Chatto & Windus, 1899.

de Cyon, E. *Nihilisme et anarchie.* Paris: Ancienne Maison Michel Lévy Freres, 1892.

Delesalle, Paul. *L'action syndicale et les anarchistes.* Paris: L'Education Libertaire, 1900.

————. *La confédération générale du travail,* Paris: La Publication Social, 1907.

Devaldès, Manuel. *L'education et la liberté.* Paris: Bibliothèque de la Critique, 1900.

Dubois, Félix. *Le péril anarchiste.* Paris: Flammarion, 1894.

Etièvant, G. *Déclarations.* Paris: La Révolte, pub., 1893.

————. *Deuxième déclaration.* Bruxelles: Les Temps Nouveaux, pub., 1899.

Faure, Sébastien. *L'anarchie en cour d'assises.* Paris: La Révolte pub., 1891.

————. *Les anarchistes et l'affaire Dreyfus.* Paris: Lafont-Libertaire, 1898.

————. *Les crimes de dieu.* Paris: Libertaire pub.

————. *La douleur universelle: philosophie libertaire.* Paris: 1895).

Gauthier, Emile. *Le darwinisme social.* Paris: Derveaux, 1880.

————. *Les endormeurs: libertés politiques.* Paris: Derveaux.

————. *Le parlementarisme.* Paris: Derveaux.

Girard, Andre. *Education et autorité paternelle.* Paris: Les Temps Nouveaux, pub., 1897.

Grave, Jean. *Enseignement bourgeois et enseignement libertaire.* Paris: Les Temps Nouveaux, pub., 1900.

————. *L'individu et la société.* Paris: Tresse & Stock, 1897.

————. *Le machinisme.* Paris: Les Temps Nouveaux, pub., 1898.

————. *La panacée révolution.* Paris: Les Temps Nouveaux, pub., 1898.

————. *Quarante ans de propagande anarchiste.* Paris: Flammarion, 1973.

————. *La révolution et l'autonomie selon la science.* Paris: A. Bataille, 1885.

————. *La société mourante et l'anarchie.* Paris: Tresse & Stock, 1893.

Hamon, Augustin. *Les hommes et les theories de l'anarchie.* Paris: La Révolte, pub., 1893.

————. *Patrie et internationalisme.* Paris: Les Temps Nouveaux, pub., 1896.

Henry, Emile. *Déclaration.* Paris: Libertaire pub., 1894.

Huysmans, J. K. *L'art moderne.* Paris: G. Charpentier, 1883.

Janvion, Emile. *Le dogme et la science*. Paris: Libertaire, pub., 1897.

Kropotkin, Peter. *La conquête du pain*. Paris: Tresse & Stock, 1894.

———. *Fields, Factories, and Workshops, Tomorrow*. New York: Harper & Row, 1898.

———. *La grande révolution: 1789-1793*. Paris: P. V. Stock., 1909.

———. *The Great French Revolution: 1789-1793*. New York: G. P. Putnam's Sons, 1909.

———. *Memoirs of a Revolutionist*. Boston: Houghton Mifflin & Co, 1899.

———. *Mutual Aid: A Factor of Evolution*. Boston: Porter Sargent Publishers Inc., 1902.

———. *Paroles d'un révolté*. Paris: Flammarion, 1882.

———. *Un siècle d'attente: 1789-1889*. Paris: La Révolte, pub., 1893.

Léger, Augustin. *Journal d'un anarchiste*. Paris: Albert Savine, 1895.

Malato, Charles. *De la commune à l'anarchie*. Paris: Librairie Tresse & Stock, 1894.

———. *L'homme nouveau*. Paris: Tresse & Stock, 1898.

———. *Les joyeusetés de l'exil*. Paris: P. V. Stock, 1897.

———. *Philosophie de l'anarchie*. Paris: Tresse & Stock, 1897.

———. *Les travailleurs des villes aux travailleurs des campagnes*. Paris: Imprimerie Libertaire, 1888.

Martin, Alexis. *Paris promenades dans les vingt arrondissements: les étapes d'un touriste en france*. Paris: A. Hennuyer, 1890.

Mauclair, Camille. *L'impressionisme: son histoire, son esthetique, ses maîtres*. Paris: Libraire de l'art ancien et moderne, 1904.

———. *Servitudes et grandeurs littéraires*. Paris: Librairie Ollendorff, 1922.

Meric, Victor. *A travers la jungle politique et littéraire (Coulises et treteaux)* (2 volumes). Paris: Librairie Valois, 1930.

Michel, Louise. *La commune: histoire et souvenirs*. Paris: Francois Maspero, 1898.

———. *L'ère nouvelle, pensée dernière: souvenirs de calédonie*. Paris: Librairie Socialiste Internationale Achille le Roy, 1887.

Mirbeau, Octave. *L'Abbé Jules*. Paris: Flammarion, 1888.

———. *Le journal d'une femme de chambre*. Paris: Flammarion, 1900.

———. *Maîtres modernes: le salon de 1885*. Paris: Ludovic Baschet, 1885.

———. *Les mauvais bergers*. Paris: 1897.

———. *Sébastien Roch*. Paris: Flammarion, 1890. *Misère et mortalité*. Paris: Etudiants Socialistes Révolutionaires Internationalistes de Paris, Les Temps Nouveaux pub.

Museaux, E. *Mission*. Paris: L'Art Social, pub., 1891.

———. *Paris*. London: Ward & Lock, & Co., 1898.

Pelloutier, Fernand. *L'art et la révolte*. Paris, Conference in May, 1896. L'Art Social, pub.

————. *Le congres générale du parti socialiste français: 3-8 décembre, 1899*. Paris: P. V. Stock, 1900.

————. *L'organisation corporative et l'anarchie*. Paris: L'Art Social, pub.

Pissarro, Camille. *Turpitudes sociales*. Geneva: Albert Skira, 1890.

Pouget, Emile. *Les bases du syndicalisme*. Paris.

Reclus, Elisée. *L'evolution, la révolution et la idéal anarchique*. Paris: P. V. Stock, 1898.

————. *L'homme et la terre*. Paris: François Maspero, 1895.

*Reformes ou révolution*. Paris: Groupe des Etudiantes Socialistes Revolutionnaires Internationalistes, Les Temps Nouveaux, pub.

Riviere, H. *Souvenirs de la nouvelle calédonie: l'insurrection canaque*. Paris: Gallet, 1881.

Robin, Paul. *L'éducation intégrale*. Conference in Paris, 1900.

Roux, Jacques *L'anarchie et la révolution* Paris.

Saurin, Daniel. *L'ordre par l'anarchie*. Paris: La Révolte, pub., 1893.

Stackelberg, Frederic. *La mesure du temps*. Paris: Les Temps Nouveaux, pub., 1899.

Stirner, Max. *The Ego and His Own*. New York: Harper & Row, 1845.

Zo d'Axa. *Endehors*. Paris: Chameul, 1896.

Zola, Emile. *Mon salon, Manet, Ecrits sur L'art*. Paris: Garnier-Flammarion, 1970.

## Collections

Bailly-Herzberg, J. *Correspondence de Camille Pissarro*, in five volumes—Vol. 1: 1865-1890: Vol. 2: 1886-1890: Vol. 3: 1891-1894: Vol. 4: 1895-1898: Vol. 5: 1899-1903. Paris: Presses Universitaires de France, 1980, 1986, 1988, 1989.

Halperin, Joan U., ed. *Félix Fénéon: oeuvres plus que complètes* (2 Volumes). Geneva: Librairie Droz, 1970.

Herbert, Robert, and Eugenia Herbert. "Artists and Anarchism: Unpublished Letters of Pissarro, Signac, and Others," *Burlington Magazine,* November, 1960.

Joets, J. "Lettres inédites de Pissarro à Claude Monet," *L'Amour de l'art*. Paris: 1946.

Lehning, A. *Archives Bakounine*. Leiden: 1967.

Lowry, Bullit, and Elizabeth Ellington Gunter. eds. *The Red Virgin: Memoirs of Louise Michel*. Birmingham, AL: University of Alabama Press, 1981.

Miller, Martin A. *Selected Writings on Anarchism and Revolution: P. A. Kropotkin*. Cambridge, MA: MIT Press, 1970.

Pissarro, L. R., and L. Venturi. *Camille Pissarro, son art, son oeuvre*. Paris: 1939.

Rewald, John, ed. "Extraits du journal inédit de Paul Signac," *Gazette des beaux-arts*. Tome XXXVI. Paris, July, 1949.

————. *Pissarro: Letters to His Son Lucien*. (Santa Barbara, CA: Peregrine Smith, Inc., 1981.

Venturi, L. *Les archives de l'impressionisme*. Paris: 1939.

Zisly, Henri. *Oeuvres et critiques naturisme*. Selected writings from 1895-1900 found at CRHMSS.

## SECONDARY SOURCES

### Articles

"L'anarchisme ici et la, hier et aujourd'hui," *Le mouvement social, no. 83.* Paris (April 1973).

Aubery, Pierre, "L'anarchisme et les symbolistes," *Le mouvement social,* no. 69. Paris (October 1969).

"Autoportrait de Jean Maitron," *Le monde.* Paris, August 30, 1985.

Benjamin, Walter. "Paris, Capital of the Nineteenth Century." In *Reflections.* New York: Harcourt, Brace, and Jovanovich, 1955.

Berlin, Isaiah. "The Hedgehog and the Fox." In *Russian Thinkers.* New York: Penguin, 1978, 22-81.

———. "Herzen and Bakunin on Individual Liberty." In *Russian Thinkers.* New York, Penguin, 1978, 82-113.

Coe, R. T. "Camille Pissarro, a Study of His Later Development." *Gazette des beaux-arts,* Tome XLIII. Paris, February, 1954.

Darnton, Robert, "The High Enlightenment and the Low-Life of Literature in Pre-Revolutionary France." *Past and Present,* no. 51 (May 1971): Also found in *The Literary Underground of the Old Regime.* Cambridge, MA: Harvard University Press, 1982.

Haskell, Francis. "Enemies of Modern Art." *New York Review of Books.* New York, June 30, 1983.

Jacquement, Gerard. "Belleville ouvrier à la belle epoque." *Le mouvement social.* No. 118. Paris, January, 1982.

Joll, James "Singing, Dancing, and Dynamite." *Times Literary Supplement.* London, September 10, 1976.

Lévy-Leboyer, Maurice. "La décélération de l'economie française dans la second moitie du XIXème siècle." *Revue d'histoire economique et social.* Paris, 1971.

Maitron, Jean. "Un 'anar' qu'est-ce-que c'est." *Le mouvement social 1,* no. 83. Paris (April 1973).

Maitron, Jean and Alain Droguet. "La presse anarchiste française de ses origines a nos jours. " *Le mouvement social,* no. 83. Paris (April 1973).

Nicholson, Benedict. "The Anarchism of Camille Pissarro." *The Arts, 2.* New York, 1947.

Nochlin, Linda. "The Unassuming Eye." *Art News,* 64 (April 1965):24.

Pritchett, V. S. "Pissarro: The Poet-Logician." *New York Review of Books.* New York, May 14, 1981.

Rewald, John. "Félix Fénéon" *Gazette des beaux-arts,* Tome XXXI, series 6, Paris, 1947.

———. "Félix Fénéon." *Gazette des beaux-arts,* Tome XXXII-XXXIII, Paris, 1948.

Ronsin, Francis. "La classe ouvriere et le néo-malthusianisme: l'exemple français avant 1914." *Le mouvement social,* no. 106. Paris, January, 1979.

Rosen, Charles, and Henri Zerner. "What is, and is not, Realism?" *New York Review of Books,* New York, February 18 and March 4, 1982.

Woodcock, George. "Anarchism." In *Encyclopedia of Philosophy.* New York: Macmillan Company, 1978.

## Books

Adler, Kathleen. *Camille Pissarro.* London: B. T. Bateford, 1978.

Agulhon, Maurice. *Marianne into Combat: Republican Imagery and Symbolism in France.* New York: Cambridge University Press, 1981.

Applewhite, Harriet, and Darline Levy. eds. *Women and Politics in the Age of the Democratic Revolution.* Ann Arbor, MI: The University of Michigan Press, 1990.

Arendt, Hannah. *The Origins of Totalitarianism.* New York: Harcourt, Brace, & Jovanovich, 1951.

Avrich, Paul. *Anarchist Portraits.* Princeton, NJ: Princeton University Press, 1988.

———. *The Russian Anarchists.* New York: Norton, 1967.

Bellanger, Claude, Jacques Godechot, Pierre Greival, and Fernand Terrou. eds. *Histoire générale de la presse française.* Paris: Presses Universitaires de France, 1972.

Boussinot, Roger. *Les mots de l'anarchie.* Paris: Delalain, 1982.

Bredin, Jean. *The Affair: the Case of Alfred Dreyfus.* New York: George Braziller, 1983.

Brenan, Gerald. *The Spanish Labyrinth.* New York: Cambridge University Press, 1943.

Brettell, Richard R. *Pissarro and Pontoise.* New Haven, CT: Yale University Press, 1990.

Campion, Leon. *Zo d'Axa.* Bruxelles: Pensée et Action, 1936.

Carr, Reg. *Anarchism in France: The Case of Octave Mirbeau.* Montreal: McGill - Queen's University Press, 1977.

Chevalier, Louis. *La formation de la population parisienne au XIXème siècle.* Paris: Presses Universitaires de France, 1950.

———. *Laboring Classes, Dangerous Classes.* Princeton: Princeton University Press, 1973.

———. *Montmartre de plaisir et du crime.* Paris: Editions Robert Laffont, 1980.

Clark, T. J. *The Absolute Bourgeois.* London: Thames & Hudson, 1973.

———. *Image of the People.* London: Thames & Hudson 1973.

———. *The Painting of Modern Life.* New York: Alfred A. Knopf, 1985.

Cobb, Richard. *The Police and the People.* New York: Oxford University Press, 1970.

Coons, Lorraine. *Women Home Workers in the Parisian Garment Industry, 1860-1915.* New York: Garland Publishing, Inc., 1987.

Cornell, Kenneth. *Adolphe Retté.* New Haven, CT: Yale University Press, 1942.

———. *The Symbolist Movement.* New Haven, CT: Yale University Press, 1951.

de Goustine, Christian. *Pouget: les matins noirs du syndicalisme.* Paris: Editions de la Tête de Feuilles, 1972.

del Moral, J. Diaz. *Historia de las agitaciones campesinas andaluzas.* Madrid: Cordoba, 1929.

Derfler, Leslie. *Alexander Millerand, the Socialist Years.* The Hague: Mouton & Co., 1977.

———. *Paul Lafargue and the Founding of French Marxism, 1842-1882.* Cambridge, MA: Harvard University Press, 1991.

Dostoyevsky, Fyodor. *Notes from Underground.* New York: Norton, 1863.

Droz, Jacques, ed. *Histoire générale du socialisme.* Paris: Presses Universitaires de France, 1974.

Dumas, Rene. *Ravachol, l'homme rouge de l'anarchie.* St. Etienne: Le Henaff, 1981.

Edwards, Stewart. *The Paris Commune: 1871.* New York: Quadrangle Books, 1971.

Engels, Frederick. *Revolution and Counter-Revolution in Germany.* New York: International Publishers, 1852.

Evenson, Norma. *Paris: A Century of Change, 1878-1978.* New Haven, CT: Yale University Press, 1979.

Fleming, Marie. *The Anarchist Way to Socialism: Elisée Reclus and Nineteenth Century Anarchism.* London: Croom Helm, 1979.

Ford, Franklin. *Robe and Sword.* New York: Harper & Row, 1953.

Freund, Gisele. *Photographie et société.* Paris: Editions du Seuil, 1974.

Fussell, Paul. *The Great War and Modern Memory.* New York: Oxford University Press, 1975.

Gay, Peter. *Art and Act.* New York: Harper & Row, 1976.

———. *Weimar Culture: the Outsider as Insider.* New York: Harper & Row, 1968.

Girard, Louis. *Nouvelle histoire de Paris: la deuxième république et la second empire, 1848-1870.* Paris: Hachette, 1968.

Goldberg, Harvey. *The Life of Jean Jaures.* Madison, WI: University of Wisconsin Press, 1962.

Gramsci, Antonio. *Selections From the Prison Notebooks.* New York: International Publishers, 1971.

Guerin, Daniel. *Anarchism: From Theory to Practice.* Paris: Gallimard, 1965.

Halperin, Joan U. *Félix Fénéon: Aesthete and Anarchist in Fin-de-Siècle Paris* New Haven, CT: Yale University Press, 1988.

———. *Félix Fénéon and the Language of Art Criticism.* Ann Arbor, MI: UMI Research Press, 1980.

Hauser, Arnold. *The Social History of Art, Vol. 4, Naturalism, Impressionism, the Film Age.* New York: Random House, 1953.

Herbert, Eugenia. *The Artist and Social Reform.* New Haven, CT: Yale University Press, 1961.

Herzen, Alexander. *My Past and Thoughts.* Berkeley, CA: University of California Press, 1855.

Hesse, Carla. *Publishing and Cultural Politics in Revolutionary Paris, 1789-1810.* Berkeley, CA: University of California Press, 1991.

Hobsbawm, Eric. J. *Primitive Rebels.* New York: Norton, 1959.

Hughes, H. Stuart. *Consciousness and Society: the Reorientation of European Social Thought, 1890-1930.* New York: Random House, 1958.

Hutton, John G. *Neo-Impressionism and the Search for Solid Ground: Art, Science, and Anarchism in Fin-de-Siècle France.* Baton Rouge: Louisiana State University Press, 1994.

Hutton, Patrick H. *The Cult of the Revolutionary Tradition: The Blanquists in French Politics, 1864-1893.* Berkeley, CA: University of California Press, 1981.

Hynes, Samuel. *The Edwardian Turn of Mind.* Princeton, NJ: Princeton University Press, 1968.

Joll, James. *The Anarchists.* Cambridge, MA: Harvard University Press, 1965.

Jones, Gareth Stedman. *Languages of Class: Studies in English Working Class History: 1832-1982.* New York: Cambridge University Press, 1983.

Juillard, Jacques. *Pelloutier et les origines du syndicalisme d'action directe.* Paris: Editions du Seuil, 1971.

Kaplan, Temma. *Red City, Blue Period: Social Movements in Picasso's Barcelona.* Berkeley, CA: University of California Press, 1992.

Kazantzakis, Nikos. *Zorba the Greek.* New York: Simon and Schuster, 1952.

Kedward, Roderick. *The Anarchists: The Men Who Shocked an Era.* London: St. Giles House, 1971.

Kemp, Tom. *Economic Forces in French History.* London: Dobson, 1971.

Kern, Stephen. *The Culture of Time and Space.* Cambridge, MA: Harvard University Press, 1983.

Kolakowski, Leszek. *Main Currents of Marxism, Vol. 2, The Golden Age.* New York: Oxford University Press, 1978.

Kunstler, Charles. *Pissarro, villes et campagne.* Paris: 1967.

Lacquer, Walter. *Terrorism.* Boston: Little, Brown, & Co., 1977.

Landes, David. *The Unbound Prometheus.* New York: Cambridge University Press, 1972.

Lecomte, Georges. *Camille Pissarro.* Paris: Bernheim-Jeune, 1922.

Leighten, Patricia. *Re-Ordering the Universe: Picasso and Anarchism, 1897-1914.* Princeton, NJ: Princeton University Press, 1989.

Lloyd, Christopher. *Pissarro.* Geneva: Skira, 1981.

Maitron, Jean. *Dictionnarie biographique de mouvement ouvrier français: 1871-1914.* Paris: Les Editions Ouvriers, 1973.

———. *Histoire du mouvement en france.* Paris: Francois Mamspero, 1951.

———. *Le mouvement anarchiste en france.* (2 volumes.) Paris: Francois Maspero, 1975.

———. *Paul Delesalle, un "anar" de la belle epoque.* Paris: Fayard, 1985.

Marx, Karl. *Class Struggles in France.* New York: International Publishers, 1850.

———. *The 18th Brumaire of Louis Bonaparte.* New York: International Publishers, 1852.

Miller, David. *Anarchism.* London: J. M. Dent & Sons, Ltd., 1984.

Mitchell, Harvey, and Peter Stearns. *Workers and Protest: The European Labor Movement, the Working Classes and the Origins of Social Democracy, 1890-1914.* Itasca, IL: F.E. Peacock, 1971.

Moss, Bernard. *The Origins of the French Labor Movement, 1830-1914: The Socialism of the Skilled Workers.* Berkeley, CA: University of California Press, 1976.

Mosse, George. *The Crisis of German Ideology: The Intellectual Origins of the Third Reich.* New York: Grosset & Dunlap, 1964.

Mumford, Lewis. *The City in History.* New York: Harcourt, Brace, Jovanovich, 1961.

Nettlau, Max. *Histoire de l'anarchie.* Paris: Editions du Cercle, 1933.

Nietzsche, Friedrich. *Thus Spoke Zarathustra.* New York: Penguin, 1892.

Nochlin, Linda. *Realism.* New York: Penguin, 1971.

Nord, Philip. *Paris Shopkeepers and the Politics of Resentment.* Princeton, NJ: Princeton University Press, 1986.

Orwell, George. *Homage to Catalonia.* New York: Harcourt, Brace, Jovanovich, 1938.

Ozouf, Mona. *Festivals and the French Revolution.* Cambridge, MA: Harvard University Press, 1976.

Palmade, Guy P. *French Capitalism in the Nineteenth Century.* New York: Barnes & Noble, 1961.

Panofsky, Erwin. *Studies in Iconology.* New York: Harper & Row, 1939.

Patsouras, Louis. *Jean Grave and French Anarchism.* Dubuque: Kendall Hunt, Publishing Co., 1978.

Pierrot, Jean. *The Decadent Imagination: 1880-1900.* Chicago: University of Chicago Press, 1981.

Pinkney, David, H. *Napoleon III and the Rebuilding of Paris.* Princeton, NJ: Princeton University Press, 1958.

Prost, Antoine. *Histoire de l'enseignement en france, 1800-1967.* Paris: Sirey, 1965.

Rewald, John. *Camille Pissarro.* New York: H.N. Abrams, 1963.

———. *The History of Impressionism.* New York: The Museum of Modern Art, 1961.

Roche, Daniel. *The People of Paris.* Berkeley, CA: University of California Press, 1981.

Rude, George. *The Crowd in the French Revolution.* New York: Oxford University Press, 1959.

Salmon, Andre. *La terreur noire: chronique du mouvement libertaire.* Paris: Jean-Jacques Pauvert, 1959.

Schapiro, Meyer. *Modern Art: Nineteenth and Twentieth Centuries*. New York: George Braziller, 1978.

Schorske, Carl E. *Fin-de-Siècle Vienna*. New York: Alfred A. Knopf, 1979.

Seigel, Jerrold. *Bohemian Paris: Culture, Politics, and the Boundaries of Bourgeois Life, 1830-1930*. New York: Viking Penguin, 1986.

Sergent, Alain, and Claude Harmel. *Histoire de l'anarchie*. Paris: Le Portulan, 1949.

Sewell, William. *Work and Revolution: The Language of Labor from the Old Regime to 1848*. New York: Cambridge University Press, 1980.

Shattuck, Roger. *The Banquet Years: the Origins of the Avant-Garde in France, 1885 to World War I*. New York: Random House, 1955.

Shikes, Ralph E. *The Indignant Eye: the Artist as Social Critic in Prints and Drawings from the 15th Century to Picasso*. Boston: Beacon Press, 1969.

Shikes, Ralph E., and Paula Harper. *Pissarro: His Life and Work*. New York: Horizon Press, 1980.

Silverman, Deborah. *Art Nouveau in Fin-de-Siècle France: Politics, Psychology, and Style*. Berkeley, CA: University of California Press, 1989.

Soboul, Albert. *Les Sans-Culottes*. Paris: Editions du Seuil, 1968.

Sonn, Richard D. *Anarchism*. New York: Twayne Publishers, 1992.

————. *Anarchism and Cultural Politics in Fin-de-Siècle France*. Lincoln: University of Nebraska Press, 1989.

Stafford, David. *From Anarchism to Reformism: A Study of the Political Activities of Paul Brousse within the First International and the French Socialist Movement, 1870-1890*. Toronto: University of Toronto Press, 1971.

Steiner, George. *After Babel*. New York: Oxford University Press, 1973.

Stern, Fritz. *The Politics of Cultural Despair*. Berkeley, CA: University of California Press, 1961.

Sternhell, Zeev. *La droite révolutionnaire: les origines françaises du fascisme, 1885-1914*. Paris: Editions du Seuil, 1978.

Tannenbaum, Edward R. *1900: The Generation Before the Great War*. Garden City, NJ: Doubleday, 1975.

Thomas, Edith. *Louise Michel ou le velleda de l'anarchie*. Paris: Gallimard, 1971.

————. *The Women Incendiaries of Paris*. Paris: Gallimard, 1963.

Tucker, Robert C. *Philosophy and Myth in Karl Marx*. New York: Cambridge University Press, 1961.

Vizetelly, Ernest A. *The Anarchists: Their Faith and their Record*. London: John Lane, The Bodley Head, 1911.

Weber, A. F. *The Growth of Cities in the Nineteenth Century*. Ithaca, NY: Cornell University Press, 1899.

Weber, Eugen. *France: Fin de Siècle*. Cambridge, MA: Harvard University Press, 1986.

————. *Peasants Into Frenchmen*. Stanford, CA: Stanford University Press, 1976.

Williams, Raymond. *Culture and Society: 1780-1950*. London: Chatto and Windus, 1958.

Williams, Rosalind. *Dream Worlds: Mass Consumption in Late 19th Century France*. Berkeley, CA: University of California Press, 1982.

Willett, John. *Art and Politics in the Weimar Period: the New Sobriety, 1917-1933*. New York: Pantheon, 1978.

Wohl, Robert. *The Generation of 1914*. Cambridge, MA: Harvard University Press, 1979.

Woodcock, George. *Anarchism: A History of Libertarian Ideas and Movements*. New York: Penguin, 1962.

Zeldin, Theodore. *France: 1848-1945: Politics and Anger*. New York: Oxford University Press: 1973.

Zola, Emile. *Germinal*. New York: Penguin, 1885.

### Catalogues and Theses

Brettell, Richard, and Francoise Cachin. eds. *Pissarro: 1830-1903*. Regarding the 1981 exhibition held in London, Paris, and Boston. Boston, MA: Museum of Fine Arts, 1981.

Brettell, Richard R., and Joachim Pissarro. *The Impressionist and the City: Pissarro's Series Paintings*. Edited by Mary Ann Stevens. Regarding the Exhibition held in Dallas, Philadelphia, and London. New Haven, CT: Yale University Press, 1992.

Dardel, Aline. *Catalogue des dessins et publications illustrées du journal anarchiste "les temps nouveaux": 1895-1914*. Paris: Université de Paris IV Thèse de Doctorat de Troisieme Cycle en Histoire de l'Art, 1980.

Darnton, Robert, and Daniel Roche. *Revolution in Print: The Press in France, 1775-1800*. Regarding the 1989 exhibition held in the New York Public Library. Berkeley, CA: University of California Press, 1989.

Tarou, Michel. *E. Armand, un individualiste anarchiste vu a travers l'une de ses oeuvres*. Paris: y Memoire de Maîtrise a CRHMSS, Université de Paris I, 1971.

# INDEX